WHEN I LAST SAW ME

JOB 11:18
CHEERS & AMEN
AZ (:)

THE MEMOIR OF
SAMMI BASS
OTHERWISE KNOWN AS LISA JENNETT

DISCLAIMER

This is a memoir, not a work of fiction. However, to protect the innocent and the guilty alike, all names of people, streets, routes, businesses, diners, fields, cities, towns, hamlets and hamsters (though no hamsters are actually part of this story) have been altered. The reality, however, remains. Resemblance to actual persons, living or dead, is because people just like this exist in places all across the world. Mothers and fathers, siblings, cousins, friends, strangers ... ordinary people all. They are remarkable because they are unexceptional. Extraordinary because of their garden-variety. This is my story, the way I remember it. The way I lived it. The way I am living it still.

ASIL

DEDICATION

As Abe laid down his boy, I lay down these pages for every James and Pete and Buck who has walked in and among and out of the prisons and war zones with little but their scars and discerns and compassions to show for it.

Isaacced also to all the Moonpies and all the Grands of anyone ... for all those who can—because we faced our dark and found some light—begin from a better place and leave a very different legacy.

THANKS TO

The Triplets

Tank

Sundy

Daniel

Golden

Turner

Lightning

Bookie

Able

Bunker

Freddie

The anonymous along my way.

The now less scary ghosts.

The dozens who loaned me their brave to be as
full bore obedient as I know how so far.

It takes a tribe. A club. A dirty dozen. A herd.
A band of brothers. A bandana-bearing gang.
An unintentional, deliberately chosen family. A belong.

It takes a kind and true altar team to walk us up a
mountain when we Isaac up our treasure.

Above all, this is a journey of hope and redemption. You will find yourself in these pages. You will resonate with the longing, the searching, the loss, the betrayal and brokenness— these things make us human. You will discover that you are found, known, seen, heard and can be healed by the only One who is able to love us to wholeness.

CHRISTINE CAINE
Founder A21 & Propel Women
Author of *Undaunted*

Contents

13   foreword

15   chapter zero

21   one
TWO AND A HALF DAYS

27   two
SKILLET LEFT

31   three
GATHERING

35   four
THE POEM

45   five
THE FLAG LET HER CRY

51   six
MR. BROWN

59   seven
CHRISTMAS LIGHTS IN 1968

65   eight
CLOSED DOORS

71   nine
WATCHING ME

83   ten
COUNTY ROADS

87   eleven
SWEET TOWNS OF JUSTICE

97   twelve
THE LIST OF WHY

105   thirteen
CARS

113   fourteen
FLATT OUT

133   fifteen
SIDEWALK DOWN THE MIDDLE

145   sixteen
SUNDAY DUSK

153   seventeen
ROUND ONE WITH A SWIMMING POOL

157   eighteen
MAYBE WE'RE ALL ALIKE

163   nineteen
ANOTHER SAME HOTEL

167   twenty
CLEAR COLD

173   twenty-one
SUMMERS

189   twenty-two
GETTING INTO THE CHURCH

201   twenty-three
GOING SOUTH

209   twenty-four
TOKENS

213   twenty-five
THE TRIP INSIDE

223   twenty-six
DIRTY INNOCENT WATER

227   twenty-seven
WHY STAY

231   twenty-eight
LEVEL BEHIND ME

235   twenty-nine
NOT GOING BACK MORE

245   thirty
ONE HUNDRED FOURTEEN

253   thirty-one
DAY OF THANKS

257   thirty-two
PETRIFIED PREPARATORY

265   thirty-three
FAKING FELICITY

277   thirty-four
MAYBE NOT QUITE FINISHED

281   thirty-five
FACE TIME

295   thirty-six
THE NEW SONG

307   thirty-seven
GETTING DEAD

321   thirty-eight
REMEMBERING HIM

Every life road has a fork where fear and faith collide.

I loved this book. I resonated with this poignant and courageous memoir of a 21st century woman who secretly travelled the life-long road of hidden fear like so many other people. The fact that she pushes forward to discover that the intentional choice of faith leads singularly to the destination of freedom is compelling. It causes me to think and to see things a little more clearly for those who have had a similar life. I believe anyone from any background will profit from reading it.

LORIANN BIGGERS
CEO of Bella Vaughan, Inc.

foreword

We are all dealt a different lot in life. Some are steeped in tragedy while others overflow with ease and joy. Not one is any less ordained than another, and yet I have the deepest respect and admiration for those like my dear friend, Lisa, who have faced the darkest depths of pain and are here to say they are truly overcomers through Him who loved each and every one of us.

Lisa embodies overcoming through the power of forgiveness like few I've met. If you ever have the gift of meeting her, you will experience a woman who exudes joy. Lisa has found a way to turn her past into purpose by putting it into God's hands.

As the co-founder of a non-profit that fights human trafficking all over the globe, I have seen the deep level of resilience required to fight back from tragedy. As the husband to a woman who has overcome years of childhood sexual abuse, I have personally witnessed what it is to battle with anger and bitterness to develop a spirit of deep forgiveness.

I believe that Lisa's journey to forgiveness will challenge you on your own journey and encourage you too to give God your past so He can use it for His purpose. Her story will remind you that you too are more than a conqueror through the Father's great love for you. It is proof that even in the darkest of times, He is light and He is good.

You and I may never understand why some have to face pain and darkness the way Lisa has in this life. But, I do know that Lisa's testimony bears witness to the fact that we serve an all-powerful, loving, good Heavenly Father who will make a way.

YET, IN ALL THESE THINGS WE ARE MORE THAN CONQUERORS
THROUGH HIM WHO LOVED US.

-ROMANS 8:37

—NICK CAIN
... my friend
... Christine's hubby
... Sophie and Catie's dad
... CEO at A21
... broken mess in desperate need of Jesus

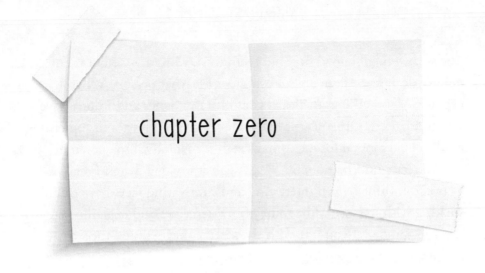

chapter zero

I am told most people skip chapter zero and go straight to the story. That's like going to the movies without having first seen the trailer. I never do that. I like having some clue about what's going to unfold and decide in advance if it is going to keep me interested enough to watch until the end.

Spoiler alert: I ran away from home. Not when I was twelve, but when I was in my fifties. I didn't put my belongings in a bandana and walk to the corner, I jumped in a Jeep and headed back to the place where I last saw me.

Wherever I go, if it comes up and I mention I ran away someone says, "I've always wanted to do that …" and their face betrays the secret that it seems everyone keeps.

But before jumping into the run, I have been advised to first tell you where I am now and what I came from. I am fifty-seven right now while I am writing this part of the story down. I was fifty-one years and nine months old when I ran away from home.

The story which follows may not seem to stay on task ... but then neither do I. Ever. I am a visual variety of learner person. When I experience something, the learn goes into my bones and I don't have a way to forget it. Other learns like auditory or reading about something tend to be temporal for me. I may catch it mentally. I may even be able to recite information, but I can't call it my own when I read or hear about things. Even interesting and captivating facts have trouble sticking with me. So, while some of my describes and explains may seem to wander, if you stay with the scatter they will tell the story because it is me beginning to experience me.

I was raised in unfailing unpredictability with three brothers and parents who stayed married for sixty-four years. My father was a combination of narcissism, brat, funny, driven, deeply troubled, handsome and violent. Long on violent. It's what I remember most about him. I have often wished he was an alcoholic so I could blame that for the cause. I never knew the cause. I still don't.

My mother was afraid and optimistic and afraid and kind and a Christian woman and afraid. Afraid of my father and afraid of most other things. The brothers and I endured and survived eighteen years each of physical, mental, spiritual and emotional abuse, affection, contorted provision ... and fear. Fear that was lightly salted with sympathy from a very few outsiders, and randomly peppered with genuine laughter inside some of our growing up houses. The laughter typically happened when my father was out of town on business.

I was sexually handled or molested or investigated or abused many times as a child. Not by my father, but by people I trusted. People I should have trusted. People that I wanted to trust because I wanted to trust someone. I wanted to be safe someplace. I did not know then that trust was a matter of worthy.

I was beaten and slapped and punished revengefully for things I did do, also for things I didn't do, and for things that never happened in our world at all because my father had a sad and bad mind and my mother couldn't stop him from his rages against herself nor her children.

I went to college and got married like most people, except I married a man who lived 5,000 miles away in Scotland. That's where I got my first genuine escape. He was old school British. Eleven years my senior. I was not immediately aware that he was pretty sure he could change me and fix me and make me more lady-like and more submissive. It took me a few months to realize that he didn't like much at all about who I was. But I was raised a Baptist, and divorce was an egregious taboo when you are from the Bible belt. So I tried from time to time to be the wife that most misinterpret from the book of Ephesians, somewhere on the right hand side of the Bible.

I lived in the west of Scotland for over seven years. It was unbearably beautiful. My house was over 150 years old, and it was surrounded by the highland hills and very close to a contented, handsome loch. I spent miles and hours and days alone discovering the less seen places. My person inside began what I now know to be a cautious restore to my original perpetual kid self.

Unemployment was very high in the United Kingdom at the time, and I was unable to find a job. So I started an export company that accidentally did very well. We had customers in Baghdad where we shipped our own label whiskey. There was a company in Nigeria where we sold frozen seafood. And then we had several customers in the U.S. to whom we shipped smoked salmon and fresh seafood to three times a week. That was until everyone lost all their money in the late 1980s and stopped paying their bills.

We went broke and had to sell everything to pay off our debts. I had such a great time with the whole adventure of finding customers and finding products and watching exchange rates and knowing how to fill out the export paperwork and creating brand names and labels. And when it was all over with, I was only twenty-nine, so I pretty much just counted it an extraordinary adventure and readied myself for another one like it.

My husband was forty when the ship sank, and his mid life crisis kicked in and he responded very differently. I was used to that. We didn't respond the same to much of anything, but this was the clear final series of nails in our marriage coffin. This was confirmed by my final act of ripping all the pages called Ephesians out of my never used Bible and slamming them into the tense horrible air between us.

During those years of living in Scotland, I had matching twin girls named Maclean and Mackenzie who did not stay on earth long enough to know me. I had one beautiful son who has stayed long enough to love me back as best he could, but currently hates me. I miscarried one child that I did not know at all, and I did not name, and I did not bury.

After twelve years that marriage was closed for business in a courtroom decree and as much as it needed to be over, I grieved it hugely.

When I moved back to Texas for good, I accidentally started a landscape company that has done well. I am still a landscaper now. I raised my son with good intentions and a poor plan and crazy love and made more than the typical mistakes of a single mom. I also did many things well, but he doesn't know that yet.

Eleven years after the divorce was final I met my husband, Tank, on an online dating site and we've now been married over thirteen years. We have a combined family of six kids. Boy, boy, boy, boy, girl, girl. The youngest is still in college. And in a few weeks when the next one shows us her gorgeous face, our grands will number twelve.

Tank is smart and kind and sometimes quiet and has fears to overcome and afraids that he has conquered. He never refers to any of our collection of children as step or half or anything except our kids. He has blue eyes and mostly he is like Santa in a shy suit.

I had no legitimate reason to run away from home. My bills are manageable and my kids are not in jail. They have jobs or classes and families, and they are healthy. My Tank is genuine and he likes me very much. I am very grateful to be in love with him.

I took an intense Ministry of the Interior variety of inventory one overwhelming morning and something inside me snapped. I could not stand the company of my parents. I had not spent time with them in years and years, but my mother had planned herself an eightieth birthday party that I was going to be expected to attend. My son had established loudly that he hated me. I was weary of the reality that I did not fit in any social circle and that I did not think like anyone else I knew. I did not like the God on any level and had not prayed since I was twenty-five. I was protected best by myself and cagey about revealing in a naked way what had made me the way I am. And the cushion of my ordinary and decent life was not a foundation that could sustain me any longer. Not even Tank could remedy my insides of crushed and confused and cower.

So, I carried a hastily packed bag out to my Jeep and drove away from my very good life.

It has been suggested to me by someone in the book business that my pages are a series of words that are not about me, but about minutia. Their take was that you might not find these chapters particularly captivating or action-packed. But, in the seeming unimportant details of the people I saw and interacted with during my irresponsible adventure, I found things out about me that I didn't know.

I could tell you more of the grim and graphic details of the various assaults on my tiny life, but those rememberings did not show me who I am. They are my facts. They are not my truths.

Until I ran away and started noticing how my think works, I did not know as much about me.

So that's what you are in for. The trivia of my travel that led to my transform. Descriptions of the ordinary that were my awakening. My notice.

There is a slow and indeliberate overcome. There is the coming to terms not with my history, but with my present—with my presence. It is not so much about what happened to me, but how it colored me. Purpose pressed by pain. Understanding wrapped in mystery.

A journey is sometimes hard. Sometimes not. Mile markers keep time and allow the grace of a reflect. Like breadcrumbs, they led me to a place I did not expect … a place so worth visiting my outlook changed. I am just another woman. I am married to a guy I love all the time and like most of the time. I am a mom and a bonus mom and a Momo. I am some people's devout friend. I am a landscaper. And I am fascinated by the human experience and its forever impact.

I think we have to ride some waves that seem daunting because the shore at the end of the foam is warm and worth a morning comb. These pages are that—sometimes terrible and sometimes familiar and sometimes amusing as they describe how I got here. Far from unusual, the instinct to flee what we no longer know how to cope with is common to us all. Maybe between these pages you'll collide with where you last saw you too.

one
TWO AND
A HALF DAYS

Dark is fascinating. It's where I can see forever if I look at the night on the sky and where I can't see my way to the bathroom door if the lights are all off.

On this night, dark is personally uncomfortable.

The window by our bed framed the city light variety of ancient dark outside. That dark. The dark of wait when I can't sleep. Tonight I couldn't sleep. I didn't particularly want to. I couldn't hush the self I was right then. I did not want to hush her. I was mildly aware. I was acutely present. I was bouncing slowly in an emotionally metal compartment of lifeless void. A vacuum. Craving a pain. Any pain that established the belief that I was losing someone. Losing something.

Minutes struggled along. It had taken a full forever to get to the last turn of a digit on the clock. Time itself had gone to sleep and forgotten to pass.

Then the ringing broke the roar of silence. I was expecting the call, but it surprised me anyway. In one motion I was picking up the phone from the night-stand and searching for my shoes in the heavy dimness of our bedroom. Tank was less asleep than I was. We hadn't been home long. We had been home forever.

We shouldn't have come home at all. I had not wanted to, but there was no room for us at Skillet's tonight. The others had arrived. The ones further up the family hierarchy had arrived from out of town. They had filled the beds and filled the house with their presence of greater importance, and I knew my job was done. I had served my purpose. Played my part. Genuinely. My needs, my wants didn't count right now. My mother's husband was going to die. My brothers were coming into town to bury their father—my father too. The father we shared biologically, but had not been unified by despite growing up under the same roof.

I had watched to see what the good thing to do was. Reluctantly. Willingly. I chose well. I left. Tank and I left. Two hours earlier.

I had straightened the bedspread where I had been laying next to Skillet. I had stopped my talking. I had stopped my listening and passed the baton to the night nurse. Before I left, I made a final trip to his side of the death bed to see what this often longed for good-bye would feel like. I had combed his white fracturable hair back with the curved palm of my hand. I had generously kissed the starved skin stretched over his forehead. I had looked a final time for the who of him.

Two and a half days earlier I had chosen this place to keep watch from. There. On his bed. Their bed. He was positioned for the inevitable. His 70 pounds of hardly alive waited, and I waited with him. I had repeatedly rearranged the blanket that covered the outline of bones his soul still called home. I had listened to his last evidences of life. I had counted the seconds between his breaths. I had watched his frozen open eyes for a blink that never came. I had watched his throat try hard to assemble a package of final words that never came to his surface. I had watched his arms never move again. I had watched his terror and witnessed his dry tears. I had changed his diapers and turned his rigidness to keep the sores at bay. I had talked with kindness that was not mine. I had told him the glories of his sons. I had played my playlist of music so he could hear my source of courage. I had loved him. I had not understood him. I had not seen him in spite of all my lookings.

I had left my last kiss on my father's cool forehead, taken my husband's present hand, and left.

Now we would go back.

Tank and I hurried out into the November dark of the driveway and drove the 12 middle of the night minutes to what had been Skillet's house only 15 minutes ago.

Linda, the hospice nurse, had noticed a change in Skillet's breathing. She had stayed with us the night before and knew the score. This was just a matter of minimizing any pain his body might be in. He couldn't tell her if he was in pain. She would watch what was left of the man and clock the time and give him drugs as both called for. This night she had seen his patterns turn for the worse and awakened my mother, Martha, who had reclaimed her corner on the bed when we left two hours before.

Tank's truck stopped in front of the brown brick house. I felt loud. Closing the door and walking on the sidewalk and breathing all seemed like bellows. Whispers seemed like dissonant clangs standing there in death's living space.

Martha met us at her garage door. We were barely past the hinges when she began explaining with some regret that she had stepped into the bathroom.

"He was still alive when I went into the bathroom," she apologized. Without looking at me she repeated herself, "Your father ... your father was still alive when I went into the bathroom."

My father. I hadn't called him a father in so many years that hearing her say it was a jar of sorts.

Her hands were awkward as she described it. Her face both sad and fearful. I wonder now if she thought I would be disappointed in her. If she felt like she was in trouble with Skillet for not being right beside him when he left. She had always been in trouble. 64 years of being in trouble. Now she seemed to be wondering what it would feel like to be scolded by the dead. A scolding to which she could not respond. A volumeless rebuke that brought her some amount of familiar cower. Comfort in the close friendship of disparage.

She said it again with her head turned a little off center, searching the wallpaper for dignity. She told us that he was still alive when she went into the bathroom.

"The night nurse had noticed a change in his breathing and woke me up ... well, I wasn't really asleep anyway. I was just dozing. I had to go to the bathroom." Her words had an elegance about them.

I reached for her but I didn't say any words out loud. I just reached for her shoulder and watched her face as the recount of events bounced out in a nervous rhythm.

"When I came out, he had already gone," she said. She paused again. Maybe picturing heaven with him in it.

I did not picture heaven with him in it. I did not say that out loud. I just knew he went to wherever it was he was going for the soul's run at everlasting time. Time with less possibility.

Skillet didn't die alone. He had the hospice nurse there with him when the chasm keepers from the other side of the veil came to take him home.

I was not disappointed in her at all. I was not disappointed for her. She had seen the dead on him a very long time. She had carried his banner to the point of exhaustion. The last exhale was between him and himself. She did not need to do this last thing for him.

As I recall it today, I think I should tell her. This now. The now of Skillet is gone and buried and everyday has moved back into position. I should ask her if she's okay with those very last measures of her responsibilities to him. I should give her some peace, give her the chance to say the thing that may haunt her. I should let her wash off any linger that maybe she didn't do this last one thing well enough. Tell her she did well. Tell her she was not in trouble this time. She would not be in trouble again. I should.

EVERY MAN MUST DO TWO THINGS
ALONE; HE MUST DO HIS OWN
BELIEVING AND HIS OWN DYING.

—MARTIN LUTHER

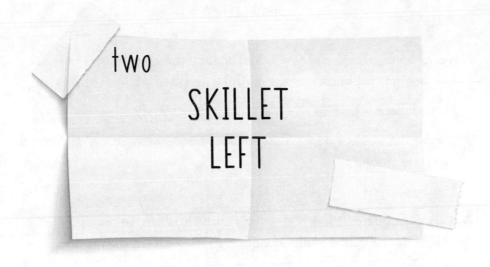

two
SKILLET
LEFT

By the time we had gotten to their house, Martha had already called the funeral home and they were on their way. They would send out men strong enough to lift the remaining 70 pounds of Skillet from his bed for the last time.

They came in through the garage so their equipment could be maneuvered easily.

They put the still mostly warm Skillet on a gurney of sorts and covered all of him with a quilt.

I liked the quilt part. It was kind. Not sterile. Not a blanket of solid white non-color. Instead it was a collection of incongruous colored cotton pieces that reassured both the dead and the remaining. Browns and tans and bland beiges. His tormented gesture made no impression through the weight of comfort laid over him. It was a gentle console for the goodbye sayers.

There wasn't much paperwork. There wasn't anything more for the graveyard shift from the funeral home to do. They offered professionally warm condolences to Martha. She smiled and thanked them. Her smile was big. They may have been taken aback by the size of it, but they didn't show it. It's their job I guess. To show up in the night and collect the deceased and be okay with whatever the survivor has to do to remain a survivor. Maybe they thought she was in shock. Maybe they just knew she was not fully aware of what was happening.

Maybe she was that. Maybe she was in some variety of shock.

Maybe she was just doing what she does best. Entertaining. Tending to everyone around her.

Maybe she was in a state of relief.

They each offered a low nod of their chins in a final expression of sympathy and rolled Skillet's body away through the garage door.

He was a garage guy. It was appropriate enough.

The house cleaning began before he left the driveway.

We took the sheets off and washed them. We pulled clean sheets off the laundry room shelf and put them on the bed that would now just be Martha's for the rest of her life.

Under Martha's direction, I gathered the unused diapers and drugs and oxygen masks. I carried them out to the garage. Some things went in a box to give away. Some things just went in the trash. I didn't try to guess what she was going to give away or what she was going to bag for the garbage collectors. She was taking clear charge of the world that was now hers.

We ran the vacuum cleaner in their room and cleaned and sterilized the bathroom he hadn't been in for weeks as if he had been carrying some transmittable infection. Maybe death is contagious.

I wondered, but not audibly, if he mostly died of a desire to depart this place. Maybe that is contagious.

It didn't take long to remove the evidence of his presence nor his departure. The house is always spotlessly clean, so we had really little to do.

My brother Buck and his family had gotten up when Martha let them know the wait was over. The awkward of death roamed around the kitchen and it helped drive the clearing. Cleaning gave purpose. It gave distraction.

Then there was nothing left to tidy and we all looked at ourselves in our clumsy griefs for a minute. The not yet dawn darkness stood watch outside.

Martha hugged us all goodnight and got ready for a few hours of sleep.

Tank and I stood for a bit. Each of us with our arms at our sides. There was no place to put them that seemed natural or courageous. Buck's family went to their beds. We went home.

I wished I missed him. Skillet was gone. I should have missed him. I didn't.

I began reconciling with the strange gratitude for these last two and a half days with him. With Martha. With the God of our making.

Now the brothers and I would bind as well as we knew how to see him to his grave.

WHEN I LAST SAW ME

three

GATHERING

Getting ready for a funeral is a strange thing. There is much to be uncertain about. Things that don't matter. Flowers and weather and people who need to be called. Did everything get said? Did too much get said? What I could be certain of was that Skillet had stopped breathing. His heart had stopped thumping. His mind had stopped racing. What remained of his human journey was inside the box he had picked out 17 years earlier when he planned for this day.

We gathered today because of the death of him, but it should have been because of the life of him. This very cold November Tuesday, words would be spoken about him, over him, for him, for his family. All kind words. Some true. Songs would be sung and prayers prayed. Today the box would be ceremoniously lowered six feet and covered in soil that workmen and a tractor had abruptly disrupted yesterday. Or maybe earlier this morning. No matter how old the hole was, it would soon be filled over with dirt and the man in the long narrow coffin would rest at the bottom.

In a little while we would solemnly enter the church sanctuary where he and Martha had long offered their tithes and presented their church faces. For now we are gathered with family and the few remaining friends in the fellowship hall.

Fellowship Hall.

A phrase that made me curious as a child.

I didn't know that a "hall" was a really big room. I thought it was just the skinny carpeted path in our house that got us to our bedrooms. I think maybe "fellowship" was one of the first church-lady words in my Sunday school vocabulary. It was an uninviting term and only church-lady men in their narrow 1960s neckties were allowed to use it in complete Sunday sentences. In my elementary school mind these Deacons of Doom had to wear glasses. They bore grim faces and it seemed to me that they only went to this "fellowship hall" to write more rules and make lists of people who didn't keep them. My early understanding of the place would change some. Later I would experience the Southern Baptist ritual of eating homemade ice cream and pot-luck lunches in the fellowship hall and fashioning words that made it sound like a fun afternoon. My belief that it was a confined space with the designation to control morally acceptable social behavior would not change, however.

Today there was food in there. No homemade ice cream.

Inside the fellowship hall there was a courteous shuffling of time and small talk. The church that wanted to comfort and support the family of the deceased had called on the bereavement committee to prepare all kinds of pasta dishes. The kinds with mayonnaise and peas and chopped squares of Velveeta cheese. I love those. There was fried chicken and graham cracker crusted pies in disposable aluminum pans for us to enjoy while the less close mourners gathered in the foyer of the "big church."

At the long tables of mostly empty chairs in the fellowship hall, we gathered into small safe groups of people. These were people we called family that we knew shared our opinions and attitudes and sentiments for the event. For Skillet. For the father. For the husband. For the late

Mr. Bass. We talked about the current. Not the past. Not about the things that had not passed. Not about things that never were.

Cousins had driven in from Pine City and Crewstone. Children of Skillet's long since exited sisters were there. A little older than the brothers and me, they had already buried their parents. The cousins were in good form. Paying respects is subjective. Some of us pay respects to the dead. Some of us pay respects to the fact that they were ever alive. Some of us pay respects to those who survived the death. Some of us pay respects to those who survived the dead guy's life, or pay respects to the ones who survived how the dead guy chose to take lives and overlook life and disregard almost everyone except himself.

> PAYING RESPECTS IS SUBJECTIVE. SOME OF US PAY RESPECTS TO THE DEAD ... SOME OF US PAY RESPECTS TO THOSE WHO SURVIVED THE DEAD GUY'S LIFE.

I had been the one to call the cousins and let them know that we ran out of Skillet.

These cousins understood. They had walked in the same war zones. They had been raised by and razed by the same darkened blood. They knew how to have parents who walked with the friends of hell. They knew how to grieve the departure with some relief and some sigh and some wish that things had been substantially different. They knew how to overcome. They knew how to see differently. How to speak differently. How to assimilate pain and distrust into fine trophies of kind and repent and prize. They knew intimately the mix that Skillet's children were feeling today.

Eventually we were told it was time to leave the "fellowship hall" and leave the conversations we wouldn't be having with people that we wouldn't be seeing if there was no funeral today. We were paraded, not yet solemn, toward the sanctuary side of the white brick building that we were trapped inside of by duty, by respect for a process. I used the march time to align the parts of me that had dashed off to other thoughts. I tried half-heartedly to wrangle the racers into an order within as we entered the welcoming corridor of the church. I was not angry. I was sad that I was not sad. I was not the sad of a daughter losing her father.

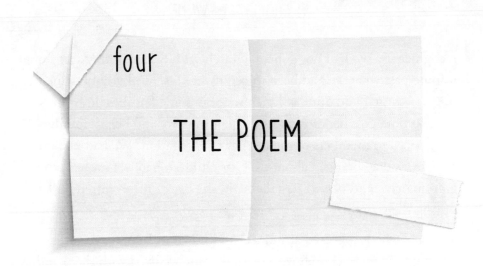

four

THE POEM

The Baptist blue paint on the walls of the foyer was subtly punctuated by the fall sun humming in through the windows. It was the backdrop of respectful as quiet people with their hushed voices collected and populated the area.

Martha came into her own as we watched her waltz about from one greeting to the next. Her clothes were perfect. They always are. She looked a bit more like she was hosting a class reunion than adjusting to loss or grief. She had grieved. She had grieved many things for many years. Grief was possibly all run out for her now. She had a job today. She had always done well when she had a job. Today she would thank everyone for coming to Skillet's funeral. She would smile and mean it and say thank you.

People commented on how well she was doing. It may have been too much gladness for those who didn't know much of the true story. I saw their eyes watch her, looking for something that wasn't going to appear. Looking for her sadness. Looking for her to break down. Even a little. There were no tears. She was genuinely pleased to see everyone who had come there.

James and I verbalized our surprise at the number of people gathering for the service. Many we didn't recognize. Just as many didn't recognize us. We had not gone to church with Skillet and Martha one minute past what we had been forced to as kids. We had not come over for church and Sunday lunch the way some families do from time to time. We had not sat near them in pews and been proudly introduced to members of the regular congregation. We had not stood near-by as they bragged about us. Our children had not sat next these grandparents and played tic-tac-toe on the back of the church bulletin during the sermon.

The ones who recognized any of us had known us from 35 years ago when we did go to church with them because we lived with them and it was required of us. Some knew us because of that. We knew some of the faces that were present only because of that small wedge of our history.

We each had a few friends show up on our behalf. Friends who knew the score. Friends who were there to see us through. Pray us to the afternoon side of this day. This event. Intercede for us. Keep us in our skin by simply being there. Offer to buy us an alcoholic beverage afterward. Watch us and report back how well we had survived later when we asked for perspective.

Taking inventory I realized that few mourners stood in the numbers.

That was disturbing.

That was reassuring.

That was true and sad and comforting and sad again.

I was not among the few mourners. I waited with intention to see if I might have some reservoir within that needed a path cleared to make it to the front of me. I asked myself to consider the gravity of this time. The father was dead. This was his funeral service. We would bury him shortly and this last opportunity would be done. I don't know what opportunity. Maybe the chance to scream or cry or inhale or spit or believe that he was sorry.

My deliberate pause remained hollow.

The un-family attenders had taken their seats inside the sanctuary. The family had gathered in a side room to get our instructions on seating and the order of the service.

Two years ago this month the brothers and I had been all together with Skillet and Martha for her eightieth birthday. That had been the first time in many years. Many years. How strange a collection of Martha and Skillet's progeny we were. Are. What a strange collection we are. Connected almost solely by our deep disconnection. So alike and unalike and so bonded by fractures. Bonded into separation by the methods of coping and integrating our pasts that we had each chosen to hold on to for a life.

This morning we were all together again. Our spouses. Some of our children. Some cousins. Some old people that we didn't know. And Skillet was there. He was already there in the "Big Church." Laying in his forever position inside the box he had picked out to spend the rest of the endlessness in.

This day we could focus on him without focusing at all. This day he had all the attention he had ever wanted and yet none of it. Today he was over. Funerals are not for the dead guy. They are for the most close of those left in the wake. The wake of a life well lived or not. The whispers and the griefs and the prays belong to the ones left to decorate the marker placed in the winter brown sod of the graveyard.

Today we are each dressed in our funeral best. Skillet was a dresser. Today we would all reflect that. We would represent that one value we had been raised in.

Sterling, Tank, all three of the brothers, and one of Pete's sons would do the honors of the pall bearers. They would also do the chore of pall bearing.

Martha would be the widow.

I would be the daughter. Not a wife today. Not much of a sister. Less even still a mother. Not at all a grandmother. None of my grandchildren would be present. None of us brought our grandchildren. Not all of us brought all of our children. We let them know. We told them so they could come if they wanted. If they were able. We did not bring them. Some did not know him. Some of us hadn't made sure they knew him. We did not want them to know the Skillet we had known. We did not need them to say goodbye with us. For us. We did not need their support. They were not there.

We filed into the church and took our places.

A prayer to open. The way things should begin. A meal. A meeting. A service. A sermon. A cross country drive. A good night's sleep. They should each begin with a pray.

I do not like out loud prayers. Skillet was a long winded pray-er and I did not like it. I like to be in the company of the prayers that no one can hear except the One who ought to. However, my last 24 months of journey had chipped at a mantel of me. There had been a few audible poems to God that I had loved being in the presence of over this recent period of my life. One or two so real that I wished I hadn't witnessed the foreignness of the affection. I felt both honored and intrusive to have been in the company of these prays. Mostly I still do not like out loud praying words.

A man in a suit had made a prayer and read it aloud and I bowed my head and let him pray his preach because now was not the time to do anything about not liking it. So I bowed my head. I counted wrinkles on my hands wondering how long they had looked this old.

But I did not close my eyes. I did not pray with him.

A man named Matthew had been asked to read the eulogy. No one in the family knew him. He read the story that Skillet had told him as true about his life. Most of it wasn't though. Skillet left out the things that were true. He named no wife. He named no children. He noted no grandchildren nor great grandchildren.

I was not sitting with any of the brothers. They were on the row for pallbearers across the Baptist wide aisle. I had no one to nudge with my elbow and say, "What the hell was that?"

I am sure my brow gave me away but no one was looking at me.

A member of the church sang a song that everyone agreed was beautiful. "I bowed on my knees and cried Holy." She may have been a paid performer. She didn't seem to be missing Skillet when she was singing.

If I could sing, I would not want to be asked to sing at a funeral service for someone I might miss because my singing voice would splinter when I realized what I was doing. My face would tear up and my cracked face would match my cracked voice. I would not do a very good job. But I can't sing. No one is ever going to ask me to sing and see my face tear up and hear my fractures at the powerful parts of the hymn and the powerful parts of the memories.

I was up next on the printed program for the deceased dearly beloved.

I had written Skillet poems as kid. I wrote many about him. For him. To him. Poems about who I wanted him to believe he was. Poems that did not say who he wasn't. Nor who he really was. He kept two. He had asked that I read them at his funeral. I told Martha that I would do that. She only found one. I would read the one that had been found.

Now I was standing there at the front of the church with a thinly posted podium between me and the forever box Skillet was closed up inside of.

I introduced myself. The daughter. I mentioned that while Skillet never had a hair out of place I always did. I pointed with my hand behind me to the words in Matthew's eulogy describing Skillet as always looking as if he just stepped out of a Ralph Lauren catalogue and made jest of not dressing quite the same as that.

A few faces smiled at the truths. The faces who knew us both.

I reminded them that despite any real evidence, I was in fact the daughter.

I looked around. I stood there about five powder blue carpeted steps above Skillet in the box and noticed my friends and some family and some people I didn't know. I explained that as a kid I had written these poems to my father. That he had asked for one to be read on this day.

I didn't tell them I wrote them hoping he would fall in love with me. Or maybe fall in like with me. I didn't say I had tried to manipulate my father with compliments and truths and lies so that I would earn his favor for even the shortest of a minute.

I knew my shame. I knew my truth. Those who knew me well knew what travesty I had committed. They didn't call me out on it. They left me to let me deliver myself. Or not.

I did say that I had been in about the fourth grade when I wrote this poem. I explained that I had written several such poems to him. That this one seemed to be the only one that survived. I described how I had laid it in the backseat of the Jeep the day before and that my own grand daughter had accidentally stepped on the page getting into her car seat.

I paused. I was thinking about not saying this next thing but the unfiltered words escaped my barely restraint. I said that when I read it last night for the first time in years and years, I realized that we might all do well to be the person our kids tell us about when they describe us to ourselves. I said that our kids will tell us the good of us. They know fresher in their memories who built us and what we actually look like. I said that we should listen to what our kids describe us as. That I should have listened to my own son. That I should listen even now.

My son was sitting there. He may have heard me. He may not have.
We don't talk much. I paused in the very silent smell of embarrassed.

Then I read my poem.

Dad, did you ever have a hero?

Well, I have this hero and I wanna tell you about him.
Now first, let me tell you what I call a hero.
That is someone who risks his own well being for someone
or something else —
maybe more than once.

My hero is something extra special.
He doesn't wear a costume like Superman or Wonder Woman.
No, that's one reason he's my hero—
he doesn't wear a costume at all.

Now he never saved anyone's life with split second timing on the battlefield.
No, he's not a war hero.
Although he's almost always in a battle
against war and hate.

He faces everything with courage.
Not wearing a bullet proof shield or even with a gun.
Sure he has protection stronger than any shield.
And his weapon won't blow your brains out. It's love.

He can speak to anyone with dignity.
Usually just a supper setting of six,
but he could as easily address a crowd of thousands
and hold his head just as high.

What more could I ask from a hero?

Love. Truth. Sacrifice. Pride. Dignity.
Beautiful ideas. And Tears.
Tears of joy. Tears of sadness. Beautiful.

Heroism takes courage.

Dad, did you ever have a hero?

I bet mine out does yours by a country mile.

I read my fourth grade poem. Emotionless.

As I finished I realized maybe for the first time that I had never said in the poem that he was my hero.

The write of my poem began as a belief that dad as hero was what I was saying. That I was going to say that. I had not. I could lie some about him. I could not lie that much. That deep. I wanted a hero. He was not it. He could have wanted to be that. For me. He didn't think about me that much. What I wanted didn't influence him.

There I stood. Black pants. Layered tops. Black and white striped shirt. Grey striped waist coat. Red jacket. Boots. Exposed. Naked. In front of the pews of people with their opinions. Laid open to their interpretations and judgments and pities and disdains.

I looked at the brothers. I looked to the brothers. We were all so young. In those years we had been Skillet's excuses for his very poor behavior. Now still just Skillet's excuses for terrible behavior and rages. They had nothing to offer me from their pall bearer section of the pew. I had nothing to offer them from my nine year old heart inside this day's 54 year old body. We knew each other. We stayed still in our stuck and graceless places of wishing it had been different. We each wondered what it would have been like to be the hero in our houses of childhood days. We had been dodgers and rescuers and hiders and liars and weepers and we had often faked laughter. We had not been champions or heroes or overcomers. But we each had a blue ribbon on our lapel for surviving.

Today we had that. Martha had one too.

I stood alone there. At the top of the steps where the preacher stands on a Sunday. I stood small and magnified. With the brothers seated in front of me and the dead Skillet still between us.

The room was funeral silent.

I didn't say anything more.

I took the very long walk back to my seat on the second row. With my physical shame I filled the gap waiting for me between Martha and Sterling's fiancée Autumn.

Preacher stood and began the preaching part.

All I can remember him saying about Skillet was that he was hard working. He didn't know that first hand. He had been told that Skillet was a hard worker. Preacher was new to the congregation and the only man he had ever known as Mr. Bass was frail and past his best before date.

A few times Preacher reminded us that Skillet was also a sinner.

I saw Martha look at her own lap. I put my arm around her shoulders. She may not have wanted that. I may not have wanted to do that. I did it anyway.

The sermon continued. Preacher spoke out of the Psalms. Number 27. Martha had told him that was Skillet's favorite passage. Preacher talked about a father who had overlooked his son. An Old Testament story that every Baptist worth his grape juice and cracker would have known. A boy called David who had been discounted by his father who would become a king despite the deliberate oversight. He talked about redemption and salvation and he seemed to hope with his tone that someone in particular was listening.

I sat. I listened. I listened for some selfless or kind piece of Skillet to be revealed that I had chosen to not remember. I sat mostly still. I tried to keep watching for the words.

The fabric of the pew was warm. I was not.

I counted chairs in the choir loft. Blue chairs.

I saw that there were flowers. I don't how many. Funeral flowers that would go to Skillet's grave with so many of his secrets. Funeral flowers that smell like expire.

The fog of un-emotion and empty settled on me. I think we sang about two more songs or maybe someone else sang. We prayed again. I don't know what we prayed for or what we prayed about or who said the pray out loud.

I was glad I hadn't worn a dress. I wished I had worn a dress. I wished I had bought a good dress to wear to a funeral on a cold November day for a father who was mine.

I had not kept watch in Preacher's words for ones that would make Skillet new to me. I had marked time in his funeral service. Today I had not been the daughter he had wanted. Again.

It was over. The words and songs and prays ran out.

five
THE FLAG
LET HER CRY

We stood and filed out with the mystery of it all on our gait. The mystery of Skillet's life. The mystery of what happens next. To him. To each of us. To any of the dead. To any of the left alive to wait our turn. To believers. To the non.

We wandered in orderly fashion back to the foyer where James and I talked to the cousins who strongly refuted Skillet's claims to poverty and sleeping on a mattress on the front porch.

Jackie's head held the angle of disturbed shock when she asked, "Who was in that casket?"

James nor I had an immediate response to match our immediate understanding.

Janet finished the sentence for all of us when she said, "The man described in the eulogy was no one I ever met. Not *my* Uncle Skillet! Those things did not happen that way ... and why was there no mention of Aunt Martha or any of you kids?"

If appall had a face, Jackie was wearing it right then.

It was a little bit funny. But not a whole lot funny.

We each tried to sort through what had been said and tried to console each other in a blend of humor and regret at the loss of life that happened long before this death.

The last of the visitors shook our hands and offered their sympathies. They nodded to us and hugged our necks and searched our eyes for grief and came up empty and went home. They each went over to the part of the day where their lives were still intact. Still in motion.

The cousins declined a trip to the cemetery to see the man off whom they didn't really know. Their agitation with his autobiographical eulogy was reason enough to get on the road to home. They were not required to stay in the company of the lies.

Most of the remaining friends and family also declined a trip to the cemetery where the bitter wind was sure to be too bracing.

Skillet's vacant life was now almost completely over. We stood and watched the parking lot empty. We drove the few minute's distance to his chamber in the dirt to bury him.

Some of us got into the limousine for family. Martha who was the widow today. Buck's wife, his two children. Me—the non-daughter. We occupied the family car, the one appointed to transport the pretend family. We tried to look like we wanted to be a family. We didn't try hard. We didn't try long.

The marines were at the graveside when we arrived in our long cold car. They were waiting to play the taps and fold the outstretched flag that had been tied to the coffin so it wouldn't blow away. Once the silence had finished being broken by the trumpet's notes, a young handsome man in uniform leaned in to thank Martha for her husband's service to our country and laid the triangle of stars in her hands.

This was the first time I had seen Martha cry that day. They folded the flag and handed it to her and she cried. I do not know what the tears were named. I doubted they were about his service to our country. I doubted that they were for the solo days ahead of her or the loss of his daily company. The grief was maybe for things we miss because they never happened except in our individual fantasies of how it should have been.

I kept my arm around her shoulders as the wind clung to its bitter. After the soldiers had folded the flag, a single young soldier handed her her husband's banner and with it her permission to cry. I sat beside her and let her. Skillet had counted the Marine Corps his greatest achievement. The most significant describer of him. His children knew that to be true. He applied Marine to every aspect of his human experience. He had liked being a Marine much more than being a husband or a father. Maybe he was good at Marine. We tend to like what we think we are good at.

Preacher held the pages down with the full stretched width of his hand and read from his Bible. It was a short read. Another pray was lifted. I did not bow my head. I did not close my eyes. I whispered my lingering screams to my insides but not to my God. I was grateful to not be mad at my God any longer. Not mad at Skillet any longer. Grief screams quietly when it is only missing things that were not.

The unjust loss. The miss. The lonesome for a grand thing that could have been and will not ever now be. There will be no restore between this father and his family. There will not be that story for the alive to tell until they are not alive anymore. The story of a father showing remorse for things done. The story of now grown children trusting the sorrow and wanting to be in the company of a new present. This collection of individuals will now be left to lay down angers and forgives and abandons on the altar alone.

At Preacher's prompting we stood. The pall bearers laid the roses from the lapels of their jackets on the forever box. A few of the few spoke to Martha again and confronted the cold trip to their cars.

I wandered off to my friends.

They looked again for my eyes. I didn't look back. We all knew we wouldn't find any funeral sad there.

The friends and I walked to the grave where my daughters are buried together. I pointed to the bronze marker that bears their names and briefly recalled the story of their short stay here. That day was a terrible and fierce funeral sad.

Martha had hoped that the brothers and I would come to her empty house and be around for a while, but no one did. The brothers made hasty departures back to their own cities hours away. They offered each other no affection. They offered no apology for their rush to escape the day. We were each empty handed. Me. Martha. The brothers. We were inside the loss we've known for most of our days. The loss of being an unclose family.

I offered nothing either. I had only stopped by her house. I had stopped to see if any of the brothers wanted my goodbye. I saw that they did not. I had no plan to stay and be the daughter I had never been.

We all left. We left and she stayed. The house empty. The remains down the road at the cemetery by now covered with dirt. Her empty now very large. Or her space finally open. She would now be the determiner of that. Would she know how?

I drove away.

Pained.

I prayed. I did not pray for courage to stay. I prayed for her loneliness. I don't know what that means. Did I pray that she wouldn't be lonely? Did I pray she would know why her children did not stay? Did I pray she would not know why no one stayed? Did not stay with each other? Did not stay with her? Did I pray that I would be forgiven for leaving her there in the ornament filled house that was so very vacant on this sterile November day? This steel colored afternoon one day short of her birthday? I know I did not pray for courage to stay. I did not pray for the want to stay. I did not pray for the permission to leave.

Maybe I wish I had.

IF YOU MEET A LONER, NO MATTER WHAT THEY
TELL YOU, IT'S NOT BECAUSE THEY ENJOY SOLITUDE.
IT'S BECAUSE THEY HAVE TRIED TO BLEND INTO
THE WORLD BEFORE, AND PEOPLE CONTINUE TO
DISAPPOINT THEM.

—JODI PICOULT

six

MR. BROWN

Two years earlier I had run away from home.

Exactly two years.

I put stuff in my bag. The bag I always travel with. So many other times I had grabbed this bag a few hours before a flight and put the weather and activity appropriate gear in it that I would need for a given destination. Some place on the globe that had draw. Some place that I had known for a day or two or more that I was going to take myself. It went with me wherever I wanted to go.

Great bag this one. I should name it I like it so much. Mr. Brown maybe. It's definitely a boy bag. Women aren't this willing to stop doing what we're doing. Not that Mr. Brown is irresponsible. In fact, he is wonderfully responsible. It's just that as women we balk at the thought of dropping what we are doing to do something that we can't immediately define as more important. Our counter gender knows when it's fishing pole and beer time. Brown gets it. He has duffle bag roominess for two pair of jeans, some layerable t-shirts and maybe a jacket, and a less casual pair of sneaks in case something dressy comes up. Big end pockets for the knickers and toothpaste and blush. The brown canvas makes it easy to spot on a baggage claim carousel and since I haven't progressed to the smarter wheel based bags, having the shoulder strap is an impressive feature.

This day I was putting stuff in my bag. This time was not like any other time I had ever put stuff in a bag to go. This time, the time had come. Some kind of time-thing that was foreign and familiar. Like a compelling moment that stopped in, stated its case, and made clear that it wouldn't wait long. Something that would haunt later if left unattended. This day and time and second where my own disabling pain collided into my strong, unstable self and the go could not be stopped.

My head was racing but the thinking was slow. I knew I needed panties. I got a cosmetic bag and a pair of jeans for sure. It's November. Late November, so I wanted a long sleeve shirt or maybe a short sleeve. Both. Tunes too. And a sweatshirt I think. And some boxers and a t-shirt to sleep in ... and my journal. There. Done. And my meds. Wondered if I got panties yet so I got some more. There. Done. And mascara. Should I zip it? Yes. Now done. And panties.

I was crying so much. Most of it the soft cry of misery and alone. Some of it that cry where I both hope someone sees me and hope that no one sees me. My face hurt where I was intentionally holding a couple of brokenness puddles just out of my own sight. I reached to touch the skin below my eyebrow where the collection of sobs gathered and realized it was to the point of dangerous overcrowding. I knew the pool was probably going to break through the skin any minute. It was a physical pain.

I couldn't stop to attend to it though. The dam would just have to give. Or not.

I took flight now. My pace was up to a clip. No feet dragging. No shoulders slumping. No full on run. My steps were heavy, but not handicapped as I followed them down the stairs.

I knew the keys would be in the ignition. They always are. We live in a quiet community where some of the casual trust of a small town still prevails. I found Tank out in the garage and told him that I had to go. I would be back. I mentioned that part too. His face probably wore stun, but I wasn't able to look up at him so I can't say for sure that's how it was shaped.

Like some kind of knight, he took the bag from my hand and walked me to the car. He asked no hard questions. Maybe he was too overwhelmed to form one. I wanted to believe that he knew more than I did about what I was doing. That his knowing of me was such that he understood any question would be too small. He put the bag in the floor of the backseat. I set my journal on top of it. Nothing would do right then except that I would have my real journal. It's giant and smells wise inside and its dog chewed where a puppy took to one corner and some pages are torn, but this was no time to be practical and take something smaller, spiraled, and inadequate. I've written in there for a decade or better. The book itself is over 100 years old and was meant to be a record of Bond Dispatching had it ever been purposefully used. I found it in a small antique store. As journals go, it's huge in size. Three inches thick with pages, a foot wide, and a good twenty inches from the top to the bottom. Taking the Giant Journal could have made either of two statements. One that I was just needing to get away and sort, or the other that I was not coming back and the journal was too much a part of me to leave behind for someone to find. It wasn't clear to me which possibility was more probable. Tank pretended to understand.

Here I slowed. I did not want him to be hurt or feel abandoned. In me there stood too little left to assure him with, so I kissed him on the chest without raising my chin and hoped I wasn't using my last breath of energy to put my arms around him. His brief hold was convincing. No neediness. No sales pitch. The genuine of him may well have

disappeared from me as I drove away. I didn't think about that right
then, but that's what a black hole tends to do with anything it gathers
that resembles love. It claims things formidable and eats them. It rids
the land of the threat of healing. Black holes are demonic. They have
no love, no light, and no god. I should have prayed maybe. I did not.

I didn't pause at the end of the drive like people do in movies when
they're about to accept some life-changing calling. This was no calling.
Or maybe it was. I didn't know if I was running away or running to.
Do I ever run away from something? Or am I running to another
something? Things were simple right here where the curb and the street
held hands. Choices basic. I only had two options and they were equal.
Left or right.

So I turned out of the driveway. Left. And west. I kind of turned west
in the barely rain and it seemed good enough.

It didn't take long to get to a highway leading out of town. I don't
remember much about those sections of road that took me out of the
bigger city next door and eventually to the fenced in browning grass
of ranch land. I'm sure I passed other cars and got passed by them.
I'm sure there were McDonald's and billboards and exit ramp options.
They must've all been painted grey that day. I don't remember them
now. I didn't notice them then.

As I drove I tried to consider if any of the other directions held better
merit. I could change my mind if I wanted. I knew south would be
limiting since I hadn't brought a passport and at some mile marker I
would run out of not only Texas, but America. No way east would help
me save myself. Trees and woods out there and if I knew nothing else,
I knew I had to breathe and be able to see a long way in front of me.
Maybe even need to run hard and fast in a direction without obstacles.
Trees would have been claustrophobic. North made me cold just

thinking about it. I turned on the heater. West was best. Maybe not good, but for sure best.

I told me that it was a completely spontaneous decision. Maybe I had wanted to run away for a very long time though. Very few ideas in the whole world are ever brand new.

I was only a pseudo runaway anyway. Real runaways don't tell anyone bye. They probably don't think about having clean underwear. They probably don't say they'll come home. They may even drink beer and shake their fists at a phantom enemy.

I wasn't following the "run away from home" rules. I don't do very many things the way they're supposed to be done. Sometimes I notice that myself. Sometimes, someone else points it out.

I was a little glad that I said I would go back, but not all the way glad.

Being in my life meant too many things I could not manage or overcome or embrace or apply my vocabulary to. And to not be in my own life meant to drive away from it.

Things were cornering me. None of them singularly significant enough to crush me. And if I had tried to garner compassion from Tank or a friend by listing them out, they would have been shamefully small things on a short list labeled trite. Maybe this was a crisis. Maybe this was just an unfortunate arrangement of elements on a time line. A crisis isn't personal. It's very personal. It's not objective. It combines facts and it collides emotions and if one person tells another person that they are in a crisis, they should be believed. I think. But I had not told anyone that I was in that much trouble. I hadn't told anyone that I was in any amount of trouble. Maybe they would have believed me. Maybe if they believed, I would have believed and then what?

If I could have listed them what would I call them? The components. I wanted to say them. Only to me. I knew I wanted to trust that saying them wouldn't diminish the struggles and the hurt, but I didn't trust.

I knew I would have to share the list with myself if I was going to raise my eyes and start looking down the road. Maybe I was ashamed of myself for running away or maybe I thought the list itself was embarrassing. Sometimes shame is in the deed and sometimes shame is just in the part where something seemingly small hurts very big. But either way, shame will keep a chin low and make it hard to see ahead.

I had no place I wanted to go. No nameable place I wanted to go away from.

Maybe the November grey gave me permission to be black and white.

Fall is the four o'clock in the afternoon on the calendar. The time of the year and the time of the day for marking time. Waiting for dinner and waiting for Christmas and the fresh start of January and another dawn. Another clean slate for restating my resolutions and commitments to eat smarter and work harder and be kinder. Fall is change when it first arrives. The wind has a different nature. It brings a certain dishevel to the morning temperatures and the lunchtime sky. Then it becomes less glamorous. The reds and caramels fall from the impatient limbs and it's not cold enough for a snowfall, but too cold for rain to seem like a blessing and it becomes difficult to love her.

This is that side of fall. This is that side of marking time. The side where I did not know things like what I wanted to do now.

Or maybe I did. Maybe running away or running to was on my list. The list I make of things I'd like to do before I go. Things I've compiled that I think might somehow add to my collection of human experiences like go hoboing on a freight train and sky diving and be homeless for a minute or join the Peace Corps or spend a year volunteering in a refugee camp. Things that might fall under the header of conquer or integrate or leave my mark, or things that have no nobleness at all. That list. Maybe this very time was on the list and I hadn't brought it to my own attention just yet.

I can do that. Not tell myself something. It's always a fascinating unfolding though, once my heart lets my head in on something it knows. And certainly there are some things on that list that don't make much sense to anyone but the core of me. The middle of my person that is less protected than the surface.

Like one time, not long after I married Tank, we were at a friend's wedding down in Gruene. A sweet, young man was marrying the most-great woman he had ever met. I got to take the pictures. Sterling was there, my son, and some other good friends. Lots of rich atmosphere and all the usual wedding air of blending families and their greatnesses and their not so greatnesses. It was busy and simple and magic.

The town also had a fantastic water tower. Old enough to have a shape that would have been modern several decades back. New enough to still be the water tower in use. It was painted silver and the name Gruene blended perfectly with the proportion of patina and rust.

Climbing a water tower had been on my list.

It had to be the perfect water tower, so I hadn't done it yet. This seemed to be her.

Tank may not have been sure that I was actually going to go through with it, but once all the wedding festivities were done and there were no more pictures to take I made my way out to the tower. He was close by and did say out loud at least once that he didn't think this was a good idea. By the time I found my way over the lame attempt to stop trespassers that some would describe as a fence and barbed wire, he knew his input had not been regarded. Tank stepped back and dealt with his anxiety about it by taking some pictures of me. For me. The police arrived soon and in an almost convincing fashion shouted orders that I needed to come down immediately. By then I had momentum and the illegal part had mostly been committed so I responded courteously that I would be right down. As soon as I had gone to the top.

Once the ascent and descent were over with, I got in more trouble with the police and it scared Tank and we were kicked out of town and the tower turned out to be taller than it seemed from my ground level view point and I didn't have on my "Water Tower Climbing" shoes. And I would do it all over again. And I may. Next time I will stay longer at the top and absorb the sweet pink sunset laying long and slow on the top edge of the soil at the end of my sight.

The thing about going up a water tower is that it didn't get me any closer to a drink.

This decision may not either, but I was willing to consider that it might be on my list.

And this departure may have the same dread effect on Tank as the water tower climbing event did. I deliberately picked to not put his fears in my bag this trip.

seven

CHRISTMAS LIGHTS IN 1968

It wasn't a lot of miles before I noticed I was hungry and stopped for peanut M&Ms® and a diet cherry Dr. Pepper®. I was surprised that I had enough presence to notice that the Jeep was low on gas, but I did notice. So I bought some gas too. West of Grove now I sat at the pump long past the need to be there. I ate an M&M. It didn't taste yellow. I tried a red one and then didn't want any more. The Dr. Pepper burned on my dry throat and I put some lotion on my face where it seemed to make crackling noises from the layers of dried up drops of flying solo. I turned the key in the ignition and let the compass on the dashboard remind me how to get faced west again and I drove. Drove toward a sundown that wasn't showing itself.

Even in the grey there were signs of dusk approaching, and I don't like dark, so I figured I would try to make Laney my destination this night. I was in no way ready for the day to be closing out and I was less grieved than I thought I should be that the further I drove, the less likely it was that I would want to go back.

The road itself wasn't turning out to be much of a companion. Not very engaging or interesting or interested. Not offering anything comforting. Not giving the respect that a runaway is due. Just rolling out in front of me like a two lane concrete yawn and taking no responsibility for the journey. Maybe this wasn't a journey. Maybe it was just a trip. Or maybe it was going to be big. Big like a quest or an adventure or a bank robbery adrenaline rush thing.

This four-hour void behind the wheel had not been enough time for me to begin to know how to break down the pains into bites small enough to chew on. I mostly felt like each new thought only added to the fear of the old ones and put me too close to the sidelines of something resembling a near fatal car wreck. The collisions we've all witnessed where for many minutes we can hear nothing but the loudly muted sounds of Detroit pressed metals whiplashing. That distance that sucks in the observer of the crash and rapidly transitions their status from innocent bystander to a forever altered victim despite not being in the wreck at all.

It's an alone thing. One more alone thing. No matter how big the crowd of bystanders.

No matter how many people in a family. My family. It was an alone thing.

I have three brothers. Two are older, one is younger. All are bigger. James is the oldest and we all think of him as the smartest and nicest and kind of sagey. Buck is the baby. Pete and I fill in the gap.

Maybe I wanted to remember who I belonged to. Ask if I belong to anyone. The brothers maybe. Where did I fit in that unit? Did I fit?

The present moment paused my thought.

A man on a ladder in front of a small house along the north side of the highway was hanging Christmas lights over the porch. A woman was helping from ground level. She was handing something up to him. A screwdriver maybe. The lights were already plugged in and on. I could see the colors from the road.

One Christmas when we were kids, Buck and Pete stole some lights. Not boxes of lights at a store, the boys had been all over the neighborhood unscrewing bulbs so that the strands would be missing colors that night when people started plugging them in to display their Christmas spirit, or to at least do what all the other houses in the neighborhood were doing. It was the 60s so everyone had those long roundy shaped bulbs about the size of a man's thumb that came in 4 or 5 painted on colors including orange and blue and no one questioned the seasonal validity of those two. It was a still a time when most things weren't questioned in a small town. Sometimes the color would chip off and expose the element inside a little—the same way life chips at skin.

You could tell which houses had which influence. Mom-run houses would have an alternating pattern or maybe all green and red lights. Dad houses and houses where moms were grateful for any help they got from the dads, were all colors with some replacements that didn't match at all, and no distinguishable pattern to the colors. But both categories always hung their lights in very straight lines along the front edge of the shingles. It was Levelland. A conservative, predictable, community of people that wanted to do things right. A sense of order typically prevailed. It was important that this message be reflected. No expense on nails was spared to make certain the cord of lights be exact by the light of day when the dark green string was visible as well as by night when the electric bulbs went on.

I don't know how the boys got to the lines of bulbs hanging on the front eaves of some of the homes of their victims. The mission of two brothers must have included the added adventure of climbing on rooftops. Some lights they just took from trees in yards and front porch decorations. Apparently they spread their Christmas capers over several blocks.

Somehow my birth order providers, Skillet and Martha, found out about the misadventures before dark and the inquisition ensued behind the closed door of the big boys' bedroom.

On this December afternoon, the yelling and cussing and face slapping had warranted no confession of the little boy crime binge and the next level of violence that they called discipline wasn't far behind. I listened closer now. With my skin and with my palms that were now instinctively pressed on the door. I listened with my words of rescue as they formed in my head. Or maybe my heart because that's where I did some of my thinking.

I heard a silence. A long gap between strikes of words and fists.

Buck broke first. He was only a first grader, but knew the score already and he knew how to avoid an anticipatory blow with a limited confession. From my side of the door-shaped barricade I could hear the pause and see his familiar pose forming. He was undoubtedly beginning to slump those chubby boy shoulders and lower the brow of his look of innocence at a slow, but noticeable rate. His blue eyes would have contain intentional levels of welling and his blonde hair would be untidy enough to be edible. Then stretching out the last bit of affordable silence, he sniffled and blurted his words out in a well-rehearsed, remorseful mumble.

"I stole a light."

"I only stole half of one though."

He may have pointed toward Pete when he continued, "Pete broke it."

Emphasizing, but not over emphasizing that he didn't break it himself.

There was another stretch of silence on the boys' side of the door. Alone on the outside of the hinged wood, I was busy straining to catch my cue to bust in and save someone when the door got yanked out from under my ear and Skillet and Martha both ran out of the room to where Buck couldn't see them laughing. So far as I knew they had never laughed anything but sinister when we were in trouble before. I was caught off guard. This was not an evil laugh. They thought this was very funny. More than likely, Skillet got a kick out of it and Martha had the good self-preserving sense to laugh with him. Either truth netted the same result within me. The sound of that moment created an indelible file in my library of reactions to pay attention to. I noted the power of humor that day. No one got beat. The terror was set aside because the six-year-old Buck had no idea how funny his lie-riddled confession was.

I relived the event. The anticipation of violence in our growing up years had been as tormenting as the physical blows themselves. The unpredictability had been the consistent theme that had kept my life in a state of on guard. The emotional shrapnel began peppering me now. I needed to stop. I shortened my goal from where to stay for the night, to the immediate need to stop and put my shoes on some piece of ground that was a present moment. I took the next exit off the highway and turned down a road leading to a nameless congregation of squared up stacks of brick and mortar.

A SUDDEN BOLD AND UNEXPECTED
QUESTION DOTH MANY TIMES
SURPRISE A MAN AND LAY HIM OPEN.

—FRANCIS BACON

eight

CLOSED DOORS

Since I didn't need gas or any more M&Ms®, I picked a parking lot that sat empty. From the front seat I thought the place in front of me looked like a mechanic had established his business there a long time ago. I liked the character of the building. Cinder block construction most recently painted white. Judging by the stains and peeling and the more gold than yellow overlay it had given into though, I decided that this most recent coat had been applied at least a decade ago.

The building beside it was less interesting. Invisible at first. I had to know I was looking to even clock that it was there.

I got out of the car to get the Giant Journal out of the back seat, but liked the way I could be sure I still had life just by the slide of gravel under my feet, so I walked away instead.

I went the 30 or so steps to the building's door and touched it. The layered paint was flaky and damp from the current weather. Before this rain, it looked like it had been a long time since any measureable degree of moisture had settled on its surface. The door had a glass panel in the top half, but the pane where view into the shop was once available was now covered with splitting plywood placed on it from the inside. A self portrait of sorts I thought. A familiar was present. Doors that I am on the alone side of. Doors that separate and protect and give undue courage to those who prefer that the dark cover their crimes. I felt the tense come into my skin.

The handle was a knob. Probably not the original door handle. Too small for this door, dark and round and not attached securely, so it was hanging left of center on the weathered metal plate it shared with a key hole. I took my hand out of my pocket and tried the knob, already pretty sure that I wouldn't go in even if it opened. It did not. The fact that I couldn't go in gave me permission to tell myself that I would have pushed it open and entered, but the locked-ness stopped me.

Usually there wasn't time to go to a room or shut a garage door or get in the house before the terror du jour began. But the dynamic had been different somehow on the day of the Christmas light thefts. It was maybe less ugly and I wasn't allowed in to do what I do in cases of emergency, so I had stood by the door ready to bolt in if Martha opened it. She would do that. To me, it seemed like she did that every time Skillet's temper went on a hostage taking trip, but good sense reminds me that she couldn't have relied on me every time. She would just open the door to a room of violence. It was my signal to come in and cushion the air and the strikes and the Hitler-like screams. Get between Skillet and the object of his impacts. Absorb some of the madness and threat and restore possible. I don't know who reached hopeless quicker in these episodes, the victim of the moment or Martha, but Martha had learned that Skillet would slow to breathe when I came in on most incidents. He might even breathe twice or just deep enough to interrupt his own momentum. Most of the time, something had to be said or done to break up the charge of his rage.

I backed away from the closed door that wouldn't open when I turned the knob.

There were several windows on the front of the building and more down the right side. They were metal framed, coated in blur, and of themselves storyless. I loaned them my observation for a minute and knew I was not interested at all in looking through them nor in them nor at them. Their browness rang soft alarms of warning. Sometimes if darkness is too far away from light I can't make myself look at it and looking in these soundless windows at dusk in the fog held the potential to reflect a face I didn't want to see. I had to take good care of myself right now and getting within range of some kinds of certainty would be another layer of weight I was pretty sure I wouldn't be able to carry.

I took a couple of steps backwards in an almost sudden kind of way and kept watch on the windows to be sure the fabric of them didn't follow me as I made my frugal get away.

Soot is thick and it comes in a lot of shades and shapes. It is neither ash nor the fire. It's the stuff that doesn't get completely burned up and rests its message on things it should pass over. I am afraid of dross and darkness that I can't get away from. I need to know that I am going to be able to switch on a lamp or reach my hands in a direction that includes light. Clean light. Clear light. Skillet figured that out about me early on and kept it as a tool to enhance the forms of punishment that he called motivation. The terrors of his insides often woke in the night and the slags began their assault on him. Violence was his great comfort. The bowl of soup that fed him in his sickness. He knew that he was one of the reasons that I knew night inside a house to be untrustworthy. He knew, but never said aloud, that his rages and his unpredictability had made me dread sundown. Maybe he didn't know how deep it would stay in my flesh and in my blood.

There are the other people who make the color of night unholy. They first visit a child when the light is dingy. Their violence is different. Quieter on the outside. They come into a child's room feigning gentle. Pretending for a moment to love. They talk sweetly. Check on you.

Then force their demons on the very small you. Later those people get braver and no longer limit themselves to shadows. The ones who linger afterwards in the dreams and nightmares of a child. The ones who leave their smells behind and stain everything. I was one of those children that those adults found. There are more of us than not. We may not all be afraid of the dark. Some of us are angry. Some of us are cowards. I am both. I am all of these.

I was little. I learned to notice that shade cloaks those two kind of adults. The adults who lurk and the adults who rage when the dark switch gets flipped. And I had learned to notice the other kind of adults who turn the other way. Adults who each feign appall when others describe the very same horror that they themselves commit or allow.

My ashamedness was visceral now. It made me present again.

I finally unburied enough courage to turn my back to the color I considered to be not quite night behind the windows that I didn't want to look into and walked back to the car. I brought the Giant Journal out of the backseat this time and clicked a pen hoping to be able to think some thoughts onto paper.

The lined and empty page stared better and longer than I. No words happened. I needed something besides lostness to wander out of me.

In the back seat sat the God I didn't like much. It felt like He was watching over my shoulder to see if I would start a note to Him. I didn't. He may have reached for my hand. It seemed like maybe He did that. My hand drew in closer to me as if it had a mind of its own. It did not reach back to hold His. I didn't want to hold some skinny, boney hand. That's how His hands seemed to me. Scrawny and awkward and frail. I did not look for Him. I didn't wish that He was hoping for me. Or maybe I did. I probably did wish He was hoping. Maybe. If I did, I only wished He was hoping for me so that I could say no. But it was okay the way He sort of let me be alone. He was staying for a while. I stayed there too. In the Jeep, in the parking lot with no other cars, in the town I didn't know the name of, in front of the two buildings.

What got me this close to the edge of a spiritual cliff where the thought of jumping off held as much invitation as it did terror? What would jumping off look like anyway? I wasn't in search of death. Maybe I was in the middle of death. Maybe the death was the pile I stood on top of now. That made a strange and small amount of sense for the moment.

It's not like I could quit. Once a thing has life, then it is. It cannot be quit. Not a decision or a marriage or a child or a turn at a traffic light. It got created and just because I don't want It anymore doesn't make it possible for me to stop it from being anymore. I can leave or try to forget or stop paying it my attention, but I cannot make it be not alive once it has been created.

I waited to see if good questions came to my heart or my mind. They did not. Nor did any words. No epiphanies. No lyrics from a song. Eventually I stepped back out into the mist to put the ledger in the backseat. The gravel sounded disturbed. It had forgotten I was there. The scent of the building seemed briefly disrupted. I apologized to both of them under my breath. I set the Giant Journal safely on the back seat and climbed back behind the steering wheel, buckled my seat belt and got back to the business of driving no place.

I listened to tunes from my ipod and watched the road and cried smaller amounts for a while.

Laney seemed to be just ahead for a long time. As if I would not get there in time. As if I would get there before I was ready. I didn't want to be driving anymore, but I didn't really want to stop. I came into town and took the loop around the perimeter where I eventually found several hotels together. La Quinta won.

nine

WATCHING ME

Dawn is there when I wake up for the last time. She was subtle. A dull rise of pink charcoal brushed drops of spider web colored water. I am relieved that the air is thick. I look out the window of my second floor hotel room onto a highway with few cars. They are all traveling in packs of four or five at that "limited visibility" speed of pseudo caution. The sky is not clear. I am not clear. The idea of a crisp dawn breaking would have been too hard today. I deem the fog a gift and say so out loud. Then I paused. I had not thanked the God and I would not thank Him. As far as I knew, He was still in the Jeep. He would not have heard me.

I laid back down after my interview at the window. I find I have lost the comfort of tears. I am not less doleful, just the burn will not roll up from my chest now. The loss of this one sure thing stops my beating for a moment. I take a short gasp and slow the march on of my life as I've known it. Then I wait a moment for the rhythm of breathing to restore itself. It was warm there under the beige blanket so I stayed longer. I didn't turn on the news or check the weather. I didn't stare at the ceiling that I know of, but my eyes were open and I was looking there.

I knew I needed a plan, but had no gumption to make one. It didn't overwhelm me to think about it, it just wasn't going to be thought about right then. I closed my eyes for a while and got all the way to seven o'clock that way.

A few times I heard a door shut in the hallway and the canned air unit turned itself off with that closing rattle sound once it made it to the 74 degrees I digitally requested.

Coffee. I went downstairs for coffee. Coffee fixes everything. I made two cups. One cup with vanilla flavored creamer and one with hazelnut. Back in my room I pulled a chair to the window and drank the stimulant while I waited for nothing.

Like me, both cups were empty. Mine was the kind that marries "busting-at-the-seams" to "10,000-pounds-of-broken" empty. Then the marriage produces children called Scattered and Distraction. The cups I drank the coffee from were just void-of-coffee kind of empty.

With nothing left to drink, I talked myself out of the chair and into the shower. I was pretty excited to find that I had a razor and my own shampoo. I had packed a bottle of body lotion and my "sticky up hair glue." From the three shirts in Mr. Brown, I dressed in the short sleeves thinking I may need the long sleeves another time. I amused myself by counting the pairs of panties I grabbed in my rushed departure. Seventeen. I smiled in spite of myself. "We're good on panties," I say to no one, but the saying felt good. Jeans and socks now in place on my skin, I gathered the goods of my past life and zipped them safely inside Mr. Brown.

I was ready to go now. Or at least I was not ready to stay any longer. I collected my stuff and let the door shut behind me before I shuffled with a medium sure foot to the elevator. I would cause myself to get on if it was empty. It was. I did.

I could travel most of western America and not find a hotel elevator that stood out from the others. Three floor buttons and space for 1,000 pounds of people. A phone for emergencies, fake wood panels, and the sound of no one getting attached to the place. Temporary the dominant color.

Then there's the lobby. Attempts at warm are stamped out in some corporate home office in some important big city and some executive sends some code to some franchise owner about creating ambiance. The result is consistent and predictable. A couple of striped fabric chairs and a couch with a low table in front of it are brought in so that management has a place to set those universally vanilla silk flower arrangements in ginger jars. A white glass dish of hard candy on the counter in a dull attempt to feel like grandma manages the place or to compete with the gorgeous crunchy red Macintosh apples that the Fairmont sets out in handsome bowls around their resorts. Seven steps later though, and it's those bisected walls of acceptable colored paint on the top half and "this season's hottest wallpaper" from six years ago on the lower section and the warm lobby feel is all smudged out anyway.

It's the kind of hotel where a person might stay during a life-changing event like on the way to Jackson Hole for the first time or the place a night was spent after a friend in another state left this life too soon. These are they. The halls of rooms filled with people who may have smarter grandchildren and busier lives than us. The hotels that participate briefly, but do not become part of the memories. The walls are too slick and the plastic too prevalent to absorb or remember things that count. They are not landmarks. They are just fine. Fine can be repulsive. Fine doesn't make it to the file cabinet of a person's history.

At the check-out desk I realized that I couldn't remember checking in, but I didn't say it out loud. The manager on duty gave me a receipt to sign and asked me with some delight and a foreign accent, "Where will the road take you this morning?"

"I do not know." I answered.

He looked up from the routine of the process, blurted his words and said, "Fantastic! Sometimes I just want to do that myself." I heard his proclamation. All of it.

I looked up at him. I tried to see his eyes without him seeing mine, but he had already glanced them down again to his business on the front desk. He appeared contrite, as if he had said something out loud that was meant to remain in his interior where he could hope to not hear it. Something sacred. And he needed now to pray for forgiveness.

I understood.

His name was Paresh. Like Perish. Like the thing that might have happened to me if I hadn't called in sick to my life.

I signed his copy of the charge slip and slid it half the distance across the counter toward his computer screen. I kept my fingers on it in case he wanted to look up at me again. Maybe go back to that thought. My pause was long and deliberate. I eventually lifted my hand from the bronze tinted formica top. The dialogue was over.

I went to the car.

I had Mr. Brown in my hand and Giant Journal under my arm. I noticed the flowerbeds as I walked through the stucco coated porte-cochere. Some periwinkles and lantana were hanging in despite November on the calendar and even still had some blooms. And there were about fifteen sun faded plastic flowers stuck in the ground to make up for the waning brightness of the live ones. I got in the Jeep. In the front seat I paused to scribble a note down about the exchange with Paresh, afraid I would forget. I do that. I forget to remember. I forget to remember what I went to the store to get, and I forget to remember who I love. So I wrote it on the notepad I had picked up from the room. Then I tore off the pages I'd written on and set them in the backseat on top of the Giant Journal until I would write them down for good where important stuff was recorded and kept from being lost or forgotten.

A strangely regular day was happening out here in front of the La Quinta. The predictably reliable hotel sitting on the frontage road of a highway. A wide roadway that takes people to and from or past people and adventures and catastrophes and the mundane and the celebrations. Outside was just like inside where no one notices that a mortal that wanted to be seen was invisible. It was not an offense. Each person was just doing the things that come with the light of their regular days. The same way it goes on every day. Minds pushing their bodies into motion while some part of them is wanting to scream or run or be anything except overlooked. Each wanting to count. Wanting to be reminded of how we each fit in and that we belong. Wanting to not have to ask to be noticed. Knowing that being important is relative. Just wanting to not have to do something important in order to warrant a glance or a longer, warmer look.

Maybe my pronoun is wrong. Maybe it's not about a we, not about a population. Maybe it's just me.

Now it is here again. My truth is chasing me and I am chasing it. And I am running from it while not taking my eye off it in the rear view mirror. No one knows. It does not matter. I have left the confines of my lonely circle. I think I do not matter. There's a liberty in that. And a responsibility. And a breaking.

I take a brief stock and decide that I am fortunate to be going after time slowly today. I can respect the dead. Most can't do that this morning. I can. I ran away yesterday and minutes are different now. I can remember the way it was before. I can look for how it can be now. I can be my honor guard or not, but certainly no one else will be.

I wished I had taken a picture of something here to mark the end of day one or was it the start of day two? I had no camera. I felt anxious.

I would be safer if I had one. With a camera I could remember the things I wasn't able to see.

I find a Best Buy in town and tried to think like Tank. What would he buy? I laugh. He wouldn't buy anything without some research. I know I'm not going to research anything right now, and I know I'm not going to ask any real questions of the well qualified blue shirted staff about cameras. I choose something small with a familiar brand name that doesn't cost a fortune and applaud myself for remembering to get batteries and a memory card for it.

It's now 9:30 and here I am again. In a parking lot. Now equipped with a camera, a compass, and tunes. I checked for my own breathing as I sat. Still doing it. Still breathing. Maybe I was glad. I don't know. Then I waited for the signal inside to tell me it was time to go home, but no urge came.

I didn't even realize that I had been watching them as I sat waiting to tell myself what to do next. Two people in a car. They were just two people in a car. Next to the site of my technological shopping experience stood a sparsely populated Target store. Their likely destination.

They had pulled into the row of spaces across from me. I saw the expression on her face first. Empty. Not sad. Not depressed that she knew of. Then I saw the expression on her hands. It was more apparent on her hands. Where she couldn't mix it with distracting features like crinkled eyes and high cheek bones. She had always been a pretty girl and mostly still was. One hand was on the wheel now. It was the dominant one she had used to ride the lines of the static parking space when she came rushing in to land her travel craft. She had that harsh flare as if she was going to win a prize for speed and agility. Her life had required it of her. Speed and agility. And now they were words not to be used separately. They were part of most things she did. In her mind there were never any points off for inaccuracy so the tires being slightly over the line was inconsequential. I think she should have received bonus points for maintaining the cigarette perched between her first two fingers from which no ash had fallen during the maneuver. Her other hand had gone to the assistance of a flexible shoulder where her cell phone was balanced. Holding the phone that way kept her head off center but no more than her life had done. She looked as if she was surely accustomed to looking at things from this unnatural angle that didn't look unnatural on her at all. I imagined I could hear it in the tone she spoke with to the person on the other end of the call. Possibly a war torn sister that had called. This was her norm. Her evolved natural where fret and energy are synonymous and as close as she gets to peace.

I couldn't actually hear her. The windows were rolled up and she hadn't gotten out of the car yet. But I could see her voice. I could see it in the tilt of her head. It was hoarse and complex and irritated and sympathetic. And I had no idea who she was really speaking to. The person had to have some merit or she wouldn't have even attempted engagement. She has no time to waste. I assigned the invisible caller the role of a sister down on her luck. More needy than the fast parking girl with the ash stacked cigarette. It was apparent that the sister she was speaking to though, needed to be careful because this patience wasn't going to last but a few more minutes. The girl in the driver's seat had dropped her right hand to shove the gearstick into park and looked in the rear view mirror at herself. Her reactive glance over her shoulder into the backseat ratted her out. She had almost forgotten that she wasn't alone. The discovery of another passenger closed the deal on the phone conversation patience thing. Her ear came off her shoulder and she grabbed the phone with a sharpness that was almost audible.

The cigarette suffered a deep draw as she reached across the width of the seat to pull a larger than needed purse into her lap. The sister would have to get a grip right now or be subjected to some low budget therapy session about standing up for herself or shooting the loser boyfriend/husband/boss/customer/father. Then the driver's side front door flung open from the inside and early winter flip flops hit the pavement one behind the other while the weighty purse travelled quickly over her left shoulder trying to settle into place. The call was wrapping up. It was already over for her, but she made a half-hearted attempt to finish listening without mocking the speaker. I saw it be over then. She hit the red button on her phone and punched it into her bag. She would be forgiven for her abrupt behavior. She always is. And as she opened the backdoor to free her passenger, she knew she'd be forgiven for having forgotten about her too. She takes being forgiven for granted. She doesn't forgive easily but she demands it for herself. It shows in her posture. Her shoulders are rolled forward that bit too much that reveals a willingness to take out any person who gets too close, says the wrong thing, or doesn't buy her bluff.

The little girl in the backseat had gotten out and used both hands to push the car door closed now. I determined through no scientific process that they were distantly related as mother and daughter. The part-time child hesitated. She knows she's supposed to hold someone's hand to cross over the parking lot lane to the front doors of the store. Her hands get ignored. Not intentionally ignored, but the ignored way people behave when they don't know any better. From where I was observing, it looked like the girl may go more places with a grandmother than this mother. The system of relationship is not translating well into this trip out with her grandmother's daughter. Grandma wasn't there to help dress her this morning either. The little girl's tan hair wasn't brushed and I had to think neither were her teeth. Her clothes weren't dirty or clean and the top she wore didn't match the pants nor clash with them nor profess poverty. Most of all though, her face didn't match her step.

She couldn't seem to look anywhere except at her mother. The mother she walked behind and below. The mother she could only see the back of in reality. At least in my reality. In her true world, she saw her mother's expression with the clear eyes of a knowing child. Children see with the air they feel and nothing changes the temperature like the temperament of a parent around a tender child looking for love. I saw all forty pounds of the smaller, sweeter person forming plans. She knew how to please this mother. She had done it most of her five or five and a half years. She was planning her pleasantness. Not too pleasant. She didn't want to become a pest. She would make sure also to not wipe her nose on her sleeve or drag her feet when she walked. And she would resist any urge to skip or ask for anything like Lucky Charms® or a Pillow Pet®. If mom tried on any scarves or held any shirts on hangers up to her chest, she would be sure to compliment her. These plans were good and proven to work. If all goes well, her mother may reach down and stroke her hair or make some other gesture of affection. She hoped she wasn't setting her sights too high. I watched her glance up again to see the face of her mother from behind.

They entered the store and disappeared. I wondered to myself if she had seen me, would she have known that I am her all grown up the way I know she is me several life changing gates ago. I named her. Emily. A gentle name. Kind and smart and pursuant of peaceful laugh. Not like Sammi. The name I carried. A name that sets up an expectation of hardy and knock about.

My own mother was self-consumed like hers. More clever in her disguise of it than this mom, but she met her own needs to be the center of the universe when Skillet wasn't around. Her approach was similarly different. She would have counted herself much smarter than the woman with the half parked car and the half smoked cigarette. It was how she fueled her will to live. It seemed that she only filled up so Skillet could drain it all out of her later. They both needed her tank to be full. He lived in the insatiably empty. She lived wanting to want to be more than a pretty face. Neither sure who they were.

Martha's clothes were high end and her cars were glitzy and she made sure her kids bore a lack luster reflection of those values. I was scolded about not being girly enough and made fun of for not knowing how. The clothes she chose for me felt awkward and looked awkward and I knew there was a fine line between looking cute enough to be with her and looking cuter than she did. It was smarter to select an appearance dimension removed by miles from hers so I did. I just stopped trying to measure up to her gold standard and grew my own. I liked hats and layers of shirts and plaid jackets and tennis shoes together. I could take the hand me downs of my brothers and manage pretty well to get dressed for school. Church was her main battle ground. She could blame her rules of dressing up on her God. By the time I was a third grader we had come to something of a truce. It began to feel like a compliment when she would roll her eyes over something I was wearing.

This is the mother I didn't know. Didn't feel known by. The years of time as Skillet's wife had made her cryptic.

LOTS OF KIDS HAVE TO BE THEIR OWN SILVER LINING.

This little girl was wearing that same future. The garments of a kid who might compete and therefore needed to be subdued. Lots of kids have to be their own silver lining.

The car the parallel twosome left parked confirmed the story the mom and the girl were playing out. It was a light brown four door that several people with marginal goals had owned in its eleven or twelve year life. It was accustomed to being parked in places that minimized the walking time for the driver. The doors had several dings in them and some chips of missing color. It sat a little closer to the ground than it should have. Not like an intentional effect where some teenage man had tricked it out to look tough, but the low look of worn shocks and low quality tires. A reflection maybe of the owner. I guessed that the seats doubled as shelves holding homework pages and directions to a missed job interview and several wrappers from gum and candy bars and a few empty drink containers. The driver's side seat was likely worn most where she often hit the side of it with her bag and the pocket of her jeans while making her hurried, landings in the front seat. The car really didn't seem to mind any of this. It remained dutiful despite the neglect. It didn't draw any attention to itself and had been denied as belonging to the owner several times. Not a car that anyone is proud of anymore, but can't be parted with because it's still useful.

I wanted to walk behind them around the store like a guardian angel and let the little girl see me keeping an eye on her. I wanted to be invisible to the mother. And I considered waiting for the pair to come back out so I could be sure that the little one succeeded. A modified rescue.

I did neither. I did not follow them around the store and I did not wait for them to come back out to the car. I knew how the story played out. I turned my look a different way now.

I had become uncomfortable sitting here. Not parked. More like in neutral with no coast. Going—actual moving—brings an assurance. Neutral is less directed than sitting at a light waiting for it to turn green. It's a kind of horizontal free fall. And parking is preferable to stalling out or getting stuck. Parking is choosing a space. Putting myself in a place deliberately and not moving until I have looked at a map or taken a rest or gone into a gas station for a pee. I was not parked.

The "stop this and go home now" signal was a no-show so I rolled out north on the loop in pursuit of west.

Where the roads intersected I noticed a sign for Sweet Creek and thought the name too perfect for a time such as this. I will maybe stop there. Maybe. If I keep going a direction that takes me there.

ten

COUNTY ROADS

There was the Interstate option, but racing in the rain alongside stressed drivers had no appeal. I had no desire to be among drivers that knew where they were going and either wanted to get there or didn't. So I drove the frontage road a while before determining through a process that was no process at all that the next county road on the right was mine for the taking. Mine and mine only actually—I didn't see another car for an hour and a half. The thought crossed my mind that I could end up in someone's barbeque recipe never to be seen again. I laughed out loud. I noticed that my laugh was a little more nervous than genuine. That made me laugh again and laughing broke loose the dam that was holding my cries back. Then the mantra kicked in where I told myself I would be okay and that eventually I would want to go home. How many of me were in the car together at that point I do not know, but I was glad we were all there.

I said one. I whispered it so softly that it made no noise at all when I nudged the air of speaking over my lips. Since I didn't break, I tried again. I said my words again with a less timid attempt.

"I don't fit."

Noise this time.

"I don't fit," came out loud enough the third time that I heard me. So from my heart I added to it, "I don't fit and I don't know what that means."

It was one truth. I don't fit and I don't know what that means.

I don't blend though. My words are usually ill-fitted and my shoe choices make my proclamation invalid in people's minds. My claim falls flat that I want to look like the others. Sound like them. Hear like them. One day I will fit into a box though. On that day they will take an inappropriate amount of my husband's money in exchange for lowering the one box I fit in six feet below grade in a granite pocked park of fake flowers on long hard plastic stems.

It's still honest. Even if honest, isn't always the truth.

I let me tell myself one thing on the list of reasons I was coming out of my own skin.

Running away from home at my age wasn't going to help me convince anyone that I knew anything about blending.

I ran out of paved road at a right turn several miles along, but just kept going the way the dark orange dirt went. It was grated off and not terribly bumpy, so I made the assumption it was still a public thoroughfare. A determination of convenience more than logic because I wasn't going to turn around anyway. The fog varied its density. I varied my speeds accordingly most likely. Things to look at didn't vary so much. More like a list that kept repeating. A windmill. Railroad tracks often parallel to my flight pattern. Tumbleweeds. Cattle guard gates. White frame houses, most with a porch. Bullet hole ridden speed limit signs. And signs indicating a narrow bridge. Cows. Horses. Mesquite groves. In *Groundhog Day* fashion they passed me by in the same order several times.

Driving in fog keeps a good distance between everything and everything else. It's confining and slower and somehow safer, like a blanket I pulled up loosely to my chin and kept my hands under.

At first I was taken by the railroad tracks and stopped to snap a shot. Then a tumble weed too damp to tumble earned a spot on the digital memory card. The gates were captivating. Gates that were closed over and none of them were blocking any road I should travel just now. I stopped to take a picture of some fog bound horses standing together like close friends and the Brahma bull in the pasture with them. He was standing close to the fence so I went down a way and took my picture of him before reaching in to scratch him on the back. He wasn't amused by my hand on his damp coat and gave me a slow motion look before trudging away to where I wouldn't be able to touch him. I wouldn't swear that he sighed some expression of annoyed, but it could have happened. It seemed to have happened.

I don't think that bulls have much attention span. It must be weird to be a large farm animal with nothing to do and have Attention Deficit Disorder. What does he do all day? He can't even scratch his own head with a hand when he considers such facts of his creation. His job is seasonal and there are only so many corners of the pasture to visit. It crossed my mind that he should have welcomed my presence as a break to the monotonous routine of just being a bull all day. Maybe he's not a real smart bull. Maybe I'm not as interesting as I think I am.

I thought about Annie. A daughter. My daughter but not. She is one of my bonus kids. We acquired each other when I married Tank. She is beautiful and brown-eyed and smart and jocular and loves horses. She would be immersed in this significance. She would know the good that was going on and I would hear her sigh at the fog and laugh at the bull and make fun of me for trying to pet him.

I clicked through the pictures I had so far. I hoped the one of the horses was going to be good. The scene was very good in real life.

It was starting to rain, but I needed the moisture so I stayed there in the tall grass next to a post that held up the barbed wire. The horses seemed to feel the same way about it. They stood still like soldiers on duty and let the rain be on them. I enjoyed watching the sprinkles happen to all of us. I saw how it changed things. Their coats darkened. Their eyes blinked back the sting of fresh water. The grass turned a darker golden. It all smelled like I thought calm would. The wood fence posts wore the sheen of a shower and the wire stretching between them gathered a very few drops. My hands protected the camera in my pocket and I wondered if I should have worn the long sleeve shirt since it was pretty cold out. Maybe I was part of the landscape for a minute. Maybe the circle of being me crossed over into this other circle for a bit of time.

I had not thought ahead about the rainfall stopping, so when it did I was just there, as before. Except kind of slushy. The crying had stopped too. My chest felt its first small relief. Like a list of "things to do" was being formed somewhere and the list itself was a progress of sorts.

I drove away. Away from the rejection of the bull and the disinterest of the rain painted horses. The fog and the drizzle and the pewter colored time followed me and led me and uncovered me and covered me.

I took no more pictures on this road and eventually the lefts and rights of red and muddy dirt turned into an asphalt road that led into Sweet Creek after all.

eleven

SWEET TOWNS
OF JUSTICE

The signs coming into town were typical, everybody was welcoming me. The First Baptist Church, The Methodist Church, The Church of Christ. Guess the Catholics were using the sign budget for better communion wine or maybe there just weren't any living in Sweet Creek, because there was no greeting from them. The words on the others said they wanted to welcome me, but somehow they seemed a bit more like campaign signs. Despite all that welcoming, none invited me. I don't like churches. And I don't like their ladies.

Main Street sported some great old buildings which held some law offices. Several law offices in fact. Seemed as if there was one church for every lawyer.

Some churches need a lawyer. Churches that pretend they don't turn away less worthy souls or the churches that settle for evangelism in lieu of transparency. And churches where people can forget Jesus and run for office by way of the offering plate. Churches that fear what they don't know and ministers that forget who they're employed by and why they took the job in the first place. They should have lawyers to defend them because no one else can. Churches where rules still rule and Grace is just a girl's given name.

On the next block I saw Paradise. A one story brown brick building with green awnings and painted on palm trees. The sign above the recessed glass door read: "Paradise—It's closer than you think. 206 Almond." Picture secured. Now I knew where it was. I made a mental note to put a check on my list next to "Find Paradise." Paradise is evidently a matter of perspective. I had to first know where 206 Almond was.

Nothing here resembled the sweet water I wanted to find. I didn't have an image in mind of what a pitcher of cool water might look like, but I knew this wasn't the weather appropriate drink I hoped for. At the corner, I waited while the traffic light cycled back to green then I drove out of town. West. Or at least mostly west.

From the driver's seat I scribbled something on the notepad about being a better steward of a gorgeous name like Sweet Creek should I ever get the chance.

This one may be a great town. I didn't give it much of a chance. I relied solely on that "initial feel" barometer that guides and guards much of my life's decision making. No doubt there are people here broken and restored and compassionate and living in small circles just like me.

Maybe I didn't want to feel the familiar of the buildings and the brick colors. They were in fact, familiar. Then there was the smell of crude oil on the air that smacked me into places I didn't want to remember and into places I wanted to want to remember and places I couldn't remember, but I could hear.

I was approaching myself suspiciously. Cautiously. I was watching me listen. I had brushed my palms across the veneer on my arms and the cold air and cool damp were coming in through the apertures in my skin. I liked it some. I liked it less than I didn't like it. But the breaking off of the layer couldn't be stopped now.

The next town siding this highway was Bristol. Grey. It was grey. The grey that matched the highway. Might be the kind of town that is grey in the bright sunlight too. Definitely grey in the fog. Several closed up businesses in buildings that deserved a long look through. Windows and doors lined up like ladies in waiting. A cotton gin stood by the railroad tracks and a train that stood still between me and the other side of the road I assumed I wanted to stay on.

I noticed that this would be a great place to photograph a lightning storm. The backdrop of a million miles of flat, flat land combined with the forefront of buildings colored in old white and the gin and the elevated railroad tracks would be brilliant with a couple of thunderstorm style bolts of airborne electricity to set them off. I held my hands up with an imaginary camera in them and snapped the shot that never happened.

I drove and looked slowly over a couple of blocks of town, maybe all three blocks to be sure nothing here was looking for me. I think I wanted to find lunch here in a café with locals inside talking about the drenched air and Thanksgiving plans and high school football. I think I wanted to order rubbery chicken fried steak from a waitress who was someone's mom and stay long enough to have my iced tea glass refilled. Hear the hard plastic plate land in a short slide on the metal-framed table top. Hear her ask me if I needed ketchup. Hear the voices, mostly men voices, making their very important farm conversations at the tables around me. Belong there for a time. Make some small talk and hear just one simple story from the waitress mom's ordinary life that proved she was not ordinary at all. Such a place wasn't there though, and with some back tracking, I found a different way across the occupied tracks and got back to the business of driving toward my not being.

For a section of several miles, the highway was four lanes wide and I had a road companion. An eighteen wheeler pulling a covered load of who knows what stayed tucked into the reflection in my left wing mirror for a while. From my driver's seat, I took a picture of the grill of the truck and the rain jumping off. I knew that he knew he was supposed to be there. If I made a travel trance induced adjustment to my speed, he did too. Maybe the God is a truck driver and this gave Him the proximity I needed. Maybe he was just coincidence. No matter the truth, once I assigned comfort to it, it was just that.

I lost him when I saw a sign that made me make a U-turn. A town called Fort Justice. Guess I didn't want company as much as I had thought.

Anyway, this place didn't have a real forgiving ring to it. I just wanted to stop there. Seemed to make me laugh. That Sweet Creek would be close to "Justice" on the map.

I took a picture of the sign at the city limits. No mention of the population count. Then drove another 500 yards or so to what seemed to be it.

Before I even got out of the Jeep for a look, my suspicions were confirmed by the posture of two rotting wood abandoned buildings. Might as well name a place "One Strike." One strike and you're out. The open sign was still up on the door of one of the buildings. Like the last proprietor might've just one day gotten tired, along with the rest of the residents who couldn't keep up with the responsibility of executing justice all the time. Might not have been the executing of justice anyway. Maybe just being executed on. Departure seemed like it might have been abrupt no matter what the reason. Nothing got boarded up. The motion of life was left to wind itself down.

Maybe the town just moved back off the main road somewhere. Maybe half a mile away there stood a series of streets named after trees where people lived in brick houses and laced up their work boots every morning that sounded like a weekday. I didn't look that far.

Instead I noticed a lost white leather high top tennis shoe had been nailed to the post of what looked like a long gone gas station. Maybe one person lost it and another saw it and hung it there to be seen and found. Maybe it was art. Maybe the hanger of the shoe was making a statement about kicking, being kicked, or leaving in a hurry. An image dashed across my mind of an animated George Jetson in those oversized white shoes, running in place a minute before grabbing traction and zooming off.

Humor departed me and a completely different pair of shoes lunged onto the surface of my present from out of my past. A recollection of Skillet's black cowboy boots spiked my body with hurt.

He loved his cowboy boots and had several pair in his closet. He almost always wore a fawn colored felt cowboy hat with tan polyester slacks, those pointy boots, and an impressive belt buckle. Button-up long sleeved shirts and cuff links were the hallmark of a smart man in his mind, only stupid men wore short sleeves. He accessorized like a woman with that whole cowboy theme. As far as I know, he had never actually been one. A cowboy nor a woman. Later, when I was older I figured out that it had nothing to do with cowboying and everything to do with appearing to be a Marshall or some such fantasy about authority. We did watch Gunsmoke every week. Maybe that was his inspiration. Marshall Dillon. I couldn't give him John Wayne as a role model. That would be blasphemous.

I always preferred Festus on that show to the Marshall anyway. He was flawed and disheveled and made forgivable mistakes that ended as morals.

At first encounter, Skillet was charming and engaging and funny and had a more firm than needed handshake for other men to take. Not tall. Probably below average in height really, but since he was the father in our houses, I kept my image of him a bit more vertical than he actually was until I was older.

91

He had this way that he would hold his teeth when he was about to shred someone verbally or physically or any other way. That shift in the set of his teeth made the darkness around his mouth go another shade meaner. The foreboding had a lifespan of its own. He seemed to use that interval of measureable time to determine how long he was going to just threaten. He had some love affair with causing fear, but he was an eventual striker too. The kind of striker that paradoxically blends dread with immediacy. Not going in for the quick kill, but more of a provoker. He preferred torture or terrorism. He never seemed in a hurry for the rages to complete once he started fulfilling his own order of violence. The place where cuss words were delivered in rapid fire and covered in spit. The kind of exertion that would exhaust anyone else seemed to be a generator of strength for my father.

Those high dollar, sharp cowboy boots were among his favorite tools.

I hated those boots. They were throw down ugly. Even when they just sat on the floor with no feet in them.

Not as much as James hated them. I hated them more for James than for me.

The thing about a physical assault is that the assaulted can only feel it. The bystanders see it. And the bystanders feel it. And the bystanders wish they were the ones being beat up. And the bystanders thank their God that they are not the ones being beat up. And the bystanders and the assaulted thank their God that they are not the beater while wishing that they were.

Martha and Skillet had kids about every three years. James, then Pete, I was next and they quit at Buck. One of those boys was supposed to be a girl. For that matter, I had been reminded often that I wasn't the kind of girl they had hoped for either. And none of the boys were the boys they seemed to hope for. James felt the most pressure of that I think. The oldest seems to have some birth right or birth curse to be larger than life and reflect all the values a family wishes they had. With that much at stake, failing comes easy and punishment comes swiftly and powerfully in a competitive, Baptist, God-fearing, God-avoiding, narcissistic house.

Skillet hid it well if it didn't delight him to kick James. My brother learned before I was big enough to know differently, how to make it look like it was something that happened to all the kids his age. He made it look like he deserved having that powerful shot of pointed boot land where no male should ever be struck. Skillet either loved or ignored the wrenching drop to the ground on first impact and just turned his aim to other targets on James body. My brother had learned that appearing to agree with the accompanying line of irrational questioning eventually slowed the force.

Parents tell kids stuff like, "Don't make that face. It'll get stuck that way." We laugh. Maybe we shouldn't. Maybe your face does get stuck. It can get stuck on silent suffer as easily as it can get stuck on funny. And maybe so does your heart. It's the China Syndrome of human soil.

It was just a high top nailed randomly to a porch column. The tumbling took me by surprise. Tiny tucked away pasts darted around me and I needed to dodge the incoming. I didn't have the resources to stay in their company right now.

There are things that I have dealt with head on. There are things I have integrated into a system of awareness. There are things that I do not speak about in an out loud voice in case they draw a breath of revival from being talked of. And there are things that no amount of screaming, or sobbing, or avoiding has healed. Then there are these things that I don't know that I don't know are even still living there until I come into the space of them. The space where they wake like a startled wasp nest.

I console myself that that's got to be true for everyone.

It's hard to know where Skillet came from. What the nightmare was that consumed him. Best I can tell, his own father wasn't busy being mad at everything. I liked Skillet's dad. We all called him Pa. He chewed a lot of plug tobacco and most of his teeth were gone by the time I started memorizing his face. He had a big, whole laugh and his overalls matched his pick-up truck somehow. I don't know what he did for a living, but it seemed to involve cows and the smell of hay. He cussed up any number of storms but it was funnier than it was scary. He didn't hug but once each visit and that was to say hello. Good-byes got a walking away wave. He let us climb trees and play checkers and shoot BB guns and disappear down the railroad tracks for whole days at a time. He seemed to know a lot about what counts and what made a kid grow. Like we were all part of a herd that didn't need a lot of managing. He burped often and loud and my grandmother had been mad at him for an obviously long time, but we were not allowed to know why.

Sometimes I've met people like that. People that have lived enough to know what tilled soil will produce and how to water without drowning the life out of a life. Those are the people I want to be liked by. Those are the people that know about freedom being obedience.

In this minute however, I was on my own. The variety of people I like being around were not around.

I wasn't wishing for anyone to be there. Maybe James. If he was there I would stand next to him. I would feel shorter than him and I would feel wider. Wide enough to offer him some still. And I would reach to hold his hand and tell him I was very sorry about Skillet's boots. And we would be children for some minutes. Children standing side by side looking at our own youth as if anything had been properly paid for.

While the truth was that the stop had only scored about a 1.5 on the Richter scale of "things I don't want to recall," Fort Justice had offered as much as I cared to endure and the time to go came.

I did not want to think any longer about Skillet or his boots or why his dad was seemingly good and kind and he was neither.

I noticed a small beige colored brick church off by itself at the end of the framed picture I was currently cast in. Pulling away I saw that it was closed and empty. I think a church should always be left unlocked and I think someone should be inside and I think there should be a phone number to call if no one can be there all the time. If I was in charge of Houses of God, I would make sure God was always in His house. A God who wears blue jeans and pours good coffee.

Maybe I would have confessed to Him. Told Him why I had run away. Described the list that I was not ready to tell myself.

MEMORIES DEMAND ATTENTION, AND
THESE MEMORIES WILL HAVE TEETH.

—C. KENNEDY

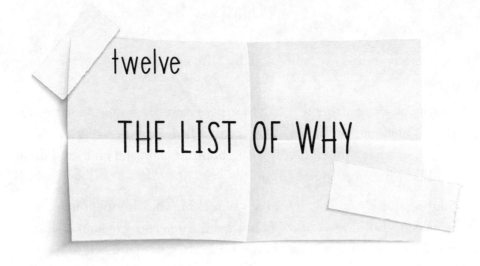

twelve

THE LIST OF WHY

I drive away from justice. Or the lack of it. And I drive away from the hamlet named for it. The Fort Justice placed here on a dust driven roadside by a well-meaning zealot. I make no noise as I speak the list.

I drive and count and wonder which thing was the straw that set my runaway-ness in motion.

In a week I will have to go to Martha's birthday party. She will be turning eighty. Skillet has not planned a party. Her children have not planned a party. She has planned her own. I didn't want to do it. But I felt terrible that I hadn't.

Or the think from a different degree that keeps me from blending? Was the last feather weight straw just believing in the awkward of being me?

Maybe the business of burying truths about myself was surfacing and I couldn't keep them under any longer. My pasts had not been overcome at all, but just covered in disguises.

The father who could not like me. The hurt of fighting so often to be seen as good and accomplished and worthy of approval had been fruitless. He would get dead and never say he was kind of proud of me.

Is it because I have forgotten courage? Has the cowardice finally won one too many matches? The golden yellow tinge in my eyes that keeps me from revealing my failings boldly? The deficiencies so apparent to my son?

Maybe it was the sting that like Martha, I had not earned the sovereign title of mom either. The one I had carried from seed to wrinkles and tears had made himself deeply clear about my damages on him. I drive. I think. I hear me think of him.

Sterling doesn't actually live in our home. He's a half grown man. But he is angry with me or at me or both and threatening to stop loving me. I have watched it grow on him for years. I have listened to his grievances and I have given them thought. Where I could see his take, I offered apologies and tried to right my ways. Where I couldn't see his take I also offered apologies, but those lacked conviction. The Saturday morning that I left had been terrible between us. He seems to believe that I am nothing but mean. I am mean. I am other things too. He seems to believe I am mean all the time. I am not mean all the time. He does not know how much I love him. He does know. He does know how much I love him. He thinks that all of it is my fault. I think it is not all my fault and I think that he doesn't know some things yet. He thinks I am unlikeable. Sometimes I think we agree on this one thing.

The morning I left he had been over. He had screamed. I had screamed back. I cried. I did not want to be unlikeable. I did not want to be unliked. I did not want to be hated so. I did not want to be hated at all.

It's embarrassing that I am so unliked.

I heard his eyes tell me again that I am pathetic. Contemptibly inadequate.

I know that I could not have loved him more than I have done thus far. It was not enough. My variety of love had not been his enough, and it was not watering to him, and my nurture had been replaced along the way with survive and protect and keep. Those are admirable things, but left on their own they are not all that a child needs. He reminded me with a slash to my maternal soul how often and how big I had failed.

I have to slow now. Slow my unreasonable. My reasonable. Ask myself these things. Believe my answers as if my truth so far is true. Make sure they are not powdery. Not falsified. Not lies that give me permission to wallow. I look around inside for admirable things. I have to write them down to myself. And my inadequacies. And my prides and my cover ups. I have to write them down so I can see them. Confess them. Reveal them. Bring a night light into the dark closet of my deceits as a parent. Cause the pitiful to wither in the exposure and the truths to flourish in the break of light. The truths that are good. The truths that are not.

Admission. It is time to admit. It is time to pay admission. Get the ticket that will let me into the big screen movie of myself.

My bench mark for being a good parent had been embedded in the limit of beating my own parents at the job. I vowed to not hit my kids should I ever have any. I vowed it young. Early. Before the breakfast of my life if the whole span of years were to be measured in one day.

I did not vow to nurture. I didn't know the word. And I did not promise to find out what was missing. Find out what values needed to be received and replaced.

I had looked all my days thus far for a different skill set of being a mom. In rebellion of Skillet, I would not hit my children. I built myself ready. Ready to strike anything and anyone that looked like assault. I would be ready to leave a marriage if it needed to be done. I would have the intestinal fortitude to not hit my kids to shut them up. Or shut them down. I would find some other way to deal with their resistances and I would try to watch for their needs as if I could meet them. I would buy them new clothes that were better than my own. I would go to their games and buy them new baseball gloves and not make fun of them if they couldn't dance. I would listen to them sing out loud. I would make their Sundays kind. I would never hit them. I would travel with them. Take photographs of them whether they posed or not. I promised that I would hang pictures of my children on the walls of my house so they would know that they are great art. I would show them safe and compassion and generosity and I would not hit them.

As I wrote I saw my own rudimentary pattern.

Mostly it seemed that my objective was to never hit my kids.

I only got to keep one child that began a life within me.

I did not hit him.

I had expected Sterling to be grateful for this one grand achievement of mine.

I also did not always see him. I did not pause to determine what safe and compassion and generosity were to him. I gave him what I had needed. What I had wanted. He needed different. He wanted different. I didn't see it. I didn't do it.

I wanted to protect him. Protect him into becoming a brave and independent young man. I wanted his environment to be controlled freedom. Give him reason to have thought. Tell him to have his own story that was rooted in having had a hardy childhood. I wanted his start to have been a kind one. I had not understood how it works. I had met one goal. I had not hit him.

Now he wanted his own story. One that required me to be the Skillet in his life. A Skillet of only a slightly different shade. He wanted his story to be bigger than his mom's story. Maybe we have the right to want to have a bigger story of overcoming than our parents had. A story of starting from a harder place and getting to a grander victory. I do not know all of Martha's story. Nor Skillet's. Sterling did not know much of mine either really.

I do not know if my story is better than theirs.

I know I did not hit my son.

I had misunderstood the job of protecting him. I had tried to tell him things. Teach him from someone else's experience. Ask him to memorize life lessons from someone else's pages and apply them robotically. There is no life in that. No mercy. No grace. No death. No resurrection. Taught material fades when it stops being used. Experiences do not. They make a home in our emotional DNA and if we are full bore about the impact, they shift our spiritual composition for every moment forward.

Even now as I write these things down, I know I have friends who would roll their eyes in some way. The friends that are mothers. The friends that know we have all done the best we could with all the love we have. So I will not say to them that my inventory is low. I will only say these things to myself on this single page of paper so that no one else can cough out a scoff at this section of my life.

And I will know that there is no pain so exacting and untouchable as this. The pain that comes with knowing that my son has taken stock of me and found me insubstantial. Inadequate. Miserable.

And the truth that I tried hard and loved deep does not penetrate the stone walls I clothe myself in when he uses his dark and unforgiving eyes to draw his sword of attack.

Sterling was on attack. He would not leave my house. I asked him to. Repeatedly. He did not. He would not.

So I did.

The list of the unacceptables of me.

My son is disgusted by me and I left to escape the disdain and because my unorthodox views scare my friends and I don't know how to stop doing that and I am not Skillet's good daughter and I have to celebrate Martha's birthday in five days and I don't know how.

The very little list brought me no validation and here I was, on the second day of gone and no charge to go back.

I LEFT TO ESCAPE THE DISDAIN AND BECAUSE MY UNORTHODOX VIEWS SCARE MY FRIENDS AND I DON'T KNOW HOW TO STOP DOING THAT.

I drove away from the closed-upness of Fort Justice and its tan void church. I looked along the line where the sky and the dirt touch each other for the enlightenment beam that should have jumped down on me like an attack of revelation.

No boom within me of understanding. No bolt of lightning epiphanies. No Wizard of Oz behind a curtain to direct a temporal moment of magic and explanation and restoration. No break in the grey. No stream of sunlight that I could deem hope. No thing I could be grateful for to the God I did not like. Did not trust.

I drove some more, but the chaos and noise inside cancelled out the listening, and concentration looked like something I imagined a Viet Nam war protestor's acid trip might have been. Then a word pushed through the crowd of adjectives in my mind or my heart and raised its hand to be noticed. Disappointment.

I watched the riots before me. They gave way to this child trying to get up near me on my stage. The chanting slowed and the protestor signs on sticks dropped out of view. She climbed up where I live and stood next to me. I looked at her. I grimaced toward her. I watched her. She spoke with bold posture. She announced her name. Disappointment.

Disappointment described herself with her whispers into my ear. She cupped her hands around her mouth and touched the side of my turned head as I listened intently trying to tune out the background blur of voices. She called herself a player in the unplanned getaway.

I began to inventory the feeling, and felt alarm at how familiar the weight was. I had known so much disappointment. I was being chased by the abominations of all the disappointments I had caused and all the disappointments I was, and there was this little postscript style list of disappointment that may not have been my doing at all but clearly had taken residence in my person.

If there was a word consistently present in my human experience this one was it. It came in packages of the embarrassment I caused and the often dirty I felt. I heard the blows and cringed from the bashes in my history. The spackle I had mended myself with these last decades was giving way as I sat there and it began to crumble like wallpaper that was being touched for the first time in fifty years.

The kid ones rushed in first as if I had rewound a video of my time. It began to play erratically toward this culmination of the value of me, now, here in the driving fog. Familiar pictures rushed by so fast I could only feel them but not actually see them or clock them or sort them. Others were new. Things that I remembered I had known but had been hidden on shelves out of reach. Then they gained on the horses called past and hit the homestretch into the recent present and the current present where I was more certain of the facts. Things I had witnessed. And things I had done. And things I had not done but had been blamed for and taken the blame for. Things done to me and things I had done to other people.

Disappointment is not remorse. It has the body of regret and the gesture of helplessness. It has no friends called redemption. It keeps company with guilt and compunction and a strain of grief that can't be healed quickly with a singular beg for forgiveness.

And now, here she was. My personified companion. Closer than my shames. Tangible and touchable and huge and in the passenger seat beside me. I knew the symptoms of soul sickness and had plastered them over for years. Now the air-borne virus was sitting here for me to put to death. She read my thoughts and made it clear that neither she nor her sisters would take attempts on their lives lying down.

I heard a nervous chuckle inside. I must've pictured myself slaying some "mighty dragon of disappointment." As if I could now miraculously be my own champion.

Disappointment got quiet. The cupped hands she had been describing herself through dropped to her sides as she saw me unravel it all. The chuckle must have unnerved her too.

I had thought disappointment was a noun. She is not. She has a life and Disappointment is a proper noun. Her name. Her description. Her purpose.

She sat beside me in the seat by the passenger side door. Here on the stage of my present. My runaway. She sat and I drove and we did not visit or sing to songs on a radio. And we did not hate each other.

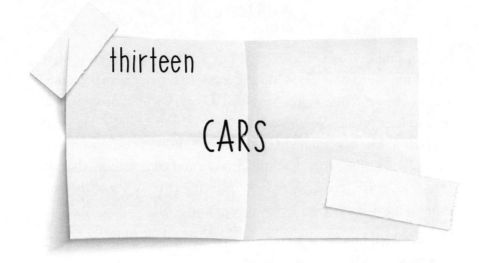

thirteen

CARS

Evidently "west" includes north on this stretch of pavement. The next town was Cotton Flatts. I had been to Cotton Flatts. I could tell that I had been here before. A long time ago.

When we moved to the valley, we must've come through Cotton Flatts. We never went anywhere on vacations except Oklahoma and we never ate in restaurants on these trips so we needed to pass through towns big enough to have a grocery store. Skillet would go in the store and get a loaf of bread and a package of bologna.

What is bologna anyway? And who started pronouncing it baloney?

Either spell it "baloney" or pronounce it bologna. I was evidently ahead of my time on the phonetics application. And what does it say about a sandwich meat anyway when its name is used interchangeably with words like rubbish and nonsense?

Martha would stay in the car with us kids. It was kind of like a break. Like him going out of town but shorter. His short absence let everyone exhale. We didn't say that we were glad to rid of him for a few minutes, we just each knew the other thought it. Maybe even Martha. Maybe most of all Martha.

No mustard or mayo or Miracle Whip® (and another thing—what is this thing called Miracle Whip®?) because these might make a mess, and no drinks. They would be spilled. Or they would mean we had to stop later to pee. Neither was acceptable, so no drinks. He would get back in the car and go back to driving and complaining about it. Complaining about doing all the driving and complaining that the bread wasn't fresh enough and complaining at the price of the bologna poser sandwich meat.

Martha would make us each a sandwich and then when everyone was finished eating, or more likely when Skillet was finished eating, she'd put all the trash and left overs in the bread bag and then into the grocery bag. Then she would crank the window down with her dutiful right hand and wait for Skillet to give her the signal. He was busy checking that there were no cars in sight. Littering, after all, could get you fined and you didn't want to get caught. He'd shout, "Now!" like it was a foxhole moment and she'd do the deed, flinging the trash out the window. We'd watch it hit the ground and the brown paper bag would either disappear or explode into a few smaller trashes on the roadside we were flying past. We usually drove fast. We drove fast because speed limits were only for people who didn't know how to drive.

If people around us drove too slow, or just kept to the speed limit, Skillet would start getting heated up. His destination was more important than anyone else's. Since he couldn't really address the other drivers, he would work himself into a lather in our car. Soon the explosion would erupt. The cussing would accent every corner of the rage. He would throw anything out of the window that made a noise. Once it was my big leather bag of marbles.

Pete had taught me how to play marbles. I had this bag full of all sizes that I brought with me on a trip to Oklahoma. A lot of them were very old. I had found them in Pa's garage and loved them! Having them meant Pete might play with me. But the marbles made a rolling noise under the seat and got flung out of the window. I didn't dare tell Skillet that some of them had been his father's. He wouldn't have been sad. I was. He would have been even madder. Pete knew. He didn't say it either.

Several times, his rage manifested with him trying to rip the steering wheel off the column while travelling at highway speed. I don't know if it just wasn't really possible to tear it out, or if he knew he would die along with the rest of us if he succeeded, so he wasn't honestly pulling with all his might like it looked like he was. It's one of his ludicrous performances that always scared me desperately. I didn't say it though. My face may have changed color with the fear, but no one was looking at me. I had no understanding in those days of being watched over. I believed no one saw me with my blood drained, white face or any other face. Unless I had on my eager face. The one that assured I would rescue. That face never got overlooked. The little girl who lived behind that face, however, always got overlooked.

If we did stop for a pee, it was most often on the side of the road with the boys instructed to stand between the open car doors and point it away, toward the fields. Martha could squat and take care of the urge. I couldn't. No matter how many times he popped me on the bare bottom. It would have been an entertaining "Made for TV" scene had it not been for the getting mad part.

Three boys between three years old and eleven, each wearing over starched jeans with knee patches and varying amounts of cuffed length, jumping out of the car and whizzing in the west Texas wind. Their lives depending on them not hitting anything but dirt with the stream of urine they had been building up for hours. Boys think peeing is an awesome superpower anyway, but in these situations they would need to focus on the elements. All pee at once, with their backs to the car, pretending that the other cars driving by didn't know what they were up to, and not get any on themselves, each other, or worst of all, the family car! Then the boys would rush back into the station wagon and Martha and I would have our turn. I'd squat with no joy. Then Martha'd show off and make her puddle. I'd decline a second attempt and crawl back into the front seat and brace for the chastisement coming in from all directions.

Kids that get bullied tend to bully, but it breaks their hearts. Doing the thing we hate most to have done to us hardens us, but doesn't make us tougher or stronger. No one in that car wanted to bully really, but for a moment it put them in the club. His club. Skillet's mean club and sometimes it is forgivable to want that much to belong to your own family.

I'm pretty sure we had a station wagon most of our little kid years. I think it was brown. It was the kind of car that every family drove. It made more sense than a sedan and no one had invented the mini-van yet.

Having four kids was not an excuse for a dirty car, it was a live-in car washing unit. Which we did. Every Saturday that I can think of for all our school years. We were good at it. Skillet led the project every time. We didn't dare try it without him there.

First the floor mats came out and got washed so they'd have time to dry and be ready to go back in as soon as the car was totally clean. If they were carpeted mats they stayed inside the car until the end when they would be removed and vacuumed separately.

Tires next. It was important to scrub the whitewalls with Ajax on a brush until they gleamed. If Martha had rubbed the tire on a curb that week, she would be summoned out to see the damage, slapped an appropriate number of times in the face, and sent away with orders to get out of his sight.

While the tires were being scrubbed cleaner than any of us were ever washed, the underside of the wheel wells were to be washed and inspected for any signs of dirt. The hubcaps were very important. They needed to be rubbed clean while the tires were being washed but they must be kept wet so they didn't air dry and get spots.

Those spots were the anxiety of the event. Once the windows and body were being washed, someone had to keep the whole car wet with the garden hose. I hated that job. I would start out okay, then I'd start day dreaming, mesmerized by the running water. Before I knew it, something was drying up and the yelling and hitting would commence. Not just me getting it. Everyone. Then it was my fault we were all in trouble and I felt the responsibility much more than I felt the blows.

We had to recover quickly. The car still had to be finished. We would rewash the dried areas and rinse them and get busy drying as fast as possible before it happened again.

Drying called for two towels per person. One to take up the bulk of the water, the second to buff up the paint or the windows or the chrome on the bumpers.

Then the towels were used on the inside to clean the dash board and the inside of the windows and the door handles and the hinges of the doors and inside the jambs. The windows were tough to clean without leaving streaks and Windex was considered too expensive even though it would have done the job.

By then the driveway was dry enough from the 100 degree sun to bring the vacuum out without getting it wet. The seats, floors, and mats all got a thorough "Hoovering" up and the car was parked in the middle of the drive so that the yard work could begin.

The family car had to go this routine before any trip and immediately on return from any trip in addition to any Saturday that was not rainy. Which would have been almost every week.

A trip in the car that included the whole family meant that the boys would take the back seat. If it was a road trip, the golden brown vinyl suitcases would be packed into the otherwise invisible luggage compartment under the rear floorboard and sometimes we would make a pallet back there for me and Buck to nap or play. James and Pete got the seats by the door and the duty of watching the baby between them if he wasn't on the pallet with me.

The baby of the family is always just that. The baby of the family. Five months or five years or five decades into life, he is always the baby. He never had to learn at the same rate as older siblings. He could take his sweet time learning to tie his shoes and how to make himself a sandwich and the expectation that he was always needing something is a life-long burden to bear. An impossible juggle of wanting to be seen as an adult or capable or independent and not wanting any of those things to be true.

I rode in front most of the time. The pallet made me feel less safe. Out of range in the event of a Skillet break down. Skillet always drove. Martha sat to my right. She looked out the window most of the time. I remember knowing that was my cue to keep Skillet happy. It was safer if she wasn't checked in. If she was reading a map or talking I had to realign the balance on my own because it was a very different universe. My duty felt doubled. If she said the wrong thing or missed a turn off, I was going to be the janitor. Messes were going to be made. Skillet was going to reach across the seat and slap her or yell at her from his position of threat with those crossed over teeth. Then it was very likely that everyone was going to get it in some way or another for the next fifty miles. If she was quiet it was easier. The less she said, the less chance there was to make him get crazy with mad. I learned to know when to speak and when to not. I kept tabs on when to remind Martha to look at the map or check on the boys before Skillet had to say something to her. I was also there to laugh an appropriate and seemingly sincere amount if he said something funny and agree with him that the other drivers were all freaking idiots.

No one touched the radio settings. No one touched the air conditioning if the car had any. No one adjusted the vents. No one wore a seatbelt.

It was an age when gas stations were full service. When the gauge got low enough, we'd watch for signs until we spotted a Texaco or an Enco station. I don't know why, but we didn't go to Conoco or Sinclair or Shell stations. Sometimes we'd go to Gulf stations, but not often.

We'd pull up to the pump and the car wheels would run over the rubber tube that activated the bell inside the small station office. Skillet would get out of the car before the attendant got there. We didn't get out unless we were invited to do so. We would just watch him from inside the V-8 powered prison with rolled up windows. He'd light up a cigarette while the man in the pressed khaki garage shirt and shiny, black plastic billed cap began pouring gas into the tank. Then he'd get all animated with the stranger while they took a look under the hood and checked the vitals. We'd hear them exchange exclusive chuckles as if they had a great secret between them. Then he'd step back away from the car as if he was pretty important, while his new best friend washed the windshield. By now another cigarette had been shaken from the green and white pack and popped into the narrow space between his lips. He'd cup his dull, tin shaded lighter in his hand to keep the wind away and barely have it in his pocket again before he had said something witty or wise to the service station employee who he wasn't even going to tip or buy a Coke for despite this grand bonding moment.

I'd watch it all from my assigned place in the middle of the front seat. I'd want it. I'd want him to talk to me like that. Friendly. Be friendly with me. And I knew James was watching too. And I'd take a fast glance over the top of the front seat to see him back there. If he caught me looking he'd thump me on the top of my head or look at something else like he hadn't even seen Skillet being so nice. Buck was little and all about the business of being the littlest and the cutest. Pete was in a land far far away in his imagination where he could mix elements from his chemistry set and blow up innocent lizards. Martha was watching for chances to smile at the stranger who checked the windshield wiper fluid so that he'd believe we were all good and okay and happy.

I think we would stop about twice at gas stations between home and the grandparent's house. Each stop was similar or maybe identical. It certainly seemed well rehearsed. I wondered now how many hours it used to take to make that drive. I think those hours were like days to an old little girl and her brothers.

We stayed quiet. It was smart. The random appearance of a father who wanted to talk to any of us was not to be trusted. The nervous voice of a mother who knew little more than how to unsuccessfully protect herself was not to be trusted either.

I could tell that this road was part of that history. The condemnation puddled behind my eyes again. It brought the deep ache. A unique hurt. Like feeling the pain of giving birth and nothing will relieve it until the baby gets here. The baby doesn't arrive. All that hurt for nothing but survival.

So here I was. The six-year-old, the five-year-old, the nine-year-old Sammi trying to reconcile with the 51-year-old Sammi. A package of people I love, fear, know, and do not know, riding down the highway together with cars passing us as if all was copacetic. We all just kept our eyes facing forward like nothing was off color. The way bank robbers behave in a low budget film when they find themselves sitting at a red traffic light with a cop car in the lane beside them. No matter what happens, we all agreed, just keep acting like nothing has happened.

fourteen

FLATT OUT

I had stopped thinking about the road and where I was going some miles ago so when Cotton Flatts drove up next to me, I just parked the car on Main Street like the robotic response of being in a trance and doing what you're told to do.

There was an old movie theatre in front of me and a great looking book store.

The sign in the window of the book store said "We're always here— unless we're not." They were not. I like that sign. I like what it says.

Just as well though, because this wee shop looked terribly inviting and I would have spent about a week in there going through books that said all kinds of very important things.

I love old books.

Their enduring truth that nothing is new under the sun. I love to touch the covers and run my eyes over the fabric or leather that holds the words in order. I love to open them and consider how many lives have been since the ink dried and I do not usually determine if I need it to go home with me until I've brought the truth of its age to my face for a deep inhale. Each page evenly steeped in the color of time being closed over it. Just fibers of years and lifetimes and being read or understood or dismissed or placed on a shelf. Concrete proof of a willingness to be vulnerable. Maybe someone said something well or well enough to escape the critic's self righteous axe.

The brave of writing things down and waiting to see the response is as meritorious as a good God would ever ask His child to be. I can't first go to the table of contents when I select a book from a line of labeled spines. Instead, I open back the cover taking a third of the pages with my grab and read the first thing in the first paragraph on the first page I find. I love how it's always the seemingly littler sentences that stick. And I love that the words are angled differently but faced the same. And I love the dog ears and the penciled notes and the underlined sentences and the inscriptions in the front that explain who gave the book to their friend. And I love that all things worth saying have been said before, but saying them again is right.

I got out of the Jeep to walk. To take a break from me and from running away. To go someplace distantly familiar and without threat.

The old movie theatre to the right of the bookstore looked like it was an operating business and it was pretty and clean and had the personality of wistful pasts. I wondered if I wanted to go in. I waited and I looked at it with everything but touch. The pause that created was short. Nope. Not just now, I determined.

I stepped left instead and up the curb to walk under the sometimes present awning of the various buildings joined together as a line and struck out slowly. A blocked stone, two-story building finished off the corner of the first street. It looked like it probably went up before the turn of the last century. Someone had tried it on for size as a museum recently, but mostly it was now vacant. Vacant but still housing a few cool portions of history. Wordless mysteries of old oak pieces. The windows framed up the invitation to see the empty and the unclaimed assortment of evidence. I tried the door but it was locked. I leaned closer to the glass to look. Dust had measurably gathered on tables and desk tops and chairs that slept in the quiet. Sort of like a too old grandmother who can't tell her stories any longer. Then the stories get lost and everyone just remembers when the time came that grandma couldn't tell her stories any longer and her last success is over because who are we without the stories of ourselves?

Several shops were closed on Sunday. This was still Sunday.

I paused. How could this still be Sunday? Not really a question.

I peered in a few windows and pulled the hood of my sweatshirt up to keep off some of the rain in front of the shops that bore no awning above.

The last store in the second block had that "chicks on a trip" look to it and I was a chick. And I was on a trip. I went inside.

The floors varied. Some carpet. Some wood sections. Mostly wavy and audible. The ceiling had some pressed tin and some sheets of paneling and a good height. The aromas from candles blended well with the smell of time. The merchandise on display was worthy of a look. They were carrying some line of items that framed up lots of words of wisdom written for "wanna be" Bohemians and people that wish they thought more. Some of the words had a valuable order to them and seemed well put. I found Christy a hair clip with a braid of leather and a red feather. She is all about the feathers right now and I thought she might like it.

I knew even as I paid for it that I would never know for sure if she liked it or not, because Christy always receives things with a big gracious grin whether she likes them or not. She's got that asset that can carve itself easily into a weakness. She makes people feel good about being in her company. She's just largely a happy person. Someday she'll need to buy another block of life and carve something that continues to maintain this part of herself but also leaves a larger surface for honesty with people she loves. For now though, she is fourteen years old and this carving is working fine. She is a delight to be with. We get to see her less often the older she gets. The every other weekend gig works fine for the split parents, but cuts in to the life of being a teenager and we've lost some of the time we used to get. She has no idea how much she has led me to myself. A bonus child-like Christy. The benefits of a blended family.

I looked at the greeting cards hoping for a flicker, or something like a hope or a direction and while a couple of them were pretty cute, the one that might save my life with some rich word of rescue or redemption was not on the rack. The antiques were not particularly patina packed with character or interest. I know my shoulders hung visibly low as I gave the walls and the shelves one last search for a savior.

My lingering gave the sole employee an opening to ask me where I was traveling to. I paused, wishing I had just gone on out into the now pouring rain. She gave me some options: "Family in Lubbock?" "You stayin' 'round here honey?" and "Are you by yourself ... really?"

"Runaway. I'm a runaway."

She searched me with her gum-chewing look.

I said it again. "I ran away from home. I didn't plan it. I don't have a destination right now."

She shifted her weight and drew her hand onto her hip as her head took an affirming angle. "I have always wanted to do that." She nodded her chin my direction.

I felt like a hero.

I remembered Paresh from the La Quinta. He knew too.

I left her store and her admiring look with my present for Christy. The rain had stopped again.

Crossing over another side street to the next block of shops, I stepped down about an eighteen-inch curb. The streets in a flat town have to be built with flash flood run off in mind since there are generally only two kinds of rain out here: none or cats and dogs. The intersections can quickly become a road hazard if no one accounted for getting the water out of town quickly and I remembered these kind of curbs from living out here before. Funny how the little things make a place more than just familiar.

Something put up in the fifties cornered the next block. Single story and going back deep in distance from the front door to the one in back, it had this hilarious invitation painted boldly on the side:

Furniture for the whole house
Your credit is good here

Countless assumptions in those two lines. The volume of my own laugh startled me. I knew no one heard it, but I wished someone had. I wished someone had heard it and let me catch them smiling about my out loud laugh.

I walked past the windows of the furniture store with a slight to my purpose. I wanted to see if there was really something in there for my whole house. Every room and my taste and good shades of red. Not so much, but it was a very long store and I was only at one end of it and I was outside so I didn't honestly give it much of a chance. I didn't want to think about a home and how it should look. But I kind of did want to think about it. I didn't want to go in the door. I barely wanted more than a glance in the windows.

My gait was a constant now. Neither slow nor quick nor directed. Just passing lives that belonged to other people. Then I passed a particular storefront that caught my eye. I recognized what it was, and went back immediately. A hardware store. Not a Home Depot. A real hardware store. Small and priceless. Opening the door was a head on encounter with the stink of fertilizer and WD-40 and paint maybe. Three aisles of retail spree before me. Or two and a half aisles, it was hard to tell really.

The man behind the counter got up quickly from a desk like he was supposed to meet some need of mine. Actually, his posture was more like, since I was a woman in a hardware store, he should take it up a notch and be prepared to anticipate what I might need. Then meet it.

I greeted him with eye contact that he watched while he made his way out to assist me. I could tell immediately that I was throwing off his otherwise predictable day of customers. I was not a familiar face in this small town and travelers don't visit the hardware store. By the time I had gotten to the back of the store by the middle set of shelves, he had caught up to me to see what I was looking at. His apprehension took on tangibility when I stopped to snap a shot of the way he had the various kinds of fasteners displayed. I roamed carefully up and down the three aisles several times without anything to say to him.

If he had access to a direct line to Homeland Security he would have been calling it right then. Probably on a rotary dial phone. A red one. Yes. A red rotary dial direct line to Homeland Security.

An important thing then came into view. A level was hanging on the wall. Multi-use with five points of bubble and straight edges for marking spots on a project wall or a blueprint. It had to be three feet long. Impressive. Useful. Important looking.

His moment of testosterone glory finally arrived when I asked him if he had a level that was much smaller. Just down the pegboard he took a little yellow package down and presented it to me with a "flex-of-the-bicep" infused seriousness. It was perfect. Three or four inches long. One bubble. $2.35. A road trip treasure. He threw in some body language directing me to the check out where he would be safe behind the counter and soon free of my confusing presence in his store.

As much as I knew what he needed, I wasn't there yet. Some of me was willing to comply, pay, and get him out of his misery. Even though I could appreciate that my company caused a strangeness, I was on a mission that I couldn't understand and I would wait again and see if I could identify it. Something in this place was mine and while the "pocket-comb-sized" level was significant, it just wasn't the whole thing. I looked for a bit at the screwdrivers and some hammers. The hammers in particular stirred up some afraidness in me, but those stories would have to go back into the vault until I could listen to them. The right now was a time for me to look ahead. There was something my future wanted from here.

The work glove selection was good. I touched the ones made of yellow leather and he did have an impressive inventory of sizes. But it wasn't the gloves either. The toggles and latches and extension cords each held potential. I knew I had spiritual imagination enough to twist them into something symbolic, but I didn't have the kind of energy required.

I stood for a lifetime or a second and wished the God would acknowledge what I wanted to ask, then present the answer on a platter. No silver required, a dime store plastic platter for serving summer watermelon slices would be greatness. My pause bore no fruit. Similar to all my encounters with the man called God.

I exhaled deeply. I took myself by surprise with the size of the air that escaped me.

Not completely defeated, I set my find on the counter for purchase and on the wall behind the register I saw it. Or, I saw them really. Not clearly in that I don't know if they numbered three or four or two, and I don't know all the colors. But so very clearly in that this was what the intention living behind my largely blind eyes wanted me to see.

On the pegboard wall behind two large desks cluttered with paper work, someone had displayed several pictures. Two were deliberate drawings of crosses.

One page had a big wide cross in the middle. Outlined and colored in, as if being built on the pages instead of sketched or copied. I noticed the green used for the woodenness on one page of white copier paper. There were four hearts colored in on the corners of the page and another cross drawn into the bottom of the vertical post of the main cross. And a heart where the two pieces of wood crossed each other. An angel with peach colored hearts for wings was sitting up on the left end. She was an outline of blue.

The other picture had three crosses. These were small and black and stark. Almost not in the picture. In the foreground of the picture there appeared to be a figure. A man in a brown cloak, facing the three distant crosses on the left edge of the paper. He seemed like a soldier might look but he was quiet. Just watching the empty crosses standing before him. Or maybe it was a rock and not a person at all. A moved stone with an opening near it. From where I stood, I couldn't be sure.

Each had that contagious dignity about it that comes from artists who have smaller, rounder, gleamier hands. A trace of the face that tilted and barely pushed out the lower lip while the child-sized fingers considered the next color to use, kept camp on the pages hanging there. I pictured the artist tapping out a rhythm on the kitchen table where he worked on his pictures as if they would change the world.

I don't like crosses. I don't like to see people wear them for jewelry as if they know what it means. Diamond crosses are the dumbest variety of all. I determined my bias by the first grade when I saw how much the gem studded lower case "t" on a chain meant to Martha and how the little children this Jesus of the cross claimed to love didn't matter. I noticed the drug dealer on Kojak was always wearing one. Some good women wore crosses too, but it seemed to have a magic spell that made good women mousey. People who wore crosses consistently shared the ability to turn the other way when wrong things were going on. Crosses tell the truth. Truth that can't be trusted. The truth was that there was no one up there watching over anyone. Empty crosses say true things about lonesomeness. These had been determinations of my six-year-old self and they were apparently still holding their grip.

I had spent tens of years hoping without belief. Praying with a barely hope and a mass of resent. Praying without faith that there was indeed a God and asking this approachable, bearded, gentle, parable-ridden man in a flowing storybook robe to speak to Him about me. I could buy into a brother type of guy. I spoke to the Son like my wanting to buy in counted for something. I would call out to the formal guy in white pretty often, but I didn't like who He was nor what He allowed. So I had waited through my life so far to see if "cross boy" would go to bat for me. All along the way, I was intrigued. Curious about the system of Holy. But I did not trust it. And I did not experience it.

And here I was captured by this kid-sized piece of light. I wasn't running toward anything yet. I was running away still. Away from the painfulness of not fitting and the fact that Martha had no one to give her a birthday party and a grown up boy son who held no punches in his disdain for me and the defiance inside me toward a God that I wanted to not like. And the Skillet who had given me Afraid as a best friend. And running. I didn't think I had run before. From much of anything. From much of anyone.

But there they were. The crosses I had felt from a dull day sidewalk half an hour earlier. The plain white paper that had been made sacred by crayons in a chubby hand. They were taped or tacked side-by-side and vertically hung, all next to each other as if they were actually one picture.

I was looking hard. Leaning in to get close. They were about ten feet away and proximity reduced the detail, but not the waxing wash over me. The other things around the collage included a print of the American flag like the one that hung on the wall of most grade school classrooms I had spent time in somewhen, somewhere. And up to the left was a wooden banner that read, "As for me and my house, we will serve the Lord," and four names had been painted on the right end of the plank.

Those signs bug me. Martha has one.

I felt the blurt of words thud out of me as I asked the middle aged man that came to work today to sell washers and spades my questions.

"Who drew those pictures back there on that wall."

"Oh those?" He said pointing, "Those are Drew's. He's not my kid. His dad owns this place. I just work here."

I looked longer and my silence seemed to make him responsible to fill the void of sound.

"See that sign about my house serving the Lord? It only has two kids' names on it because Drew came after they got that made. Those drawings have been up on the wall a long time. Drew is about nine or ten now."

He was out of information and turned to see if I was satisfied with what he'd given.

I reluctantly broke from my long look.

"Can I take a picture of them?" I said.

"Oh, yes ma'am," he responded with a mix of triumph and relief. He knew that his world of ordinary would return as soon as I got my picture and my level and got out of his hardware store. I think he would have let me take a picture of the open cash drawer and alarm code if it meant I was going to leave his safe zone of brass tacks and maintaining.

It was simple and rich and profound. The crayon drawings on business purposed paper were a father's prize and an electric look from God. A "this-world-glimpse" at what is good. A reminder of how a huge God will use very small things to calibrate His love down to a size a kid could look at. A reminder of the Pardon granted. I felt the tender nudge of a proper humble. I accepted His gift but it did not make us friends. A boy drew God and I saw it.

I lowered my camera. As the store clerk rang up my level, I unpacked it from the paper and plastic and saw myself place it in the palm of my right hand and closed my grip gently around it. Then I unfolded my fingers and held it up to look at it like a precious gems merchant might hold a ruby to the light. He handed back my change and gathered my trash from his orderly counter top.

I said goodbye. I should have thanked him. I did not. It wasn't intentional. I just forgot to be grateful. He nodded in the fashion of an old school cowboy to close the exchange. I wish now that I had done something, said something to ease the confusion that had blown in through the front door with me.

I walked out and started to cross the street. That was the last building on this side. I remembered the camera and turned to take a picture of the place. I needed to know that it was really there.

I don't know everything that I think about predestination and things preordained. I know this though. The heavens that lined up right there in that three aisle store had been in motion for ages. Along the way they had affected many people for the good. Some part of the purpose of this store and this little boy were to add weaves to me. But today a God opened every door and a dozen windows in order for me to see Him like I hadn't before. I saw His Fatherness. Briefly. It wasn't mad or angry or disgusted. A clear, mostly unwelcome and short glimpse.

He could have laid out this plan for me years before. Or minutes before. I didn't care when. Pictures drawn in crayon hanging on a wall in a hardware store are my language. Maybe this God guy speaks fluent Sammi.

I went toward the fascination end of the spectrum where the pure kind of engagement keeps house. The value of me didn't actually go up, but my want to see how I count did.

I clicked the camera and let it lower from my face. The hardware store was real. The image on the camera confirmed it.

In a very sweet, small-town way, Main Street separated the direction of traffic with grassed medians and trees down the middle. Either the design was implemented before electricity was commonplace or city planning failed the citizens a bit because there were no power sources in the islands of the downtown street. One evident result laid out on the top of the ground was a spaghetti bowl of extension cords going from one lighted Christmas decoration to the next. Had to love it. The determination of some resident or city councilman to light up the town was not going to be thwarted by a little detail like a lack of accessible plugs and power. The trees and the wreaths and the lights and the chaos of cords bore the intended Christmas cheer.

As I finished my way to the south side of Main, the rain picked back up and I felt for my two prizes in their respective pockets to be sure they were safe. Level and camera. Running for the cover of a storefront, I found a menagerie style exhibit of retail that seemed open, but not well lit. I went in to get out of the rain.

Two narrow, high ceiling places of business had become one with a bit of dividing wall removal.

A woman who carefully blended two signals of existence was working. She was wounded and she was watchful. I walked ten or fifteen steps into the retail clutter that was not hers. She was obviously a conscientious employee, but took no real ownership in the success or failure of the venture. I spotted something I was willing to want to know about and she went to great lengths to bring it down from its unreachable point of display. A long vertical fabric sign. It was brown and listed out about a dozen English towns. A train station schedule to be displayed at the proper platform. I like anything to do with trains and Britain for that matter. She said she didn't want any help to retrieve it while complaining about the dust it stirred up. Low key martyrdom, one of the obvious safe places of living for her. She had reasons to feel like a victim that had high profile residence on her skin and in the way she operated her fingers. The reasons were her secret and had to be kept in the closets she packed them in to generate the energy she needed. I did not want to upset the balance of her moderately painful world by having her catch my stare.

I walked on to inspect any other possible finds and let her get the sign down on her own.

I knew I was going to buy the train station list she was currently wrestling with just because of the bother she was going to get it down for me. I also found a note pad I could keep in the front seat to write on while I was driving. The selection of random purchasing possibilities was big for a store this size. The quantity was overwhelming on the heels of the "basics only" hardware store. Once she had the depot sign down I was almost past being ready to go.

Checking out took minutes instead of seconds. She was frustrated that I tried to pay with cash. She had nothing in the till to make change with. I gave her a credit card instead. The swipe machine wasn't in the store that day. She explained in one of those shaky voices that grow inside people who have smoked cigarettes instead of crying hard, that the woman who owns the store had gone somewhere with it. Maybe she meant to a flea market or another store location. I didn't understand and it didn't matter to me so I didn't ask for further explanation. Explanation came anyway. It rolled out like a murmur of embarrassment as she placed my card on an old style slide that would take a carbon imprint of the card details. The owner had an event sale some place that ended yesterday but she hadn't made it back with the essentials for running this store yet. Essentials like change and the credit card machine. There was a mild resentment on her tone of information that I hadn't asked for.

This new activity did get my interest. She would rather have given me the merchandise than finish this transaction and we both knew it. I didn't blame her as I watched the thought cross her face. She wanted to be doing something well anywhere in her life. But at this moment she mostly wanted to be a good employee and close a rainy Sunday sale that might be her only.

The first attempt to run the press over my credit card ended in failure as the contraption hit the ground. She collected the components and assembled them on the counter. I saw her take a deep breath with her hands and try again to look equipped for the task. This time the handle suddenly broke loose, slid over the card and paper, and she looked like she almost broke out in applause on the inside with the success of it all. I thought I heard some of the silent celebration escape between her smoke seared lips when they gave way to a tiny smile. She picked up the rectangular paper and spotted the next hurdle. Nothing of importance had transferred in the effort to copy my credit card. The sadness of another setback manifested into a kind of calculable slow, smooth motion whereby both hands lowered themselves to the counter while her look stayed straight ahead. The sides of her palms held the weight of this latest near defeat as they made an inaudible impact with the painted wood. It only took a tiny second, but the eyes scolded the hands and they reached for a pen to push on and find a way to finish up this round of comical disgust. She was used to things being harder than they had to be and she was used to being the only one who was going to help her.

"Oh my," she graveled out audibly, "I think it's best that I just write this all down and I'll run it through when the owner returns with the credit card equipment. If that's okay?" She added apologetically.

By now I had become the benefactor of her attitude about staying alive in a life that didn't really seem to want you.

She wrapped my items in tissue and tied the handles of the bag with ribbed turquoise ribbon. She looked at my face this time. Like I was now her friend.

"Where are you from Sweetie?"

I answered with the name of the town my home address was in. I wasn't honestly sure that I was from there but it would be sufficient in this moment.

"I've never been there." She responded. She didn't know of the town I named.

Sometimes when we don't know anything about a place that we think we should know about, we act like we do. We might throw out impersonal or ambiguous information like a landmark or a general vicinity or we tell a story we heard from a friend who has been there. We think it makes us part of the conversation.

We do it with music and places and people's names and books and the God. If we have no experience, we toss out a concept or a scripture or the name of a better book as if we are giving directions.

I think if we give directions, it should only be to a place we've been.

It is funny that when we ask directions we want to believe the person who gives us directions. We ask because we are ready to go there. We trust and we follow because follow is more active than accept. Someone tells us a way and we understand or trust and then go and do it. We go their way. We go on the path they described. They directed but did not lead. We still get to lead.

I think I should always know north. If I know true north, I will find a way. Except now. This trip. So far I have gone west. Or at least mostly west. Some north.

If she had asked, I could tell her about my town. And how to get there. She did not ask. She seemed to wish for something to contribute about my town. A way to have us belong to a common thing for a minute.

I watched it strike her as odd that I was alone in Cotton Flatts, Texas on a rainy Sunday four days before Thanksgiving.

"You on the way to see family?" she asked.

"No Ma'am," I said. "I ran away from home and now for no reason that I know, I am here."

That's when it became okay to listen closer to the other signal of her. The one she gave when I came in to the store. The silent glance of resigned panic. The knowing that she was never going to change anything about how her life was, jumped out from under the layers of colored t-shirts and various leather bracelets. She made no effort to stop the look from hitting the surface. She didn't care to hide it right now. Her longing had become more of a colander than a bowl.

She looked downward and just said, "I see."

She did see.

I spoke a last time to thank her and she extended her final politeness. Then she asked me to move on by reaching to start the vacuum cleaner she had been running when I came in the door. She knew I wanted something for her that she could no longer want for herself.

I went out the door and noticed the bells living on the handle were far too loud. Marking every departure doesn't need to be written in sound with capital letters and bold print. Nor every entrance.

I looked in the window of the next shop as I moved past it. I saw displays of nothing I can now remember. Just that the window was there and that while I walked I looked in at some retail void.

Just windows and doors. So far my running away had been about windows and doors. As if I was a small town myself.

I continued along the wide and empty and temporarily stained with dampness sidewalk. I saw the box office of the local theatre group and I caught the glimpse of a hat laden old gentleman sitting in a metal framed chair between the window and the front table inside the diner that I passed next. I walked on wishing I could forget the skinny woman I bought the notepad and train station sign from. She was not forgettable though.

The rain was now a drizzle.

The Jeep was still parked in front of the bookstore that was still closed.

I stood at the back bumper and looked along at the whole of Main Street. The rain was not snow. Just a few degrees makes a big difference. Definite cold is better than almost cold and this was definite but not freezing. Snow is good. It makes things quiet and a little crunchy. I didn't much like the way the rain looked on the ground.

I put my purchases in the back, except for the level. I took it out of my sweatshirt pocket and set it in the cup holder by the stick shift so I'd have access to it if I needed to look at it. The treasure from the hardware store. The hardware store where I was facing forward when I spotted God looking at me. He was not in the backseat there. Nor driving a truck. I had not successfully crushed him between the pages of the Giant Journal. He was hanging on a wall compressed down into one dimension. A crayon drawing of a cross with hearts to accent it. A cross with life standing in the gap between two dark empty trees of despair. He made sure I didn't miss Him.

Cotton Flatts had been my doorjamb. I could get on with leaving to a further away place now.

The fog on the air protected me again as I drove out. It limited my sight and my thought and the veil of it still comforted me somehow.

I purposely attended to the privilege of noticing more cotton fields as I left town. Some of them had not gotten picked this season. Most in fact. I pulled over soon for a closer look, taking my level out into the scene with me. I walked to the close edge of the field and touched one of the drought bitten plants standing there at the end of a row in the drench of a too late rain. The wool was still hanging on to the burrs. The straight rows covering countless acres looked forgotten and worthless and thin and brown and waterlogged.

I stood for a long few minutes looking at all the flat and all the lead colored air. I listened to the road behind me. The sound of wet tires on a mission. I didn't consider myself lost, but I saw my motionlessness. Eventually I leaned down near a rigid sun murdered stalk and made a photograph. I felt the level in my pocket and took it out. It only had the one bubble in the center so it wasn't exactly postgraduate physics to see that I could hold it in perfect balance with the horizon. Perfect balance is rare.

I studied it for a moment and found myself looking up over it for the whoever who said the thing I heard. Maybe I heard it in my own brain. Levelland. The level was extended horizontally from the end of my fingers and the bubble lay perfectly centered. It was level. I took another photo and stood to hear better.

Levelland's a less than medium sized west Texas town north of wherever I currently was and maybe a bit more west. It's a town where most things are even with the earth's edge. I knew that's where I wanted to go now. I had lived there some as a kid and that's where I needed to go to now. I wanted level.

GOD IS ACTION, COMPLETE WITH MISTAKES, FUMBLINGS, PERSISTENCE, AGONY. GOD IS NOT THE POWER THAT HAS FOUND ETERNAL EQUILIBRIUM, BUT THE POWER THAT IS FOREVER BREAKING EVERY EQUILIBRIUM, FOREVER SEARCHING FOR A HIGHER ONE.

—NIKOS KAZANTZAKIS

fifteen

SIDEWALK DOWN THE MIDDLE

I searched for it using the map on my phone and found out I could use the highway I was already on to go north into Lubbock and then turn west on 114 ... straight into Levelland.

I gave the level a spot on the dashboard and took another picture of it.

I was in no hurry. It felt good. The slow felt right.

Maybe I drove another hour or maybe with the pauses it was more hours, but as I got closer to Lubbock I decided not to overlook it. It too was a part of the story of me. We came here when the sixties were barely three months old.

I knew we lived on 79th Street and that James had gone to Denson Elementary School and that the name of our church was Second Baptist. I was four when we left to move to Levelland and I didn't know if I had been glad to move or not. We had moved to Lubbock when I was about six weeks old because Skillet had gotten a job at a cotton gin. This was the full diameter of the facts I had in my recall. It wasn't so much information in my memory, but rather what had been given to me about moving here and living here.

James would have been about six when we picked Lubbock to live in and that would have made Pete about three. Buck was born a few years later. It would have been three years later ... two and a half actually ... before Buck joined the family.

I saw a sign for the loop around Lubbock and one that said the exit for 80th Street was coming up. I took the exit and turned north on Bennett because my phone map said that would put me near James' school. I accidently passed the elementary school while trying to figure out where 79th Street was exactly.

In Lubbock, streets generally go north/south and east/west. All the numbered streets go east and west, so I figured that finding my old house on a numbered street would be a no brainer. What I didn't know was that 79th Street was not continuous. Blocks and sections of it were parking lots and such for businesses on 80th Street.

I drove around Denson and took a couple of pictures of the school. I could definitely remember the building that had fought to keep looking the same and won. There were long white bricks on the outside with little odd colored diamond shapes mortared around them and large blue panels of something that wasn't brick or stone under the groups of the windows. Fifty years had not phased it.

I'm sure I must've gone in the school with Martha at some time, but I couldn't remember anything about it. The playground felt familiar and I could definitely remember being pulled in a wagon to come here. Maybe we walked James to school or back home sometimes. I didn't really know.

Martha would have been about twenty-nine years old. A walk of most distances was feasible for her. She was always on the go. Always in motion. Energetic. Hair always done. Pulling a wagon with a three year old and a baby girl would have suited her definition of an afternoon adventure. She may have been less used up then. Less worn down. Less worn through.

I drove to find our street from here and realized I was a muted buzz with thinks and the impressions and feelings of a time that was both long gone and deeply current.

The first block I drove down didn't seem right, or the second. Then I had to detour around and come back to 79th several streets later when it returned. I could remember the house pretty well. Brick, with the driveway on the left side and a concrete walkway to the front door down the middle of the front yard.

I was certain about that walkway.

One time when Buck was just a baby he was sitting on that sidewalk and maybe I was supposed to be taking care of him, but I can't remember if I had been told to keep an eye on him or not. What I can remember is that Skillet was spraying chemicals, like probably a bug killer, on the lawn and there was a puddle of water on the concrete where Buck and I were playing or sitting. Buck wasn't walking yet so he was probably about eight or nine months old at the time. Skillet saw him drinking the water in this little puddle, but before he picked Buck up out of the water, he grabbed me and went to slapping my face, screaming at me for letting the baby drink the poisoned water. I was sure Buck was going to die and that I was going to die too. Him from the poison and me from Skillet killing me because I had killed Buck.

That's how I knew the house had a sidewalk up the middle of the yard. The poison puddle would still be standing if I found the house. I would still be three. I didn't know how little three years old was. Even then, at the time of the puddle disaster, I felt old. I felt responsible. I felt small, but old and responsible.

I knew the garage and the driveway were on the left end of the house and so far that combination wasn't on the parts of 79th Street I had seen. In fact, not one house had a sidewalk to the front door that started at the street.

I passed behind a brown-bricked big church and recognized the parking lot immediately. We had a go-kart when we lived in Lubbock. I saw it. In that parking lot behind the church that wasn't the church we went to, I could see and hear that little go-cart from five decades ago. We didn't go to church often in Lubbock anyway, but this was a Methodist Church and no way would we have gone to a Methodist Church so we must have only used this parking lot because it was close to our house.

I felt an enormous pull tighten in my chest. The certainty that I didn't want to find the house was engaged in a round of tug of war with the certainty that I did want to find it and look at it. Just look at it.

My knees weakened when I tried to leave the asphalt approach of the church. The feeling of being pinned to the ground by a 300 pound professional assailant that comes with breaking the same heart countless dozens of times made me stay stopped there.

I didn't try to slow the memories or categorize them or sort them. I only really know them by their shade of dread.

It became apparent that even if I could find it, seeing this house was likely going to be more gruesome than great.

James and Pete and I had lived in a room together there. The boys had bunks and I had Grandma's old four poster bed. Buck slept in Skillet and Martha's room. There was a grand piano in the living room and I have seen a black and white photo somewhere of me sitting at it. I'm wearing a red velvet dress in the picture. I know it's red and velvet because I still have the dress. The backyard wasn't impressive. There was a gate to the alley where the trash trucks drove. We had a swing set that I think was there when we moved in. The TV room was called the den. It was small and the TV was small and the couch was small and the closet door was small and inside the closet was small. I was small.

And once I held the back screen door open while Martha rushed out of the kitchen with a cast iron skillet full of grease that was on fire.

I remembered the outside of the house. It was grey and brick and had some siding and the trim was painted dark. Green maybe. There was one step up the porch to the front door and the porch was narrow and ran the length of the front window of the room where the piano lived. The other window was on the right. Skillet and Martha's bedroom window.

Martha's station wagon was kept in the one car garage. I don't know what color it was. Skillet had a pick-up. He parked on the driveway.

And I remembered that Skillet had a button back by the license plate on the bumper that would start his pick-up truck and put it in reverse. He used it to move the truck where he needed it at the cotton gin. I pushed that button one time. The truck was parked on the driveway when I did it. I don't remember much, but I do remember that I got into a terrible amount of trouble for doing that. The Skillet kind of trouble that makes the whole world physically different once the flesh has settled.

I think that truck may have been green. Shiny light green. Like a blue colored green. I just know that the blood from my nose showed up bright on the paint and he hit my face again when I cried about the blood. I saw Martha look out the front window but she didn't come outside. James was out there with us. He must've been sick with helplessness watching it happen. He was nine years old by then, so maybe he was learning how to protect himself a little from how it felt to be the watcher. I shouldn't have pushed the button. I shouldn't have cried. It made James helpless for me to push the button and get hit and cry. It made Martha hide behind the curtains. The curtains that covered the long front porch window of our lives.

I realized that I was sitting in the car now praying that James had found a way to not feel everything he watched happen when we were kids. He was the oldest and saw it all happen to us. None of us had been there to know all that had happened to him.

I looked at the parking lot now. The Methodist church parking lot that I forgot I hadn't left yet. We had brought that go-cart down here to ride. Skillet wanted to drive it and our lives were all about him so we were probably all down there so we could watch him perform. I don't recall Martha's face in the picture so she may have been at the house with the baby. I know I was quite taken with the go-cart and wanted to ride it. I wanted to do most anything that Skillet wanted to do for as far back as I can remember. Doing things that he liked to do was the safer side to live on. He knew how to have fun. He did fun big. Rarely, but big. Selfishly, but big. Exclusively, but big. I prefer fun that has company.

He put me in his lap and that alone would have been enough. I don't remember that any of us ever sat with him or even close to him if there was any other place to choose from. But on this day, he was going to include me in his fun thing. He told me to hold on tight to the steering wheel and we took off. It was loud and rough and I think we were going about sixty miles an hour, or ten, but it was very fast for a three year old and I held on for dear life. So tightly in fact that he apparently wasn't able to turn the steering wheel where it needed to go. We crashed. I cried. I had ruined his fun thing. He cussed and kicked and I stood there wearing summer clothes, taking what he delivered in the church parking lot. I could make him that mad when I was little. I could make him so mad that he broke things he didn't want broken and scream things that he said he didn't want to scream. And kick kids that I hoped he didn't want to kick, although he never said that part. I was three and already responsible for his behavior. There would be other times later that I would ruin his fun thing. This may have been the first one.

I was through with remembering. I left the church and drove to another section of the street in search of anything that might be gentler. Or just have some light.

I knew that there was a red brick house on our block. It was across the street and several houses down and two boys lived there who had a spaceship in their backyard. Pete played there some and James less than Pete, but I had gotten to see it once too. It didn't take off or anything like a real spaceship, but it was fantastic! I think their dad had built it for them. It was made out of wood and painted grey with some black and red on it. It was like a playhouse, but it was a spaceship. I'm sure James and Pete didn't like having their little sister tag along to play, so I may not have gotten to see it but that one time. I only remember once. I liked remembering it. It felt like it all happened on a good day. Or made that day good.

I drove down these next two blocks and knew it wasn't the right place either. No houses with the right sidewalk. No red brick house with a spaceship in the backyard.

I thought about Mr. and Mrs. Barrow who lived next door to us. I didn't know them very well, but I know that they were crazy about Buck. They were old and drove a very big, mint green Cadillac car and they gave my little brother a red rocking chair one time and me nothing. I wanted to get a red rocking chair. Or any other present. But they didn't know me nor buy me a present. That's about all I could remember of them. That and wishing very much that they would have seen me and liked me the way they did Buck.

I was impressed at how nice most of these houses still looked fifty years later. I was trapped again between two distinct feelings. One was the feeling that I must find the house and the other was the feeling that I must not.

Must won.

A brick house on the north side of the street, with the driveway on the left and the lead walk to the front door running right through the middle of the yard was there in the next block.

I stopped and got out. I was still there. Not all of me. A portion. A portion larger than a memory. More defined than a smudge. The me that learned to toddle. The me that faced some dooms like a squared off John Wayne and some fates with an unheard sob and some fruitions with a deep punishable grin. The me that learned to talk and to not. The me that would never be feminine enough and the me that was both glad and ashamed of it. Maybe this is where my inadequate daughterness began.

> I WAS STILL THERE. NOT ALL OF ME. A PORTION. A PORTION LARGER THAN A MEMORY. MORE DEFINED THAN A SMUDGE.

The three-year-old Sammi who had rushed to put on a swimsuit when I saw Skillet spraying the neighbor kids with the garden hose. I didn't want to get into trouble for getting my clothes wet so I had run into the house as quickly as possible and changed clothes. I was too late. He had already made everyone laugh and he put the hose away before I could get in on the fun thing. So I had hidden myself around the corner of the garage so he didn't see me be too late. I felt naked in my swimsuit. I had no way of getting back into the house without him seeing my embarrassment. I stood behind the wall like a hostage until he disappeared. Then I ran in through the front door and didn't cry like I wanted to and changed my clothes before the bullies could have a go at me.

The baby sister who liked James' football helmet more than he did and who liked to peel all the leaves off the mimosa tree twigs and decorate mud pies with them was still here too.

The Sammi that was supposed to keep her father from leaving her mother and the Sammi that thought Pete was the funniest kid ever to be around were both here on the front porch and standing in the grass. Not waving to me and not ignoring me. Just being the girls of my story that hoped to be seen by me.

The lawn James would mow with a reel push mower was not being cared for as well as we had kept it. The bushes in the planter box built in front of the living room window hadn't changed much. The big window behind the planter box was familiar with the rectangular multi-pane arrangement. The same big window that kept the street from seeing where our unplayed grand piano once lived.

The concrete sidewalk and driveway had broken surfaces and were not smooth the way I remembered, but they were where they belonged, not betraying my recall.

Martha showed me how to pull weeds and dandelions in the backyard one time. She wanted some help with the chore so she taught me how to get all the root out. It didn't make any sense at all to be pulling up the only green thing in the yard, but she said that the grass couldn't grow as long as the weeds were there. It made even less sense to me to be pulling up anything that had a yellow flower! And when I found out that dandelions were also the little guys who made the beautiful seed tops I loved to blow, my internals got very stressed out about taking their lives and tossing them into brown paper bags for the trash man to carry off. But I did. I dug them up. I pleaded for them to stay and I dug them up because that's what she told me to do.

My present is now one morning when Martha put Pete and me in the wagon and pulled us down the street to each house. She invited every mom on both sides of the street to come over and have coffee cake in the backyard at our house. People made friends with their neighbors in those days and Martha needed to have some friends. Not real ones who might know what goes on inside her house, but coffee cake friends.

This November day I stood on the sidewalk. I watched where she had pulled the wagon down the street. I stood and watched the places where she kept her days moving. Where she strived to hide from who she had become. Where she clamored at the dream of being a very good wife and a very good Christian and a very good mom and a very good neighbor. Not just a pleasure, but popular. Like the class favorite she had been in high school. A place in her mind where nice was more valuable than kind and impressions more valuable than truths. I felt her lostness. I felt it as my three-year-old Sammi self. I felt it from the semi-adult spot on my timeline. Her ambitions were bold. But they were crops planted in clay and most of them drowned.

I had to leave. I had to go away from here. I had to go where I could get a better view of what she had taught me without knowing what she was doing. I was beginning to understand why I was a terrible mother and a terrible daughter and a project for church ladies to pray for.

The mist on the air had become rain again and I got back into the car. The soggy was on my skin and on my clothes. I realized I was cold. I turned on the engine and the heater and soon I left the place along the curb where I had stopped the Jeep. It was a slow leaving with an edge of urgency. I left, and the sidewalk Sammi came with me.

Other memories lined up, but I didn't want to remember anything more so I just kept driving away from them. Much about those children called Sammi and Pete and James and Buck will need to keep living on 79th Street. I can't take them all with me. My rescue days are winding down.

I have wondered about that whole rescue thing. If I had stopped protecting what would Skillet have done? Some behaviors get permission or get promoted just because they know that someone will stop them.

I have seen them. They have lives. The children of this past and their conventions. I remember that I know them. I turn my heart for them forward and drive without looking back anymore. Without listening back.

I needed to breathe. I needed a deeper draw. A longer minute of breath than what I had taken over the last couple of hours. I needed an inhale that would fill out my shoulders and almost hurt my chest. I needed one of those breaths that would make a statement to myself. I drew the air in hoping to appear strong to myself. I didn't get all the way there, but I marked it as progress even if it wasn't success.

WHEN I LAST SAW ME

sixteen

SUNDAY DUSK

I was going west. Chasing another sundown slowly. I had no hurry.

I had driven a dozen blocks before I remembered I was looking for a gas station. Standing where the loop intersected with highway 114 was a 7-11. I almost mindlessly pulled in and got out of the car. The rain was falling ten feet away, but I was sheltered by the metal roof above.

I put the handle in to fill the tank and realized I was probably pretty close to the orphanage we used to drive by on our Sunday afternoon drives. People don't do that anymore—take a Sunday drive.

I thought about trying to find that children's home. Mostly all I could remember was a scene of several small, bricked houses on a large piece of hot looking ground with few trees and a playground and maybe a church or a school. There were often kids out playing when we would drive by. I don't really know why we drove that way at all.

As a kid, I had wanted more than anything to live there and be an orphan with no parents at all. In my fantasy the brothers would live there with me and we would all be orphans until we were old enough to be our own parents. I wanted it so much that I was afraid Martha and Skillet could read my mind in the car and I would be punished for thinking it. I would be caught praying for it with all my tiny kid might. That cycle of thought had only made me want to live there even more, but that deep plea pray was never answered. Never granted. By the time the family moved away from Levelland I had learned that the God doesn't hear prays so I stopped.

Finding it now didn't seem as important as getting to Levelland to spend the last few grey hours of this day's sunlight.

I remembered that I needed the restroom and took care of that while the gas tank was filling.

It was late in the day but still a good distance from the night, and the air still had a murkiness to it that dulled the sky and made the ground muggy and shiny.

Skillet's demons tended to come out in the evenings.

Sunday night was the worst. Dusk on any Sunday night. Maybe every.

It didn't matter how good we had been or how beautiful the weather or what town we lived in, dusk was our horror movie.

The boys too. We clocked it together separately. Each of us watched the other as the dread approached and we waited to see where the danger would lite.

This is where I learned about aloneness in a house full of people. It's where I learned that no one could stand between a person and their pain. Where I learned that protection would not come. Where I grew a home sickness for a place that I only believed existed but had never been to.

While other families watched Walt Disney on Sunday evenings, we watched Skillet come unglued. He would start remembering everything we had done wrong. Each thing. Either that day or that week or in our whole lives. He would begin with the crossed over angry teeth, then the screaming and the slapping and the kicking. The belt with the evil metal buckle would be yanked from the loops of his tan polyester pants and impacts of steel and leather accompanied every case being brought against us. Unsatisfactory report cards from school. A glass of spilled milk. Mud on the family car. Not saying, "Yes sir" with Marine Corps conviction. Not flushing the toilet. Getting sick. Being loud. Losing a tool. They were all death row acts of insubordination.

Today was Sunday. The town I most called my childhood home was less than three dozen miles ahead of me. The time was less than four dozen years behind me. The collision of them was now within me. The deep middle earth core of me.

I believed we would not outlive this town. I assumed the brothers and I would be written about in the local newspaper when we were killed by Skillet. One of us or more. The crime would possibly seem small to an objective reader, but the survivors in our family would know that the infraction was punishable by death. We would know that we had been warned. We would know that our death was deserved somehow. We would be like a page three story in the *Levelland Daily News*.

I knew a lot about reading the paper because I had been a paper girl. James and Pete and I had all worked there at different and some overlapping times to throw the paper in two of the neighborhoods on the south side of town. I had 135 customers and the paper went out five days a week. No Monday and no Saturday printings. The stack would be on the sidewalk when we came in from school, tied together with some crossed over twine. Before we did homework, we would do the dirty job of rolling papers and throwing them on front lawns.

Before it was my paper route, I'd help James roll his papers and I was always volunteering to throw them for him for money. I didn't quite understand what volunteer meant. Most of the time, the weather was good enough to load them into a big white canvas bag that said "Levelland Daily News" on both sides and throw them from a bicycle.

I wish now I still had that bag. It had made me feel important. It had changed me. Having that bag over my shoulder full of responsibility had shown me how to escape and impress myself and underwrite my own ambition.

It was a very small paper, except on Sundays. Those would come early in the morning and we'd all chip in to get them done. Well not all. Buck was never much on paper rolling. He didn't like shelling black-eyed peas either.

It was about the same event really. We'd divide the stack of newspapers onto the den floor, each fold them the same certain way, roll them closed, and wrap the rubber band around a couple of times and put them in a pile. If we were shelling black-eyed peas, we'd spread old newspapers out and dump heaps of peas in the middle of the floor. Everybody sat in about the same place in the room for both activities. We'd each have a pan to drop the peas into and a common mound in the middle for the shells we had emptied.

No matter which was going on, Buck was getting out of the work somehow.

The Sunday paper was supposed to get delivered before we went to church, so sometimes Martha would drive us around the route to save time. No matter whose route we were throwing, I wanted to be in on it.

After the papers were thrown, Sundays usually took a nosedive anyway, so it was kind of like the only sure shot at a good thing for the day. The beef that Skillet had with that last day of the week began at the first light of day. He got up to a slow kind of mad and spent the day getting madder. Martha would try to take us kids to church, but no way in hell was he going and by the time church let out, all that hell that kept him from going with us had usually taken up residence at our house on Mesquite Drive.

Church wasn't the problem, it was just the book mark. Every once in a while Sundays would trick us. We would almost think Skillet was good. We'd drive to Lubbock and eat at the Zuider Zee and then drive around town to look at the big houses or drive through neighborhoods of people less fortunate so we could feel rich. And very often we would pass the orphanage I went to in my mind whenever I wanted to pray to God for something very specific. Either way, the drive would eventually incite Skillet that poor people didn't take care of things and that rich people had things he deserved more than they did.

The ride home was always longer than the ride over. It was longer and more dangerous. And the business of almost thinking Skillet was good was closed.

If we didn't take a Sunday drive, Martha would try to make the day seem redeemable by putting a pot roast on to cook before we left for church. We'd get home and she would start serving up a very nice Sunday lunch with gravy, bread, and mashed potatoes. I think now that Skillet used up his "not going to church" time finding stuff to lose his head about when he got some targets back in the house.

I was very cautious on Sundays. And the boys were very scarce. We couldn't all disappear though. Skillet never did well with being by himself. I would stay in range so he wasn't left to deal with his unpopularity. I would start the day out vowing to myself to not make any mistakes and to not say anything stupid. The vow itself impossibly stupid.

Sundays required more concentration. We each had to be on our best game in order to survive. Maybe the fact that the weekend was almost over played a part in Skillets opinion about that day. Or maybe that we had done most of the chores on Saturday and there wasn't as much to make us do on Sunday. Maybe that meant he had less bossing around and yelling to do. The NFL wasn't much of a Sunday afternoon factor and he wasn't a regular golfer even though we had a membership at the

149

country club. He didn't seem to have other men to call for a golf game. Maybe the other guys at the country club knew Skillet better than we assumed. Maybe his lonely showed up as bored. The bored may have brought on the irritability and then before we knew it, one of us had said something or done something that sent him into a free for all. Well, not a free for all. Maybe a free for one and his one was enough for all. He threw his violence down and we received it.

Sundays carried a huge anticipatory blow to the mid-section of our bodies and our hearts and our minds and the remnants of our displaced souls.

I had wandered too far into the labyrinth again.

I noticed I had gripped the steering wheel a little more tightly because of the meteors of memory pelting the windshield. I drove slower, but I couldn't ease the bombardment. It took a few minutes for me to realize that most of it was flying past me instead of into me and the mix of painful and funny and sad and intense had a small amount of balance to it.

I relaxed my hold some as I passed the city limit sign. No real change to the resident count. No one noticed that we left town all those decades ago. Or maybe some family of six moved in to claim our spaces. Or maybe it wasn't in the budget to change out the sign until the number changed by a greater amount.

The turn at the first traffic light past the cotton compress took me south on College Street toward the side of town I lived on until we moved away when I was in the fourth grade.

Half a mile down, I drove through the parking lot of the now old, Levelland Motel that was built in the 60s when we were living there. I had spent some time here because my friend Kim Campbell's parents owned it, along with the Spot restaurant and the dry cleaners and the beauty shop and a huge chunk of farmland northeast of town. She went to the same church that I did and on a few special occasions I had gotten to go home with her from church and play at the Motel pool while her mom managed the restaurant. The motel had aged well. I stopped for a look but I didn't check in. Didn't get out.

I circled back out onto College and kept going south. There were too many places I wanted to stop, but didn't until I got to our old neighborhood and Mesquite Street where our second house in Levelland was.

We had lived on Aspen Street when we first moved there after Skillet took a job at the compress. By the time I started school in 1966 we had moved to the Country Club addition and the boys had changed over to Henderson Elementary from Joshua.

Mesquite was the house I counted most as mine. Just an age thing I'm sure, but it had the most to offer as far as information about who I was and who I am and now it was there in front of me for the first time in forty-two years.

It seemed benign enough in the filmy damp of a Sunday evening. No demons came charging out onto the street to carry me off. No flashes of laughter brought a grin to my face. It was still orange bricked and one story and the front door was the same.

The house and I looked at each other a few mild minutes. We would have to visit more later.

I had a couple of other things I wanted to see before dark, so I put the Jeep in first gear and drove slowly to the end of the block to make the turn to Lori's house on Sycamore.

Driving the length of Mesquite Street I realized that I could remember a lot of the names of the neighbors. I had been the papergirl for this neighborhood, so I had known who lived where. It made me small. I was eight. Eight in 1968. Eight again right now.

FORGETTING IS PAINFUL.
REMEMBERING IS PAINFUL.
BUT NOT KNOWING WHICH TO DO
IS THE WORST KIND OF SUFFERING.

—PAULO COELHO

seventeen

ROUND ONE
WITH A SWIMMING POOL

Lori was that friend we each have in our yesterday. The proximity of our houses meant we went to school together. We were in the same grade at school. We were both blonde-headed and I liked very much playing at her house.

I found the house. It was on the corner. When we moved to the Rio Grande Valley, I wrote Lori letters and even now I could recall her house number and the zip code.

Her dad, Bryan, was a farmer and her mom, Sandy, stayed home with Lori and her little sister, Mary Jane. I think I spent more time here than I did at our house. They seemed to like the way I laughed and their house wasn't all gossamered up with surprises and anger. I thought about going to the door and asking if anyone knew where I might find Lori or her folks. If I knocked, I would have had to explain myself or something. I did not want to do that.

I didn't get out. When my pause ended I drove away.

I read the street names out loud and noticed the newer houses. I went on up to the country club which was closed. I had mostly known that I would eventually go there.

The dark was almost in sight and I felt the anticipation of another alone night start to bear down on me, but it would not be well with my soul to stay in the car. No one was around, so I wouldn't need to avoid anyone who might make conversation. I turned off the engine and cautiously opened the car door. Crude oil air and a chill comforted me. I crossed the few marked spaces between me and the familiar concrete ramp to the swimming pool entrance. The wood fence around the pool was rotting out along the lower border of some of the wide planks. I peered in between the gate panels and saw that nothing had changed.

Buck and I came to the pool more often than the big brothers. Pete would be out doing something with Donnie or a kid named Chris from Sycamore Street and James was always busy mowing yards or doing whatever boys in junior high school do. But Buck and I would put too much zinc oxide on our noses and ride our bikes down here to play in the pool.

Buck was the better swimmer even though he was younger. I could only swim under water, so whenever I ran out of air I had to be near the shallow end or a side to grab onto. Buck could swim with his head under the water or out of it.

I couldn't remember the circumstances, but one day Skillet came down to the pool while we were swimming. My best guess would be that he had been there to play poker inside the club. I know for sure he had not come solely to check on us.

Skillet noticed what a good swimmer Buck was and I noticed that he was quite proud of him for that. Skillet also noticed what a limited swimmer I was. He tried to make me a better swimmer that day in the summer of my seventh year. I didn't want him to teach me. I knew that I was going to disappoint him and since I knew what that would translate into, it paralyzed me and I fulfilled my prophecy. Each time I failed to swim like Buck, he'd tell me to swim over to the side he was

standing on, then he'd grab me by the top of the head and hold me
under driving home his point. Later he told my brothers how stupid I
was that I couldn't swim and for years after that I had dreams where
I would hold my breath until the panic of not breathing would wake
me up. He was always holding me under in the exact same spot in the
exact same pool in those dreams. This pool, that was just on the other
side of the damp coated, wintery gate.

I might have been standing there looking at my memories for an hour
or maybe three minutes or five, but now it was best to go. I mentioned
a thought of comfort to myself that maybe I'd feel braver later.

There are varieties of courage. Like when I know I have nothing to
lose. That may not be a valiant kind of courage but it works sometimes.
And maybe I'm answering a question with my move into face a fear
on occasion. Maybe I'm looking in to see if I have something to gain.
It takes courage to do noble things and it takes a courage to do some
things less noble and self-serving. I think courage is harder to come by
when I'm alone. And I think courage is a completely alone thing. An
alone thing that seems more gallant and more possible when I am not
by myself.

There is a whole daring category of people who hold the brave in place
with their courage. They are the strong who tuck in close beside the
bold and keep them wrapped in the skin they live in. And then the
brave don't have to be brave and bold anymore, the holders of the brave
let loose their hold just long enough to shop vac the puddle of pee that
escaped when the scary moment was all told.

Maybe I'd go inside the gate when there was more light on the day.
Bright daylight kind of light. I knew the unfinished would get finished
but not in the dusk light of a Sunday evening.

I filled the grey empty in my chest with breath and forged a flimsy pace
to the Jeep.

I drove up Brownfield Highway on the west side of town to the courthouse square in downtown and found a diner.

eighteen

MAYBE WE'RE ALL ALIKE

Stepping up the curb I looked into the diner. There were no customers even though the sign said they were open until 10:00 pm and it was barely 7:30 pm now. I pulled the door open, letting warmth out and cold in, and asked what time they were planning to close. The two girls working confirmed jointly that they would be staying until closing time.

I went back to the Jeep and collected Giant Journal, a couple of pens and my iPod. There were about fifteen tables and everything was decorated in red and white and black. In the corner stood a cardboard cut out of George W. Bush. There were pictures on the wall of local football heroes and John Deere tractors and all things small town farming. The white was bright, the red my favorite shade, and the floors clean.

I chose a four top table along the wall so I could spread out and catch up with myself and listen to the melancholy that grounds me at times like this. The times that come along where I think I have to reach my full unmeasureable weight of 10,000 pounds before I can start shedding any of the mass. I wanted to set things out in front of me and count them and appraise them. The journal, the iPod, the unfiltered thoughts, the lies, the true things, and the purchased aluminum colored level all needed to be laid out on a big flat surface so I could order them and see them.

As I arranged my closely guarded paragraphs on the very public tabletop, the cook girl went into the kitchen and the waitress girl brought me a menu. I ordered a cheeseburger and some chili cheese fries and a Coke. She asked me every which way but straight what I was doing in Levelland with this very old book and no friends. I kind of wanted to not be talking to anyone because I had so much to hear and remember and record before it escaped me forever. I dodged the inquisition.

When she brought my glass of Coke back, she brought a different approach to the query. I put my pen down and found her eyes looking for mine.

She knew that I was letting her pose her actual questions when she said, "You're not from around here are you?"

I smiled on the inside and thought to myself, "Yes, I am."

"I don't live here now," I said. "I lived here about forty years ago." I continued because she was still listening.

"I ran away from home a few days ago." The words sounded lame and bold and I felt my emotions slouch some. "I didn't plan on coming to Levelland but now that I have ended up here, I'm just visiting some familiar places and doing some thinking."

She pointed to the Giant Journal on the table. "Is that what you're all writin' down about?"

"Yeah." I hesitated, hoping she would hear me protect the experience from invasion. "Yeah, I just want to remember some things better than I used to so I'm writing them down as I go."

I had just set my hand on the pages and finished my statement when she said, "I've done that before. I didn't ever go back though and that's what I'm doing in this town now. Seven years later, I'm still here, but today I got a call from my dad and he's getting out of prison after serving twenty years of his sentence."

Somebody's always got a better story than my own.

It seems like everybody wants to say some of their story to a brand new stranger and then, the story teller wants to almost immediately minimize the horror and damage and go on about life with the posture of faux heroisms as if they are not even wounded. The limp is obvious though, no matter how subtle it is, and then when the limp heals up we still have the story about the limp we used to have.

I think I prefer to listen to people who still limp. And I think I prefer to keep limping. Like the trophy is in being the walking wounded instead of the recovered. The life that the healthiness brings changes our responsibilities too much. I will likely lose friends and the sympathies that I've fed off of if I mend. It sounds too isolating to be among the fixed.

I wondered what her dad had gone to prison for. She saw me wondering. I felt my face scoot back that half-inch way it does sometimes when I want to hear someone better. The not very bright of her eyes dimmed one abandoned notch. It didn't matter now why he had gone away.

I watched her walk away repeating my order to the cook girl and noticed her step was a mix of disgraced and the short-lived pride of being seen.

There are so many like her walking around upright. Like me. We some how appear unique. But we are not.

I wonder if she or I got here with any built-in abilities that really count? Count in a make-a-difference kind of way? Or do those usually get conjured up from life experiences? Invented in the moment when we needed another variety of competence just to stay in the adventure.

I know that I can catch flaming arrows as well as most and fend for life—mine and anyone else's that the moment deems worthy. I can assess danger and delight pretty fast. I can see things I don't want to see and know things I don't want to know. Did I arrive that way?

I did get here with lots of energy. I'd rather do than not.

I know sad from a pretty good distance. Seems like I've always known sad from a pretty good distance. And fear. Sometimes I know fear is in a room. And sometimes gentle pieces of people that are not as hidden as they think make eye contact with me.

I can protect and defend and I don't remember a time when I was too little to do those, but I don't know if that's a built-in feature or just something that was circumstantially required of me.

I know I prefer writing things down to not. Maybe because the page is my most available friend. When I speak to explain what I see I usually complicate things or give birth to a glassy eyed look that reminds me that most flights are solo.

Maybe my only built-in ability is to cling to my own character arrears and liabilities as if they were the excellences of me.

We are connected. Me and the waitress girl. I should thank her for her being visible. She gave me permission to be the same. Disgraced and proud and seen. Purposed.

I knew her. The young waitress that ran away to here. I knew her and she knew that. Maybe that was my built-in ability. Maybe that counts.

I put my earphones on and started the music I brought in with me. I opened the journal pages and wrote the day down quickly; motivated by the fear that I could forget something I needed always to remember.

Shortly my newfound little sister arrived with my requests from the kitchen. The chili cheese fries were a gorgeous pile of perfectly sized strips of fried potatoes, freshly grated cheese and loads of greasy, ground meat, chili. I lifted the top bun of the cheeseburger for a look at the anticipated toasted texture that I was about to crunch down on. I didn't have to eat it at all to know it was perfect.

In no hurry to go anywhere, I ate French fries and wrote my words and took bites of my burger and wrote more words and let the music complete the fantasy that I didn't matter to anyone anywhere. Not in a blue way. I'd call it deep woods green.

An hour blew by and then another hour after that. I was still the only customer. My visits from the staff of two had been scarce. I didn't need anything. They didn't need anything more from me than the initial exchange had merited when I came in.

I looked at my watch. It was time to pause.

Picking up my treasures, I left the plates I'd eaten from on the counter with my bill and a good tip and a distant prayer in a faithless way for the girl who would soon be called on to visit an unfamiliar face reshaped by prison time. I had written a day's accumulation of considerations and still I was behind. I was behind and I was okay and I was not okay.

Across the street from where I parked was the county jail and the metal barred front door was partially opened. I remembered when they built it there and Martha told me that people in jail only got bread and water to eat. Seemed okay to me. I loved bread. I took another picture and in the darkness the flash popped up. That made the dingy jail door look pristine. I was pretty sure this was no longer a jail anyway, but I couldn't tell what it had become.

In the camera was the digital image I just recorded and I recognized that it was another self-portrait. I am no longer a jail with a barred door locked from the outside. The door is open. I opened it from the inside. It was a choice I made. And now the prisoners could go free. Some had. Some were afraid. Afraid of halfway houses and parole and freedom so they were still drinking water and eating bread and wearing prison stripes. They were also choices I had made.

Now I would need to find a hotel to be in while the darkness crept by. The day had resembled a week, but would wait no longer to end.

I clocked the growing cold gathering on the county court house parking lot now and shivered a little from the chill hitting my not yet dry clothes. The rain had stopped and the stars moved into the vacancy left by the now gone clouds.

nineteen

ANOTHER
SAME HOTEL

The Best Western on the corner of College and Highway 114 seemed nice enough, so I took a room there. Mr. Brown and the Giant Journal and I went into the same room we had been in the night before. Someone had moved it, and the lobby, and the elevator to Levelland. I brushed my teeth and sent Tank a text to say good night. He didn't try to tell me to come home where he may have thought things were better. In a similar courteous fashion I didn't tell him that the further away I went the harder it was becoming to picture going back.

He continued to prove my belief that he was the greatest find ever in a husband man. For now, he had his very smart eye on me and knew that pulling on the rope wouldn't bring me closer.

There was Levelland all over my surface, so I took a hot shower. I found the memories to be soap resistant but the heat of the water resembled rest. The Giant Journal laid quiet on the table so I left it there.

I talked to Sundy for a time. She is my friend. The good kind. The rare kind. The kind of friend that would think running away fell short of reason, but not short enough to warrant a scolding.

We may have talked a long time. She may not have talked at all. I had to say about this one series of torments out loud. It felt like it would kill me if I did say and it felt like it would kill me in my sleep if I didn't say it. A forgotten or buried collection of obscene that had risen into my present runaway Sunday like a striking snake.

A shame I had not caused nor provoked, but one that had been sunk into a dark pour of cement and today had taken life as a liquid specter and escaped my packing job. It came up from the ground tall and vertical and it sought me out. It had surprised me and frightened me and I denied it initially. But it was tangible in my know. The truths that had charged out as I drove around inside my past.

I was small when it had started happening. Small and young and it made me feel little and old. Little and old and no longer a child. Less able to make eye contact. The first couple of times he acted alone. He made certain that it was dark. Maybe he thought the dark would blind me. I wouldn't see. Wouldn't know maybe. But I did see. I did know.

I am one of the millions. Crowds do not bring comfort. Solitudes do not bring comfort. Neither will temper the deep red on a face nor the deep treachery behind it.

Over time he got bolder. The disdain and nausea and contempt were alive within me. I had no vocabulary. Now still I have no vocabulary. I have my disrepute. And when my six-year-old self was absolutely certain that nothing could be worse, he made it worse. He added a girlfriend to the confusion. She was without conscience. She said things worse than him. She did things more loathsome.

It went on for four or five or more years. I do not know. I wonder why I don't know. I wonder too why my timid declarations had been dodged. Why my protests had been so easily discounted. I know this man's affliction on me was evident to anyone like him. Some other men got to me once the seal had been broken. Some did not. The one that took away the chance for a hold to ever feel safe lives in more lives than just mine. His name changes. The family changes. The story is the same.

THE ONE THAT TOOK AWAY THE CHANCE FOR A HOLD TO EVER FEEL SAFE LIVES IN MORE LIVES THAN JUST MINE. HIS NAME CHANGES. THE FAMILY CHANGES. THE STORY IS THE SAME.

I had buried them somewhere. The invasions. The trespasses. In a deep hole. Inside a coffee can in a deep hole that I dug. Inside my own bones. Away from my recall. Out of the sight of my awareness.

They had not suffocated beneath the surface. They seemed to like the darkness for all those years. Today they had burrowed their way to the surface somehow. Out of the can and out of the bones, they surfaced as if depth charges had been lunged at them. At me.

I said it. Out loud. I mentioned about them at first. Then I told one out of its life in the dark. It didn't kill me. They didn't kill me. The events nor the saying out loud of them, nor the rememberings took my life. And they did not judge me. The terrible moments themselves did not judge me. And Simply didn't judge me.

I put the phone down then.

I didn't want to cry anymore. I cried some more.

I knew I would not write them down.

I wrote them down. The trespasses and their trespassers.

I wished that I hadn't promised to go back. I wished that I wanted to go back. I wondered if home was forward now or back.

I dozed off and woke shortly with the nausea of a migraine. Mostly the night went on that way until dawn. Some sleep, some wake. I took something for the headache and it began to curtail before morning. I took some more about an hour before light and the pain cut itself down another notch.

The quiet helped the headache. The quiet underlined the glaring blanks in my silent sentences.

twenty

CLEAR COLD

Despite the headache, the day that got born by the spin of the axis seemed different. Better. I went to the window and the red beige of the town was crisp. No spongy sky. No fog blanketing out over the landscape.

This day was cloudless. Sometimes the sun shines. Sometimes the sky shines. Sometimes with me. Sometimes for me. Sometimes in spite of me.

I put on a baseball cap and my same sweatshirt and went downstairs to find the coffee. That would be enough to push the remnants of the migraine out and make room for the rush of thought I would soon need to figure out how to file. Two cups should do it.

Same breakfast area with the same waffle mix. The same hotel was over in Laney somewhere.

I visited with the lady in charge of the morning and eventually confessed to being a runaway. The delight on her face was confirming. It made the knowing within her surface.

I took my pair of coffees up to the room and drank most of one before laying back down for a while to close out the headache.

The hot water felt giving instead of draining this morning as I showered. I chose the long sleeve shirt and put my things back in my bag. I noticed a Best Western mug on a shelf and picked it up for a closer look. It said Levelland on it. I liked that very much. I liked seeing Levelland written on something that I could hold. Something as valuable as a coffee cup.

I took it as if it was my holy grail and went downstairs to check out.

A teenage girl sitting in the lobby noted the Giant Journal I was carrying and invited herself over to look at it closer.

"That book's gotta have some pretty important stuff written in it." She said

I stopped and showed her the pages inside. Some blank. Most not. The lady from my earlier exchange was now behind the front desk and leaned over the counter to have a look at the years of me. I looked at the blond framed face of the young girl as she tried to take in the book. Questions that smelled sincere were on her frown, but she did not pose them. I waited until her gaze became a glance and shut the pages over.

People may have lost the art of explore. I'm not sure. It's as if curiosity had been left up to the hippies and war protestors and the Beatles and people who like to travel to Washington DC and march against things and do LSD. In the 1960s we still believed that asking questions created problems. Now we seem to believe that asking questions exposes them. Maybe one day questions will stop being blamed for creating or exposing problems and we will fall in love with posing questions for the pure that they are. The true they awake and the adventures they lead and the connections they reveal and the blessing of dependence they hand out like Halloween candy.

Setting Giant Journal down on top of Mr. Brown, I showed the cup to the woman at the check-out counter that I had confiscated from the room and asked her to put it on the bill. She said, "Forget it," and handed me a permanent marker to write the date on the bottom of the cup with. Her gesture let me know that she wanted to be remembered as part of my quest. A good part. A small and good part.

In the parking lot I caught the thick scent of oil before its refinery experience and put Mr. Brown, Giant Journal, and the coffee cup in the backseat. Then I took the level out of my jeans pocket and held it in line with the roof of the closed cotton gin across the highway. I found that I could raise my chin easier today than yesterday. And I could look from a higher place. Maybe this would be the day that I would finish understanding why I had even run away in the first place. I rolled the level into the middle of my palm and paused before putting it in the empty cup holder for safe keeping. I knew there was a want to look for the eyes of God but it wasn't huge, so I didn't. He cleared his throat in the back seat to let me know He was there. I still hadn't thought of anything to say to Him. I still didn't reach for His hand. I was still mad at Him. Still shunning Him. Still punishing Him.

Expectancy was forming a barely life near me. It was small. Like a measure of the light from a burning matchstick came with waking this morning and I knew I wasn't on board the same train I arrived on. The weary making of my encounter with Disappointment hadn't been permanent at all. I thought about how to describe it to Tank and a picture of a pressure release valve being turned a bit to the left came to mind. A metaphor that an engineer could indulge. Embrace.

I headed south on College Street across the railroad tracks and found myself anticipatory of a warmth that illuminated. I accepted the loosen. Disappointment kept her seat. Her posture changed. Less slumped in the seat now. Shoulders approaching the back of the seat incrementally.

Aimlessness prevailed. I remembered about Levelland having a "colored" part of town and how far away that kind of thinking seemed now.

I thought of my two little friends who we called Mexicans before political correctness set in, and who had been given all manner of derogatory slang names. Now we have "Hispanic" as a poor substitute to label a kid's history of origin. We were not allowed to be anything except classroom friends. We were not "spend the night" friends. I never really wanted anyone to spend the night anyway. If they knew about me and the inside of my house they wouldn't want to be my friend.

Gabriella was very smart in school and Nadia was the one that Martha had told me was beautiful. Then I remembered the age I was when I realized that no one had ever called me beautiful. I was no one's princess girl. Almost no one's daughter.

There are no unbeautiful little girls in the world and everyone should hear that word right next to their name. Beautiful. It's not the same as cute or sweet or smart or funny or other lesser things.

The pause was brief. More fact than pain.

The mindlessness returned. And I went back to Nadia and Gabriella and playing on the playground at school.

I remembered that I played better at the boy games at recess than the girl games and often I was better at them than some of the boys. And how bad I would feel after hurting some kid's feelings when he didn't beat me. And how many times I vowed without conviction to let him win the next time.

I remembered the skateboard James helped me build when we were living on Aspen Street. We found a foot long plank of 1" x 4" wood and attached parts of my skate to the bottom. I loved that I could stand on the little "sidewalk surf board" and skate down the pavement like the big kids. I was four or five and in my imagination, James was proud of me. He was the only person I remember trusting to do that. Be proud of me.

The other girls my age were busy loving their brand new Barbie dolls and their dress up clothes. Dress up clothes made me hot. I didn't play dress up very often. Dolls were prefabricated girls that I would never be like. They were made of plastic and had owners who managed their feelings and their clothing and their destinations. Not like managing a skateboard, but like making the bigger hands the boss or the god over their perfect empty profiles. I wanted to know how to play dolls, but I did not. So I pretended that I had other things to play with. Better things. Smarter things. Things that would change the world. My world. The whole world.

I didn't learn to ride a bike at the right age. I didn't have a bicycle anyway so I used that as cover for the fact that I was embarrassed that the other kids in the second grade knew how to ride a bike and I didn't. I touched my cheek now to see if I felt the same flush of humiliation. Yes. Shame lays a heat on a face and shades it a red that is beyond the agility of the rainbow to replicate.

Little memories. Not little impacts. They rushed back and forth. The crossings of ages and minutes and stories.

CHILD ABUSE CASTS A SHADOW
THE LENGTH OF A LIFETIME.

—HERBERT WARD

twenty-one

SUMMERS

I was driving past the now closed, full service gas station as a recall of Skillet getting mad there raced into mental view. I had made him mad. I slammed my own thumb in the car door. It happened while we were waiting to fill up the car with gas. I'm sure I had been told to stay in the car, but I didn't stay still much so I must've gotten out of the car when I wasn't supposed to. Somehow, getting back in the car I caught my thumb in the door. I did not cry and that saved him from having to hit me, but he was mad and I was stupid and he did not thank me for saving him the bother of having to hit me upside the head.

Sometimes we get beat up. Sometimes the beater takes something. Sometimes we get beat up for nothing and it's much more insulting. To get beat up and know that we had nothing they wanted is disgrace.

Sometimes I fight back from my core. Sometimes from my extremities. They look different. They feel different. They are different. One achieves a victory—even if I lose. One does not. Getting beat up doesn't always look like a fight.

I stopped across the street to look longer. The view of the station shot me back to the last time Aunt Mary and Uncle Carter stopped here for gas on their way back to Pine City. Maybe 1966 or 1967. They were driving a dark blue Thunderbird or something Ford and two door. Pete and I were both going home with them this time. We got gas and drove away from Levelland like Pine City was a great place to go. Later that night we were in a terrible car crash that involved four or five cars on a dark stretch of highway and some people got killed. Aunt Mary had cried most of the trip before the crash and Pete and I had stayed very quiet in the back seat. We both knew how to stay quiet when there was trouble even though we knew that Aunt Mary wasn't mad at us. She had cancer and maybe she was going to be sad about dying. Anyway, the big wreck had just made her cry more.

I was the lucky kid that got to go to Pine City in the summers and stay with Aunt Heather and Uncle Arthur or Aunt Mary and Uncle Carter. I don't know why Pete got to come this time, but I was very excited to have him. I had pictured myself showing him around all the houses and neighborhoods as if they were mine. He probably wasn't picturing it that way at all.

Aunt Mary was Skillet's oldest sister and she lived in several places around Pine City over the time I knew her. She wore small black glasses with "diamonds" on the sides and sometimes-outrageous sunglasses and she dressed in loud clothes. She had thick chestnut red hair and wore scarves around her head and her voice matched her style. She smoked like crazy and was always carrying a glazed ceramic ashtray in her hand like a bejeweled accessory. She wasn't tall really, but she seemed like it. And all conversations needed to be focused on her if we hoped to keep her engaged.

Aunt Mary could make Skillet look like an amateur when it came to fit throwing. She loved to play a board game called Wahoo but she didn't do well with losing so we adapted to making sure she always won in order to minimize the game table tantrums. Tangents that included throwing iced tea glasses against the furthest wall and swearing that made the Bible on the end table shudder. She never directed the frenzied conniptions on us so it was more entertaining than threatening.

I think it's a good thing to find things fascinating whether they make sense or not and my Aunt Mary fascinated me.

Uncle Carter was nothing like Aunt Mary. Big. He was a big man. Quiet. And his laugh was muffled and he opened his mouth in a narrow parallel line to set the tiny expression free. The rim of hair that corralled the bald spot was dark and his ears seemed small which probably protected him from hearing everything that Aunt Mary was going off about. His glasses were black and descriptionless. He wasn't a terribly motivated man. He didn't need to be. Aunt Mary had enough drive to cover the lifetimes of about a dozen grown men. He spoke softly. His voice was about a tenth of his size, but it made me want to look at him when it did make an appearance. I knew he loved me as much as he was allowed to love anyone besides my aunt and my cousin.

I'd stay a little while at Moma and Pa's in those summer trips. They always lived in the same house. Always.

There was a railroad track close behind their house that I loved walking along. No one seemed to think it was anything but okay for a little girl to go there on her own and maybe it was. Sometimes I'd go down there and lay rocks or sticks out on the rail for the train to crush. Or I'd line up a row of overlapping pennies that I'd stolen from Pa's dresser jar for the steel wheels to melt together when they rolled over them. I'd carry the penny plank back to the house to show Pa or Moma and we would all pretend that we didn't know where I had gotten the coins. That's generosity. To forgive a thing that was only barely a crime even though no confessing took place.

Moma was never a very warm woman. I think she had never been young. No teenage years I could imagine. I never discussed it with myself. I just knew that she had been born a grandmother. For me her hair must have been grey all her life. It was short and flat on top and curly on the sides. Her face was almost always still. A flesh tone of grey. She rarely wore ear-bobs. Maybe to church. Or to the Safeway®. The rare appearances of them would be small collections of colored plastic octagons that clipped to her ear lobe, accompanied by a single strand necklace that matched exactly. Her dresses were plain and lanky like her. She was tall and her hands were tall when she held them up to express anything. She was skinny and serious and probably not all that glad to see any of the four us coming. Her other grandchildren were older and much less rowdy, but she seemed to do okay with one or two of us at a time.

She would take me to church when I was in her house on a Sunday. Her church was small and pretty boring and smelled like old creepy songs and old wood and old people and old pages and the preacher pounded his words out on the podium as if it would make a difference.

Pa was shorter. He wasn't round but he had strong on his bones. Forearms and calves that were statements of strength. He always got dressed in the large hall closet. The closet was like a safe cave. Not painted inside. Slats of dark wood for walls. Walls that smelled like his overalls. A window on one end. It had enchant and intrigue embedded in it. It was like a silhouette of my father's father. Because of it I knew that not all closets were dangerous to a no longer innocent little girl.

His bed was in the TV room and his chest of drawers was in the hall next to his closet door. That was where he kept some of his pocket change and there were two pictures in frames up there that someone my height could only barely see. One of Pa and Moma when they got married. One of my cousin and her husband on their wedding day with Moma and Pa.

The whole room arrangement was a mystery that we never talked about. It was just understood that Moma slept in the double bed in the one bedroom in the house and Pa slept on a single bed in the room where the TV and his smoking chair were.

He cussed in front of us often and laughed more than Moma and never apologized for himself about anything. He had this truck with no doors that scared me to death when we had to ride in it and his garage was engaging and frightening.

It smelled like very old grease and rat bait and all his stuff was filed randomly in King Edward cigar boxes stacked on buckling shelves. It was always darker in there than the sunlight through the open door could beat and had great amounts of treasure to be found and held and investigated. Pete was totally captivated when he was in Pa's garage. His busy mind for all things scientific would quiet his voice and awake his mouth breathing. Pete was born to forage.

Near the clothes line that was strung up behind the hedgerow there was a fig tree that James would eat straight from. They had three cottonwood trees in the backyard that offered shade for the adults to play dominoes under on a Sunday after church. The screen door to the backyard swung out over a small patch of concrete that resembled a porch. They would set up the card tables and chairs on the lawn and drink iced tea from not tall glasses while they shuffled the dominoes across the tables. The uncles and the neighbors and Aunt Mary and Aunt Irene. Irene was Skillet's other sister and she wore her anger differently. More like someone who wanted everyone to pay for how her life turned out.

We all had BB guns and sometimes we'd walk together down to the store at the end of the narrow asphalt road they lived on to buy our packages of BBs. They cost a nickel. One of the men who came to play dominoes always wanted me to take his nickel. Sometimes I did. I sold my eye contact for a nickel.

I stayed with Martha's sister, Aunt Heather and Uncle Arthur the most. They lived on the south side of town and didn't ever mix it up with my father's family. My cousins Amy and Bonnie were a few years older than me, but at least they were kids—which were non-existent at the other relative's houses. They had a bookshelf in the hallway and it was stocked with Nancy Drew mysteries and they would buy Lay's potato chips, which I loved. Actually I really loved Ruffles, but the plain Lay's were a treat too. I did not ever mention that I liked the Ruffles chips better. Aunt Heather looked strong but was actually fragile in my mind so I would have never wanted anyone to hurt her feelings. She bought the Lay's and always showed the bag off to me so I would know they were for me. To let her know that Ruffles were better would not have been an education. It would have been ungrateful. Sometimes information is redundant when motivation is pure.

They went to a Baptist Church like us and like Moma. Guess the whole family was Baptist, but they weren't quite as bent on being there every single Sunday. I was glad for that because I hated petticoats and dresses and patent leather shoes.

I was the lucky kid that got to go to Pine City in the summers.

I was also the less lucky kid that had to go to Home from Pine City after the summers and be around with other people who were not Uncle Arthur or Uncle Carter. They should have been jailed. Now they are dead. They deserved worse. I want very much to turn the pages in my soul and skip those chapters. I cannot. The barreling in began like a flame to my skin. My face. My palms. My whole outer self. My whole inside self. The burn made me unable to drive away from my spot across the street from the gas station.

The other boys and their friends should be revealed when they scrape layers of life and innocence from the eye color of a child. They are the people who should not be allowed to check either gender box on forms that we all fill out over the course of our lives. Every identifier save one should be stripped from them until they repent and break and see what they have done. See and feel and know and bury their faces for a piece of eternity in the stench they created. Breathe in the pain until it runs in their veins.

Those assassins of clean who lure both the loved and the unnourished alike into their dark caves of barely visible death. Those who choose to touch children, take their clothes from them, hold them captive in mental and emotional shame, and make themselves a part of a child. Enter them physically. Spiritually. Eternally. Make them hold parts of a body that the littlest of us should not have even cast a glance toward yet. As if it will be as easily forgotten by the victim as it is by the uncaught felon. Those who delight in the destruction of purity and crave the control of tiny hearts and minds. Those who crush forgiveness in children. The most malicious of all spiritual Berlin Wall builders. They are the those who should smell nothing but decay in every breath they take until their last gasp.

I bounce like an inflated beach ball now between the walls of this mixed history. The redeem and the carnage run side by side around the track of my life. The remembers of kind feather pillows and snores of a grandmother run along the path next to the exhale of the darker people. The ones who created the uncertainty of any invite to sit on someone's lap. The alert in my soul if someone wanted me to go for a ride in the car with them on my own. Parking lots behind any building the possible destination disguised by a return with a pack of cigarettes. The Lay's potato chip purchases made just for me and the compassionate know of trust must blend its residence in my memory with that of fear and wondering if I was enjoying the crimes against me. Is the shame that these kept happening or is it that I didn't know how it felt or is it that no one heard the changing shape of my no longer young face.

The remembering of the initial timid shame-filled speaking of it to those I still believed wanted to care about me. The realization that they didn't care about me as much as they cared about themselves. Being a parent is very different from having children. Being a parent should include the courage to listen to difficult sentences that a child has to figure out how to form.

> BEING A PARENT SHOULD INCLUDE THE COURAGE TO LISTEN TO DIFFICULT SENTENCES THAT A CHILD HAS TO FIGURE OUT HOW TO FORM.

All these belonged to the summers in Pine City. The collisions. The care. The compassions. The chaos.

I found no comfort in realizing that I am not little anymore and that they are dead now.

It was time to stop looking at the closed down gas station where we filled up Uncle Carter's blue Ford car in 1966 or 1967.

I had travelled forty-seven years and two blocks.

I took a long breath and rolled the shape of the steering wheel in my hands.

It's a day-to-day thing being here. Here on this gorgeous painful warm planet. To have breath and to be human. To have a day when the summer heat has been interrupted by a sudden thunderstorm and to have to choose between feeling startled and feeling cooled.

True greatness doesn't get credit at first. The alarm has to wear off and not all greatness is permanent. No rain stays falling forever, and no sad and no sun. Nor a laugh. Just like a snow cone and a brain freeze. Most things stay a length of time that I assign them. If I decline to give it a value measured by time, it may flee too soon or it may stay forever. I have to choose first to be aware of a thing. The accumulations that make up a day. See them and ration them a value. I will do this today.

I moved deliberately from my stopped stare at the filling station to a search within for things that may need to be uncovered and brought out into the light.

I looked at my hands again, put the Jeep in drive and drove to a park we had been to a few times on the northwest corner of town.

I knew we had a birthday party for Buck there one time with an orange cake. I thought it then and I think it now, "Who asks for an orange birthday cake when chocolate is an option?" The baby I supposed. And he got it.

Once I got there I could only remember one time besides that birthday party that I had been there. Some kind of church party. Maybe like a Labor Day potluck picnic kind of thing and a girl from my school got crushed under the seesaw and broke her leg. I don't think I knew her name, but I know I had wished it had been me so I could get away with some stuff for a while and get all that sympathy.

The park held no unfinished business in its picnic tables and broken asphalt parking spaces. It was empty. No hurdles. I thanked the wind. I looked at Disappointment riding shotgun and she gave me the "drive on" nod as if she was in charge of me.

I drove past the Allis Chalmers dealership building where Skillet had worked. It was now some other business to do with farm equipment. I slowed to a pause or a stop without pulling over and looked at it. Still brown. Still small town industrial. I did not know the windows. The door did not recognize me. I eased my foot from the clutch and drove on. Beyond and behind the building stretched out the big red flat of forever.

The dirt roads west of here began to appear on the screen of my mind's eye. Unnamed grated ribbons of packed red dirt the width of two pick-ups. They outlined the farms and made their way to barns and houses and past plowed rows of soil. We used to get to drive out

181

of town this direction sometimes and go into the sundry unmarked fields to pull corn and pick black-eyed peas. Those trips seemed like such a party. Especially the corn gathering adventures. We all loved corn, but nobody loved corn like Buck. I don't know if anyone actually likes black-eyed peas, but I learned from them that if I eat enough of anything I could acquire a taste for it. I think that's why no one wants to eat much humble pie.

Farmers were the good guys. They seemed unnaturally tall and their hats were put on their heads purposefully. I would watch their paper sack colored hands push the brim back when they spoke to my mother as a gesture of "ma'am." And if they spoke directly to me, they'd push it back a little more to grin out a "Well, aren't you cute," without any words. They evaluate herd animals quickly. They always picked out the lead in our pack. Then I'd see them put a hand on James' shoulder and point with two or three indirect fingers out over a general area and tell us to pick as much as we wanted. Quiet, over-sized, no nonsense men who worked with land would show a dignity toward James that he recognized. The pause those exchanges cause will stop even angels in their gait of protection. Then James would take it from there. He'd make sure we had our grocery sacks and rush us to match his stride to the lines of plants sagging with their fruit.

It takes a lot of people working together independently to save a life. Any life. The reaching out with a look or a nod or some iced tea in a glass. It's the making of a grand mosaic where many artists place bits of themselves on the canvas. Farmers whose names I can't remember are part of the saving of the brothers and me. They didn't even know it. Or maybe they did.

James and Pete got to make money sometimes from the farmers by chopping cotton. It seemed such a glamorous thing when I was little, to go chop cotton and get paid. The boys argued my perspective at the time, but I knew about the farmers being kind as much as I knew about the money. I just didn't know much about August heat and a hoe and blisters and short-sleeved shirt sunburn.

I didn't go to any of those roads this day. I drove toward downtown and passed the Piggly Wiggly. We didn't buy our groceries there usually, but I had been in a few times. We shopped at Furr's over by the church. I loved going to the grocery store. It was an outing. An outing and an important chore because we had purpose. A list. A week's worth of meals and cereal. Two days worth of milk and bread. Nothing to get in trouble about unless we couldn't find the right roast. The aisles were safe. Buck usually went too. He always went on his own trip to look at the toys on the shelves. We didn't have to stay with Martha in the store. I wanted to though. I could talk to her and help her and get things and remember things she might have been forgetting. Martha was good at the groceries. She was good at making food go a long way. She was good at making things taste good. She was in her element with all things kitchen. She was easy and focused and attentive to me and to herself when we went to the store. Then we'd load it all up the back of the station wagon and drive it home for the unpacking and I'd have more jobs to look forward to. Taking all the bags of provision into the house in their unprepared forms. Putting three gallons of milk in the refrigerator and bags of potatoes in the pantry and finding out if we might get to eat spaghetti that week. A rare indulgence that was fully dependent on Skillet's absence from the dinner table. That was always my favorite food night.

The next block was the county courthouse square. When I lived here, there were two movie theatres. One was right across the street from the courthouse on the corner. It was either called the Wallace or the Gary and then there was one off the square about half a block called the Rose or the Rosie. The Wallace was for the white people and the Rosie was for the black people, but the same man owned both of them. That confused me as a second grader. Why didn't the black people want to watch movies with us?

I saw the *Story of Hank Williams* there. And the *Parent Trap* with Haley Mills. I wore a pair of green plaid pants and a matching vest over a white top to the movies the night we saw the *Parent Trap*. I had been given strict instructions not to use the public bathroom at the theatre. The movie was over and we were waiting outside for Martha or Skillet or both to pick us up. The urge to go long passed the ability to hold it and I wet my pants standing by the light post. I cried. James got mad. He knew. He knew that this was going to mean trouble for all of us once Skillet found out, so he had to yell at me. He was as scared as I was about what all would happen that night. So he had to yell at me. It was my primer. It was his chance to build up courage and to strike out at the anticipatory pain with his words. I cried more. My quiet cry. He didn't see me. He didn't look. I would not let him look. His carry was already too big.

I parked the Jeep and got out to take a picture of the place. The building has changed and the light post we waited by that night has been updated. The humiliation seemed to be alive though. The night I wet my pants at the picture show was still very real. I held the camera up and got the shot. I lined up with the soaped front doors of a ghost. Then I took another. I looked at the camera to see what shape the disgrace took. I was surprised to see that something so real was invisible and the shape was only within me. I consoled myself that some things are just too dark to show up in a one-dimensional image.

I stepped down the concrete street stairs, took a seat on my bumper and thanked the brilliance of daylight for being my warm company.

I walked the perimeter of the downtown square one time.

The bank we always went to was now a law office and the shoe store was an indistinctive gift shop. There was a dance studio and the diner

I had eaten at about a week ago, or the night before. The post office for 79336 was south of the corner on the right and across from it was the store where James spent his money on model racecars and Pete bought Matchbox toys. The S&H Green Stamp redemption center was as forgotten as the third verse of any hymn in a Baptist church.

The JC Penny where most of our clothes came from was closed and shut up.

Martha bought Pete a pair of black lace up tennis shoes there once when he was in the fourth grade. They were not boy shoes. I knew that by looking at them. She may have known too. They might have been on sale so she bought them. He had to wear them. Everyone made fun of him about his shoes. They were his though until they wore out. I felt very bad for him. The JC Penny didn't have much inventory and unless your family drove to Lubbock to buy clothes, you were dressed like all the other kids your size.

The *Levelland Daily News* office now housed something called the *News Press*. I wondered who had all the archives of the paper. I was once on the front page. I was Levelland's only papergirl and someone must have found that newsworthy. It was one of my finer moments in the "childhood achievements" column, but now those records are all filed away. Or not.

I had my picture in the paper another time when I was at the Halloween carnival at Henderson Elementary School and a reporter wrote an article about it. A kid named Brent with red hair was in the picture too. I don't remember liking him much, but I had cut out the black and white photograph and put it in the scrapbook that I started keeping in the third grade.

I had wanted a scrapbook because I found my mother's one time. It seemed a thing that could make a life seem worthy. I didn't know what one even was when I found hers, but there was this page that had all these small black and white pictures of me on it. I was so excited about the discovery and ran into show Martha what I found. She laughed and told me that they were school pictures of her as a kid.

I felt heavy at the delivery of those words. Rooted to the linoleum I stood on. I eventually backed out of the room with the page still opened wishing I'd never seen it. She had told me many times what an ugly little kid she had been and I hadn't known until then that I looked just like her. Maybe no one had ever called me beautiful, but worse than that, they had forgotten to warn me that I was ugly.

I decided that if I ever had a scrapbook I would collect pictures and things that made me seem important if I couldn't be pretty. So I put the carnival picture from the newspaper and a report card on the black paper between the blue shiny hardback binders that pressed the records of me together.

My feet back in step and I crossed the street past the JC Penny and the news paper office to the next block of business lives.

The Wacker's Dime Store on the southeast corner looked like it had become a thrift shop maybe, but Atchison's jewelry store was still open as was their competition, Thoman's on the north side of the square. The Rexall drug store chocolate brick exterior still in place disguised that the insides had changed purposes. Maybe more than once since the middle of the 1960s.

Just off the other side of the square was where the Gibson's store used to be. It was a variety store with more stuff than a dime store. I don't know what all they sold, but one year I got to purchase a Halloween costume there. I picked something called "Sleepy Sam." I added my own hat and was certain I would win the costume contest at church. That was before churches got all of those witchcraft phobias and started banning Halloween due to its evilness. I didn't win though and I let

Martha make me a Casper costume the next year because the store bought costume had proved worthless.

In those days, mothers often left their children in the car while they shopped. They probably lingered in the bank or the pharmacy a little longer than need be. It would have been a break from the kids. They could visit about bridge groups and how that certain woman had dropped out of circulation after her husband caught her in an affair. We spent our time getting bored and restless and usually got into some kind of fight while Martha was inside Gibson's or wherever her shopping errands had taken her once she parked. We never felt abandoned or at risk being left in the car. It was normal.

I made the final side of the square and thanked my country that the Rosie theatre had been torn down.

The tour of downtown ended there and I got back in the Jeep.

twenty-two
GETTING INTO THE CHURCH

I drove a few blocks more east, past the Furr's grocery store that now seemed way too small, and the Levelland clinic where we had all been hospitalized once for a flu or something. They had put all four of us in the same room like a ward. Buck was in a baby bed. I was on a cot. James and Pete were in real hospital beds. We didn't make much noise. The nurses complimented us for that. They didn't know the whole story. They didn't know Skillet and they didn't know about the threat of him.

We were at this hospital often. Buck had to get some gravel cut out of his forehead and stitches one time. James had gotten a huge nail in his foot once and they patched him up. But most of the time we had been here to visit Skillet.

When I was six, Skillet was supposed to die. He was in this hospital. We would come to see him and mostly we'd sit out in the hallway because he was too sick to have anyone in the room except Martha. He told Martha he was going to die and Martha told us. I don't know what it was that time that was going to take him away but it didn't. It was neither the first nor the last time we were threatened and promised that he wasn't long for this life.

Most recently, Martha had told me that Skillet was going to die from some issue with his stomach. When she called me about her upcoming eightieth birthday party, she had let me know that I needed to come see him because his days were numbered. Again. She didn't say again. I added that in my mind while I was listening to her.

He will die sometime. Time is on his side for this wish. His wish. Maybe my wish. We have no relationship. I do not visit or go to lunch or call. I wonder sometimes if I will be okay with that decision once he does leave for good.

I am not the daughter they wanted. I am also not the daughter I wanted to be.

I had stopped to listen to the sun warmed brick of the hospital. I didn't get out and try to hear better. I took the Giant Journal out of the back seat and wrote the revelation. The reminder that being a daughter is a role. That actors get replaced when they don't play the part as directed. That we were all disappointed but not surprised when the critic's reviews came in on my performance.

The notes were longer. The inventory growing. I had gone rogue because I don't blend and I never will and Sterling can find nothing to be glad about between us and Martha's birthday party is going to happen and Skillet is going to manipulate me one last time into visiting him and I am no one's good daughter. And I have now accidentally come to Levelland to intentionally dig loose the roots of some of my current anguishes.

I put the pen between the pages and closed the book. I set it in the front seat. My friend called Disappointment cringed a little when I laid it in her lap. I did not apologize nor offer to put it elsewhere.

I wished I had a drink. I wished that I drank so that I could wish that I had a drink. Not a colorful umbrella laden drink. Maybe a martini.

A drink that would be old and smart and have impact on my mind and my body and my soul.

I drove across the next intersection north of the clinic to the First Baptist church.

We went to church here. This was our church. Everyone had a church and most were Baptist. I didn't even know a Catholic or a Methodist. I didn't know anyone who didn't have a church. Not everyone went every Sunday but having a church was part of the unspoken condition for living in a small town.

People make friends in their church. They seal business deals without contracts. They determine who is to be trusted and engaged. It's where people go to look like they are trying. They do not go there to weep or reveal or confess.

I parked in front of the main building of the church in the end space and turned off the engine. I wanted to go inside. I needed to go inside. I opened the Jeep door and stepped out without taking my eyes off the second house of God I could remember.

I stood out front and took some pictures of things I knew I would appreciate even if it hadn't been a piece of my own story. I was stalling I think. Trying to know what I wanted to do here.

The steeple had inconspicuous metal screens or shutters fastened to the lower sections. They were a little rusty and even though I couldn't understand what purpose they served, they did look like history between the leafless limbs of the Red Oak. I took a picture. Still taking it all in from the front lawn, I looked at the windows to the preschool age classrooms that were built about half a story below grade. I remembered churning butter at some time in the room on the end. When it was ready, we all got to spread some on a saltine cracker. It tasted like the best candy ever.

I took another picture. This time of the outside window of the room where we had eaten the buttery candy on saltine crackers.

I remembered asking when the "next" testament would be coming. I guess I thought a New Testament that was 2,000 years old wasn't all that new. My teacher laughed. Then she told Martha. Martha didn't laugh. Her only daughter was obviously blasphemous.

Epic fail. For both of us.

I walked around the buildings three times looking for a way inside. I asked a man sitting in the back parking lot about getting in but he assured me that no one was there because of Thanksgiving week. I decided to not believe him because of the half dozen cars near him.

I knocked several times on a door I found and eventually a lady named Jo came to let someone else in. I explained to her that I really wanted to go inside. She was guarded, but not defiant and I continued to describe that this had been my church forty-six years ago for about five years. I paused. She was thinking about it. What I really wanted to see was the Sunday school rooms, but I knew that I was going to have to reel in my list if I wanted to go in at all, so I didn't mention that.

The sanctuary would be my compromise. Could I go in the sanctuary? She said she would take me. I knew it was a stretch for her. Letting me inside made her look anxious and proud and anxious again.

I wanted to sit in the pew where we sat as kids, on the right hand side by the windows. And I wanted to see where the grand piano was. I had played in a piano recital there when Catherine was my piano teacher. Her Mom was James' sixth grade teacher and I would mow their yard with James sometimes. He'd let me walk in front of him behind the mower. I'd help by pushing from the middle bar on the handle. And the ramblings of the chronicle of me poured forth like chicken and dumplings in winter. Hardy and substantial and good for the insides.

One time Catherine told me I could sit on her horse after my piano lesson. I was barely in the saddle when I fell off and badly sprained my wrist and missed piano for a wonderful many weeks.

I got my first "composer bust" here in this sanctuary. I held it in my hand that day and thought it white and plastic and unimpressive. I did not say those things out loud but my face may have betrayed me. My opinions were already strong at seven years old even though I kept many of them in a nondescript box behind my good eyes.

I remembered wearing those clothes to church that were designed for the specific purpose of making little girl children miserable. And I remembered how one Sunday after a lesson on the old woman and her two pennies being a greater offering than the rich merchant and his bag of gold coins, that I put two pennies in the big church offering plate. I felt quite elegant and self-righteous about my contribution until Pete scoffed. I said rather loudly over the top of my left shoulder that "every little bit helps" and the adults for three pews busted out laughing.

I don't think I put money that made noise in an offering plate ever again.

I could sense the rush on Jo the tour guide and decided not to go sit there. I looked at the pew. I wanted to wave at myself but my hostess would have been freaked out by such a motion of the hand.

I took a picture from the front and one from the back and told her how much I appreciated it all. She didn't respond with equal measure of passion, so I repeated my gratitude hoping she would know this was a really big deal. She did not. She could not. She was on the outside of my journey looking out.

We might be better at being in the human condition if we stood behind each other once in a while and looked at the view from over another person's shoulder. I will want to do that more now. Now that I have spent these alone and anonymous days.

I thought out loud to myself on my way out that most of the time churches seem hard to get into.

Except for the horrible clothes, I liked going to church as a kid. It was a reprieve. We were probably the only kids in Big Church that didn't want it to end. Once the service had been amen-ed we were going to be at home with Skillet.

Now I don't actually like church. And I don't actually like God. His boy is not too bad. He did a remarkable deed. He did what he said he would do. His Father however, was not very good at His job at all. He might be on watch for some, but He had not protected me and the brothers anything like He should have.

I wished that He would leave me alone now. He'd done it all my life. Why was He on my trip now.

I backed out of the parking space in front of the church and turned left toward College Street. The east side of town is where our first house was. The cotton compress where Skillet first worked when we came to town was over there.

I knew that to get to the compress I would just need to turn at the intersection that I was now stopped at and go east on Joshua. That was going to put me right on top of Aspen Street and Joshua Elementary School. It all felt very familiar and the streets that hadn't changed much in all my years of absence took me right back to the house we lived in when we first moved to Levelland.

Buck and I had a playhouse in that backyard. It was red and white and had a very steep roof in the shape of a capitalized "A." It was the only color in the backyard, unless the dusty dirt counted. We played hide and seek and kept captured horny toads and lizards in shoeboxes inside our playhouse. Skillet and Martha would let that painted plywood building babysit us for hours. There was no fence in the backyard and there were no more streets to the neighborhood so we could see the pumpkin colored nothing for miles from there. It was paradise.

Sometimes Pete would take off by himself down to this big pit they dug dirt and rock out of from time to time. I would go too when he let me. I remembered a time I walked down there with him after a rain and we got stuck in the mud and I was sure that it was real quicksand like I'd seen in the Tarzan movie and that we were going to either die there or get killed by Skillet for going out in it. I remembered that we lost a shoe in the mud that time, but I don't know if it was one of his or mine. The pit seemed huge and very deep and I had felt very brave going there before I got all afraid about the "quicksand." Then all my brave had withered and I had to focus on not getting dead.

I was still sitting in the Jeep idling in front of the house with the heater on when the entire memory finished coming to mind. I arrived back in my present and looked hard at the front door of the very small golden brown house.

Martha and Skillet had the bedroom that sat on the front of the house. James and Pete's room had the same bunk beds as our room in Lubbock. Dirk and I shared a room and the same double bed that used to be grandma's. This was a very angry house. This had been an especially angry time.

The quiet sobs of Martha as she whispered that Skillet had broken her arm rushed out onto the street and into my chest or my throat or my gut or all of them. He had broken more than her arm in those thus far fifteen years of their union. She felt the break in the arm though. She could point to it and know it was real. Valid enough for tears.

I looked at my own right hand and put the stick into the first gear position.

I couldn't stay stopped in front of 1964 any more today.

Driving away I saw James again, plaid shirt and jeans, walking along the curb. Me beside him. He was always that way. Inclusive. He wasn't a hand holder. He would kind shove me in the shoulder if he wanted to show affection. My very good oldest brother.

I circled past Sharon's house and remembered getting bit on the wrist by a medium sized brown dog in the driveway of the house on the opposite corner. The tetanus shot hurt more than the dog bite and I got an unusual amount of sympathy from the whole event. By this age, I think I had already figured out that sympathy was a good substitute for affection.

> I THINK I HAD ALREADY FIGURED OUT THAT SYMPATHY WAS A GOOD SUBSTITUTE FOR AFFECTION.

Skillet tried to teach me how to ride a bike down this street. I was four. The bike would have fit me in about four more years. He bought grips for the handlebars, but they were too big and fell off easily making steering difficult and giving me too much to have to concentrate on. I sat up on the seat, but couldn't reach the pedals from there so I stood on them instead. Then he started pushing the bike and I started pushing the pedals down to keep up. I got my balance and got some speed and took off. No one had explained how to stop. I couldn't stop pedaling and I couldn't sit down and I ran out of street and had to crash into Sharon's garage door in order to stop. I was a mix of glad to stop and feeling very embarrassed. No injuries sustained really except for being yelled at in front of Sharon's dad and my brother James. They both looked down while Skillet delivered his message of disgust with my failure so I just assumed they agreed. Now I mostly believe they felt bad for me and not about me. Time has a way of filling in the perspective gaps.

It was kind of like learning to swim. Or rather, not learning to swim. I may have already learned how to be the great disappointment before the embarrassing day at the pool. Maybe this day. Maybe one sooner than this one.

I was banned from bike riding after that.

I drove the short block to Joshua Elementary School where the bigger brothers had gone and the next mile to the cotton compress

Dozens of long, corrugated metal buildings side by side. There were roads between each building making easy access for shipping.

Not too far into the complex, I located the office and walked in asking the first person I saw if she knew where I would find Lori Robinson.

She looked right at me and the shock took hold in her expression. She stuttered about one syllable and told me that she was Lori. Then she beat me to saying it myself when she said that I was Sammi Bass. She was genuine and surprised and her reaction made everything okay.

We talked and she didn't get much work done for the next two hours. I asked about her mom and dad. I told her that I had run away from home and that I had bought a level in a hardware store and decided I wanted to go back to Levelland.

She told me about her two kids and that she was living in Whiteface and her dad had already passed away, but that her mom lived just down the road and was doing great.

It was authentic and kind and hurried and all the things that come with friendship, even, evidently, friendships that have been in a holding pattern for more than forty years.

I told her about stopping into the Levelland Motel that morning and asking the guy at the desk if he knew Kim Campbell. His quiet Elvis smile had let me know that he knew her well and he gave me her phone number. Kim Campbell didn't remember me at all but asked me if I knew Lori Robinson and that was how I found her. She complimented Kim and described her as one of the sweetest people ever.

She told me about her little sister Mary Jane and going to Ruidoso to see her pretty often and that when her youngest graduates from high school in the spring, she plans to make time to travel.

She tried to remember my brother's names. I tried to remember if her dad was actually a good man or had just seemed that way when we were kids, but I didn't try to remember out loud.

We filled in the gaps of our last forty years in general ways. Nothing too specific. We didn't know each other that well anymore.

Her boss came through and he and I talked for a minute. I told him that Skillet had worked at this compress in the early 60s and he figured that would have been when his grandfather ran the business. I said that I always loved those miniature cotton bales when I was a kid. He found a couple and gave them to me. I smelled them and held them and wondered to myself why I liked getting that gift so much.

I needed to leave. Lori had work to do and needed me to leave. I took her picture on a porch swing outside of the office and hugged her good-bye.

Going out I stopped to look inside some of the warehouses. It struck me as a strange business to compress cotton into 500-pound bails and inventory it until the farmer sold it. A profitable business that had sustained since 1949 in this location, but still odd.

I thought about the variety of jobs Skillet had held since leaving the Marine Corps.

Restaurant owner and cotton business and all kind of sales jobs that never lasted long.

He was a man who seemed to want to be impressive and smart and run in all the right circles. A man who was pretty good looking, except for those boyish sticky out ears, who could be charming and funny. A man who seemed to find his own reflection both repulsive and dashing.

I knew from the time I was very small that we were not the real source of his rages and disgust. I had to believe that we were though. The alternative left me with no control. As long as I owned that I was the reason he was always so volatile, then I could believe that I could make him be better. Then all of us stood a chance.

Some days I did make things better. I could think in sync with him and I knew how to make him laugh or hand him the right tool at the right time and I could slow his wrath on occasion.

Just as many days happened though where I was the cause of his meltdown. I was never able to master the skill of knowing when those days were coming. I let my brothers down and Martha down when the "Crazy" of Skillet would blast past me and get to them.

Martha wasn't the reason he was a disappointed, disappointing man either, even though he described in detail and a loud shrill of a voice often that she was. He never actually came out and called himself disappointing. That's just what I secretly wished he thought about when he was honest with himself. Then I had to secretly wish that he would someday decide to be honest with himself.

So now this monster named Disappointment was my haunt too. She had been Skillet's great guardian and now she was mine.

Before he got robbed by someone or something or a collection of both, Skillet was likely a palatable presentation. I can imagine that he was smart and as handsome as most boys in the 1930s. Charming, winsome, and aware of how to get what he wanted. Probably he even had a formidable amount of care and compassion. But I think maybe something else got a hold of him and stole the assets of his Maker and the tarnish was eventually galvanized and he stayed mean and selfish the rest of his days. When did he depart from the business of "being made in the image." I assume that to be very different from facial features and appendages. I believe the business of the image to have been a list of personality descriptors. Was he a victim of some crime or tragedy or lie like me? And did he just graduate from innocent to assaulter and judger as I have done?

It gives me a hair's breadth of compassion and a smaller measure of empathy toward him these days. I don't know what to think that will make it all forgivable or good. I know that I have reaped good crops from this ground. I am aware of the system where a rocky life gives a person a variety of credibility that makes them both someone to be avoided and someone who can be trusted.

The grateful of me had kept its head above water so far.

twenty-three

GOING SOUTH

I knew the kids were out of their classes by now and I wanted to go over to Henderson Elementary School. I parked the Jeep and walked around the school building trying every door without success before I found the custodian and knocked until he came to the door.

He stood on the inside. I stood on the outside. If he knew he had something I wanted, he hid it well.

"Hey there!" I shouted lightly with my best warm voice. "Can I come in for a walk around?"

He continued to look at me. Emotionless.

"I'm from out of town and I used to go to school here."

At this I'm sure he was thinking, "That had to have been like a hundred years ago lady!"

"It would mean a lot to me to get to come inside for a few minutes," I sort of pleaded.

He punched the horizontal lock on the door lightly with his palm and opened it about a foot wide. "You can't come in here." That was it. That was all he said.

I waited for more of a sentence.

"It's against the rules," he finally added.

He had no more said it than he realized rules didn't mean much to me and he knew I was going to persuade him to let me in. He hung his head and shook it. This time all principles had left his face and he opened the door enough for me to get through.

"Thank you man! You have no idea how important this is to me. Thank you so much for this. I went to school here as a kid and I just needed to see some things again."

My ramblings were being ignored. He really didn't care and he wasn't trying to act like he did.

I pointed to the first door we passed. "That was the janitor's closet when I was here. He had a vacuum in there that was specially made to clean chalk board erasers. It was always the best job to get out of class and come down here to clean the chalk off the erasers."

"They don't use chalk boards anymore ma'am. Haven't for years." His matter of fact tone almost hurt my feelings.

He went back to his work.

I went back to my past.

I walked first to find Mrs. Vaughan's classroom. She was the strictest of the third grade teachers. The room was something administrative now. Mrs. Vaughan had demanded much of her eight and nine year old students. She had an unusual and well-hidden tenderness that made a child want to be her favorite. She noticed things. Good things.

She noticed quiet and she noticed smart and she noticed difficult.

I went to find Mrs. Fowler's room next. There were three teachers in each grade. I remember being glad that I hadn't gotten Mrs. Greenall in the first grade. She was tall and had short blonde hair and looked very strict. Mrs. Fowler was short and already old and a little bit roundy. I don't remember that third teacher's name. She was young with brown hair and was talking every time I saw her.

I loved school and I loved writing my numbers out on the pages of the Big Chief tablet and I loved reading.

Standing there in the now narrow hall. I thought about a day that Martha had come up to the school. She didn't come up to the school very often. We all rode the bus to get there and to get home. If we missed the bus, we just walked home. My first grade teacher, Mrs. Fowler called me to her desk on this particular day. I never had gotten in trouble at school but I knew she wanted to tell me something as important as bad behavior. I showed no hesitation walking up to the front of the room, even if I was going to get in trouble. And I wasn't entirely certain that I wasn't. She told me that my mother was wanting to see me just outside the door. That wasn't a relief. I went out in the hallway and she was standing there crying. I needed more information to know how to take care of her and I asked her if my father was dead.

He had been in the hospital again and I thought he was going to die. I assumed she had come to tell me that. She looked quite mortified and said, "No, I just missed you."

She must have been staying at the hospital a lot and not been home I stood still. Thinking she must want to look at me. Remember me or something. Check on me. Push my hair back with the palm of her hand and touch my cheek. She did not. She did not come to the school and do any of those things. I would have. If I had been my mom, I would have squatted low and hugged me like I was my little girl.

I don't know why she had actually come to my school that day. I don't know if she stopped in at the classrooms of the brothers. I know when she left I was sure I had failed to respond with whatever it was she needed from me. That's all I know for sure.

This wasn't the first time I had thought Skillet was dead. He was always threatening or promising to die or shouting that he would be dead and it would be our fault. I don't know if I was glad that he was alive or not. I'm sure I acted glad.

I stood in the place of that exchange for a while. She didn't hug me that day. I was probably supposed to have hugged her, but I think I made the jump too quickly to what I would need to do if he was actually dead and what I would need to do if she was actually sad. By the time I figured out that he wasn't dead and she wasn't sad about that, hugging her must have skipped my mind. Gotten buried in the attempt of a six year old to intellectually evaluate such grave adult informations. Make reason of the unreasonable.

Now I reached for the shiny wall, to a tile about three feet up where my six-year-old height might have measured. The tile was cool. Present.

Then I opened the door to the room that held my first year of school. It didn't have desks in it and looked too different to have any impact. Round tables with small chairs stood scattered around the room now. The low windows were the same, but no line of beige and grey desks and no blackboard and the tan vinyl squares of flooring had been replaced with institutional grey carpet. I didn't need to go in. It didn't smell like first grade. I let the door wind itself shut.

I went to the other end of the building where elementary schools historically separate the little kids from the bigger little kids. I had Mrs. Rainey in the fourth grade. She seemed old and strict at first, but she taught us some French and always called me Salty because I never actually sat in my desk. She said I was like the salt shaker standing in the middle of the dinner table. Mrs. Fowler had said the same thing, but it seemed nicer when she said it.

I walked to the windows of what had been Mrs. Rainey's classroom and looked out on the playground. I looked out of this window one day during school and saw a tornado and shouted for her to come see it. We all had then been marched out of the room and into the cinder block and tile hall to sit against the wall and tuck our heads down. Then she ran to tell the principal, Mr. Rishel, and soon all the kids in the school were lined up against the glossy walls. I felt like a hero that day. Mrs. Rainey brought Mr. Rishel to meet me when the near disaster was all said and done. He shook my hand and thanked me for spotting the tornado. I wanted to tell him that I only told her because it was fascinating and that I hadn't really planned on saving any lives that day, but I liked the attention so I didn't say any of those things.

I won the spelling bee for fourth grade in here. I remembered standing at the blackboard to practice writing the words and a girl named June got caught copying me spell the word "gigantic" and kicked out of the competition. But, as Daniel the custodian had mentioned, they don't use chalkboards anymore. There is a dry erase board where the blackboard hung. Blackboards are never completely free of the writings on them. They hold the fine silt of words written the day before and the year before and they smell like homework. Dry erase boards are always new. They smell like nothing. They can't make the snap noise of angry chalk being tapped hard on the blackboard for emphasis and they make science seem cheap with their rainbow colored illustrations. They are not to be taken seriously. I turned from the wall behind the teacher's desk and saw the desks from my ninth year of life as if they were still there. Tan tops and grey painted frames and three heights for different sized kids.

I had to go to school one day in the fourth grade after my Aunt Mary had died the night before. We were leaving that afternoon for Oklahoma, but we all got sent to school while Skillet worked and Martha packed the car for the journey. Mrs. Rainey told the whole class about my tragedy and I turned red and smiled in my nervousness and a girl named Meghan told the whole class that I must not have loved Aunt Mary very much because I had smiled. I wasn't ready to say that Aunt Mary was dead. I hated Mrs. Rainey for putting my sadness out there in front of a whole room of kids who couldn't possibly understand my loss. I didn't like the fourth grade when we came back from the funeral. I had not known what to do with grief. I had not known what sympathy looked like. I felt awkward and out of my control and embarrassed.

I didn't know at the time that she was offering me her sympathy. In fact the sympathy of the whole class. All I knew was I had done it wrong. I had gotten nervous and smiled and not done grief right.

I did not know how to receive her offering. Any offering of affection that wasn't tied to an expectation was beyond my capacity to recognize. All I knew was my social stupidness was glaring that day.

Blinking back my present moment shaming tears, I walked to the classroom door and stood for a very long time. We moved away from Levelland that year. I was excited to be moving away. Maybe relieved. No town of my childhood ever brought the same attachment as Levelland, but I couldn't have known that then.

Much like my stop in Lubbock, a long line of businesses unfinished had lined up. Memories of things I had done wrong and things I had done well that were never noted. The school stop was the right and hard and wrong thing to do.

My brow was heavy with the dark of turning on the light behind so many forgotten doorways. I wanted to sit down. I wanted to walk away. The walk that says I will never be back. I wanted to run. The run that says I should have never come here. I wanted to not be alone. I saw him move.

Daniel the custodian had been stalking me a little as I walked all over my own memories and was now standing here in the elementary school sized hall. I smiled at him and told him I was leaving.

He came over to see me out.

"I can't thank you enough for letting me in today. It means a lot. I so needed to do this man! Thank you!" I said.

He just nodded a "You're welcome" with his blank face and closed the door after me.

I wasn't completely ready to leave yet. My stride felt heavy and tempted me to regret both going and leaving the school. I took the long way around the school back to my parking spot out front. A long very last glance of not wanting to remember anything else. And not wanting to forget who I was then.

THE REAL JOY RESTED IN POUNDING TWO
ERASERS TOGETEHR, THE UNALLOYED CHILDHOOD
LOVE OF MAKING A SANCTIONED MESS.

—LEWIS BUSZBEE

twenty-four

TOKENS

I wanted another souvenir of this Levelland.

I drove over to the college and looked for the bookstore. I thought they might have a t-shirt or ball cap that said Levelland on it. I asked a couple out in front of one of the newer buildings where the bookstore was. They pointed across a campus of mostly one story, latte-colored brick buildings to another building, but assured me it was already closed for the Thanksgiving break. I drove over there and parked and asked a girl if this was indeed the building that the bookstore was in. She said it was, but that she was pretty sure it had already closed for the holidays.

I thanked her and hoped that she was wrong because now I was on a mission to find my something that said Levelland on it.

It was only about a two-minute walk to the entrance, but I rushed anyway as if cutting that time in half would make some kind of difference. Sometimes I do that. I don't want to miss something but I really don't want to "just" miss it even more, so I hurry to avoid feeling the loss of not getting there in time. Could be a control issue. How can I feel guilty unless I tried really hard to achieve a thing and lost.

The door was open and the bookstore was open and they had some t-shirts and everything was going to be okay.

I had time now so I looked at every shirt and pajama and bag and cap on display but nothing said "Levelland." The woman working there was about my age and made a lot of conversation about the new inventory of books for the spring classes starting to come in. She was busy describing the details of her approaching workload for the next couple of weeks getting them out of boxes and onto the shelves. My responses were polite and I feigned a courteous interest level, but I knew that was just jabber and she was mostly warming up to find out what I was doing there.

I slowed my search to give her time to form her question perfectly. She asked if I was in town to see family and I dodged the real question by answering no and offering no more. Maybe I wanted her to ask again so I could determine if she really wanted to know or if I was the object of small talk to pass the time. By now I knew beyond my own bones that my travel was holy and should not be marked down like an item on Saturday morning garage sale table.

Brave is greatness. It reproduces quickly and makes itself multiply. It's like the amoeba of character traits. She had cleared the vocal hurdle and was now feeling all hardy about it. With a new surge of engagement might, she pressed again.

"Not a hot spot for shopping, the South Plains College bookstore," she said aloud.

I went to the counter she was standing behind and handed her the t-shirt I was ready to pay for and let her look me in the eye for an answer.

"I ran away from home actually. A few days ago, I got in my car and drove west and stopped here because I had lived here a long time ago and it seemed right."

If she was surprised by my response she hid it effectively. She just laughed a gentle, resilient sigh and said, "I should do that. I want to do that."

Another pause.

Her look now on the transaction and not my face. "I will do that one day," she said to herself with an audible shamed spirit.

If I had stayed there any longer, I fear she would have prayed over both us.

I thanked her and took my purchases to the car.

Driving away, I realized the exhales were easier again. The crisp in the air had lost its cut and identifying the companion called Disappointment had begun undoing the deeds I had put in charge of me. I believed now that I could take an inventory and find an end to the list of blows and piercings.

It was time to return to 802 Mesquite street for the longer visit I had promised me.

ALWAYS FIND IT FASCINATING
AND IT WILL BE.
—BONNIE MALLONE

twenty-five

THE TRIP INSIDE

Nothing had changed. Nothing was particularly different. Nothing was especially the same any more. It had been foggy and strange here when I came into town. Now it was clear and the orange brick of our house looked less vibrant with all the moisture dried up from its surface. The driveway wasn't nearly as steep as I had made it in my child-sized mind and the yard we all fretted over was actually scrawny and small. The vacant lot next door had a house on it now and more than likely no one even remembered the dirt go-kart track we worked on so diligently those forty-five years ago.

We had a midget racer as kids. It belonged to us. It was painted royal blue and had a red and white egg shaped STP sticker on it. We built a little oval shaped track on the lot next door to our house and James would drive us around on it.

Buck and I were young and less smart enough to have considered it a great honor to be appointed to the "Track Maintenance" team. We got to rake the track over and over and over. We were especially important to the cause when James and Pete would have us stand on the back of the rake while they drug it around to knock down the more difficult bumps in the path.

James would speed around and we would play chicken not jumping out of his way until the last possible moment. One night Martha and Skillet were out and James, the fifth grader, was our babysitter. It must've been a summer night because we were wearing shorts. James was racing around the track. Buck and I were standing in the middle of it waiting for the exact moment to jump out of the way. I jumped. Buck forgot or something. James flattened him in the dirt. Ran right over the top of his little round body. I think the unconsciousness of Buck was short lived, but lasted long enough for James to think he had killed him.

Pete sent me running into the house to get a towel. I came back with the dishrag. He yelled that he wanted a washcloth and I ran back in for it. The panic now was to rid the injured of any evidence of the event. We did eventually get Buck cleaned up. He was mostly fine. The promise was to not mention it ever to Skillet and Martha. An unreasonable pledge quickly betrayed by the victim. We were all getting into trouble over it and then James made a big deal out of telling Martha I brought the dishrag instead of a washcloth. She got onto me for doing such a stupid thing. I'm sure I felt deeply repentant for an extended period of time. I always did that.

I was almost six. Buck was about three and a half. Skillet and Martha left four kids in charge of each other with a go-kart and I was the stupid one. I have no response to that.

Still, today it made me laugh to picture it all. I had not laughed at it ever before.

I liked the laugh. It came out loud and had manners.

The noise of the laugh returned me to the front seat where I sat in my Jeep, parked across the street from the house. I waited to see if any of the brothers came out through the front door. After a respectable pause, I determined they would not.

In my mind I went in instead and looked around.

The hallway to the three bedrooms ran down the east side of the house. It was the first entrance on the left after the tiny entry way. The front room and bathroom were Skillet and Martha's.

Down the hallway, after the double doors to the hot water heater, there was a yellow rotary dial phone on the wall. I could reach it to answer, but not well enough to dial. I didn't have anyone to call anyway. Phones were for grown-ups. If I wanted to talk to someone, I walked to their house. The brothers and I shared the other bathroom with its long corridor shape and pale blue half tiled walls.

At the end of the hall, James and Pete had the room on the left and Buck and I shared a room on the right. The same beige sculpted carpet ran the length of the hall and covered all of the bedrooms.

The first room on the right of the entry was always the formal living room. The grand piano that we had in all of the houses we ever lived in was in there where I practiced as little as possible for each lesson. The couch was white. Martha loved the idea of elegance even if she did have four children. And there were two end tables. Walnut Queen Anne legs with marble slabs for tops and one drawer with a single pull in the middle. All of these possessions that had moved with us to the Valley and then to the next house had their start here. The carpet was the same off white with a curvy design sculpted into it that ran in the rest of the house. Since no one ever went in the living room, it didn't show any signs of wear. Or warmth. Or company having sat there. The niceness of the furniture in the living room lent itself to the fantasy of a nice family. A black and white television family.

What this room really had though was the stereo. It was walnut as well and had two brown and tan speckled fabric covered speakers. They were built into the console and I knew how to start the records on the turntable without scratching them. I would play Floyd Cramer's *Last*

Date over and over to hear the piano notes and we had a 45 rpm copy of Bobby Goldsboro's song *Honey* that I loved. I think I loved it. Maybe I loved it because Martha loved it.

The den was the next room and it was nothing like the living room. No one lived in the living room. Everyone came to the den. The floor was a coffee colored pebble patterned linoleum. The couch was gold and shimmery and Skillet had a reclining style chair that was a dark leather. The sideboard that my grandmother had designated to be mine was against the south wall. It was oak and resonated of legacy to me. The mirror had lost most of its silver so I could never see my face in it, but that fascinated me. I would tell myself that just because I couldn't be seen didn't mean I wasn't there. I shared that little kid revelation with Martha and she laughed at me. I was right though and determined that she might not be the best person to hear what I thought about.

I may not have been right. Now I take count for her. In her thirties. Four kids. Skillet. She may have been consumed with trying to breathe.

The TV was at the east end of the room. Actually, I don't think the room was big enough to have ends. The TV we had wasn't one of those fancy console units like the Inman's had. It was on four short, posted legs and had rabbit ears on top.

The walls in the den were white on top and thin wood paneling on the bottom third. The pictures were of birds and landscapes and there were no people pictures hung anywhere. I asked about that once. I wanted pictures of people up on the wall. I did not like the watercolor red birds or the dull prints of flowers. They were not true. They didn't tell anything and they didn't really hide the things we weren't telling. They were not pretty or happy and the frames were flimsy.

I think Martha would have hung family pictures if she had been married to someone else. Skillet used to break apart once in a while about the preacher that had performed their wedding ceremony. He would lunge into the bucket of jealous he carried around and scream about that preacher wanting to marry Martha himself. Then the hurt in the air he had dispelled turned into the routine physical strikes.

I had seen their wedding picture and thought it was beautiful. She wore a long trained satin gown with dozens of looped buttons on the sleeves. He was skinny and dressed to compete and very handsome. Right between them stood the preacher. Martha showed me the picture one day and explained that she had never been with that preacher, but him being in the picture meant we were never to have it out.

I didn't want that information in my brain. No one ever seemed to know I was little. Too little for words like these. Too little to always live in a world void of an occasional thunderstorm of tender or affection or being known.

There was a single large window in the den. Martha had put a love seat on each side of the curtained edge of it. The miniature couches weren't soft or inviting. They were wood seats with tied on cushions. Skillet broke the little seats in a rage and glued back together several times. She put a small table between them and created a place for friends to sit when they came over, but no one ever really came over much. I knew she wanted friends to come over. And I knew she did not want friends to come over.

When Skillet and Martha would go out, we would all congregate in the den as they left. We'd be reminded that James was in charge and that there was to be no arguing or fighting and Skillet would cross his threatening teeth over to make clear his revenge should we do so. Then they'd leave through the front door. I'd run to the living room window and look through the diamond shaped panes until their car was far enough down the street that I couldn't see them. They looked happy when they were going out. Happy enough that it was okay to hug them good-bye, as long as I didn't wrinkle anything in the one sided embrace.

To see them smile or laugh was thrilling. It was as if our lives were all fixed and now things would be good forever. I bought into these moments. I wanted to believe that they had gotten dressed up and seen themselves as beautiful and made some secret pact to not be unpredictable anymore because beautiful looked better. I didn't know for sure that such a thing couldn't happen. They didn't consider themselves brutal. They considered themselves the victims. It was us that caused them to get so mad. People don't make pacts about change when they like things the way they are.

We ate all of our meals in the kitchen. It had a built in bar top that was table high and we mostly could all fit around it. It was more comfortable if Skillet was out of town. For lots of reasons.

Our kitchen was for eating and for getting busted up. Most trouble started at the supper table. Either school got brought up or Skillet came home and found a bicycle on the driveway or maybe no one had done anything wrong at all and Skillet's balance was just not balanced. Dread and dinner shouldn't go together hand in hand.

Skillet smoked all the time. He'd finish eating his dinner before anyone else then use his plate to ashtray his cigarettes. I sat next to him and the smoke always flavored my food since I was last to be served and the slowest to eat. I had better things to do than eat. I was watching for the signals and managing topics to better our odds of surviving the cornbread and red beans. He smoked and cussed and complained and bragged on himself at the table until something set him off. Sitting by Skillet had benefits though. I got to be the one to refill his glass of iced tea when he wordlessly shook the ice in the glass and sometimes he'd look right at me if he said, "Thanks," I'd swell up a bit inside my chest and hang there on the exchange that made me feel like someone's favorite. I'd be on duty and forget about eating. I'd watch his tea glass for the next chance to fill it up and earn his rare notice.

It was a very basic house, but Martha tried hard to make it fancy and we certainly kept it very clean. All Skillet wanted when we moved into that house was an address in the country club addition. Image was huge to him. To them. We had certainly bought the smallest house in the neighborhood. But it was the right neighborhood.

I sat in my Jeep with the heater running, watching the dinner table inside the house that I used to live in from across the street. I smelled the flavor of cornbread and the flavor of afraid and the flavor of children coping more and hoping less. The breaking of bread and the breaking of limbs and the breaking of innocence.

I recalled bringing home a rabbit I caught one time. In the cotton fields near our house. I brought it home and let it run around this backyard. Skillet had grown weary of me bringing home strays all the time. Dogs and horny toads and turtles. Anything that needed a home was my new best friend. The rabbit must've been the final straw. So he yelled about it for a while and slapped my face a bunch of times as part of the predictable routine. Then he said he was going to make sure I never brought home another stray animal. He put the rabbit in a box and gave me a loaded rifle. He told me to go out to the field and kill the rabbit, then bring it back so he could be sure I didn't just let it go. James went with me. I couldn't do it. I couldn't shoot the box with the rabbit inside. He was kicking against the cardboard like he knew what was about to happen to him. I cried so hard. James knew what would happen if we didn't come back with the dead rabbit, so he took the gun and shot the box until it stopped making noises.

Being a championer must make a heart heavy.

I didn't want to have to kill any more animals. I stopped bringing strays home.

There was a big porch on the back of the house. A covered patio actually, that we built ourselves. Skillet and Martha had promised to take us all to San Antonio for the 1968 Hemis-Fair, but then later convinced us that we would have more fun if we built a patio that we could use over and over and all the time. The boys and Skillet dug the area out and set up the form boards for concrete. I don't know who helped pour it, but we got a cement patio. Then they framed up posts and a roof and we shingled the cover to match the house. My job on that segment was to walk along the new roof and press down the shingles onto the tar with my feet. I was having a grand time walking around on the roof like I was old and important. Then I got distracted. I was walking where I shouldn't have been when Skillet threw me off the roof. Buck got my job and I went in the front yard to cry by myself. More for being fired than getting hurt.

The now me looked for the then me in the front yard. She wasn't there anymore. It was cold today. It had been hot the day I ruined the new roof forever. I don't know where hurt hides itself until the weather is right.

The patio down and the roof up, Skillet built a bar on one corner with a bamboo covering and put a record player in it. He bought several 45's and wired up speakers and he and Martha had some friends over for dancing. It may have only happened one night that people came over to drink and dance. Skillet sometimes forgot to be a Baptist. I stood inside the house by the far edge of the big window with the wooden love seats and watched them all. I did not want them to see me see them.

I loved watching them dance that night. Skillet and Martha knew how and they were better than most and they moved together seamlessly like they might be in a different world than mine. I don't remember the songs that were played. They were not what I heard. I heard my parents dance with no words between them. I heard them be kind to each other. I heard them being enjoyed by the other couples who also watched them.

Tender varieties of memories make up most of the pain in the world. The depth of the gentle of them matches the severe on the other end of the spectrum I think. If we have no sympathy we cannot measure injustice. If we have no compassion we cannot descry abuse. We can defend ourselves from many violences but few mercies.

The house that concealed so many injuries also kept the boys and I out of the rain and the elements and we ate very well and I knew I should be more grateful than I was. More grateful than I am.

Some needs have nothing to do with need. To want is holy. It takes admission and request and vulnerable. We needed the roof over us, but we wanted to be covered. We needed the food, but we wanted the meal.

Still sitting across the street from the lost decade, I tried to remember some funny things or some events that seemed regular. Like an ordinary family might laugh about later. We didn't do those really. We got our repose at school and finding jobs and staying at friend's houses. I don't know where Martha got hers.

I looked for Pete in my search over the lost decade and saw his freckled face come into view. He had that crunched up grin that he carried around with him and it usually meant he was up to no good. He was the explorer who was largely invisible. Invisible by choice. His clothes never fit as well as James or Buck's but he honestly didn't care. He didn't know. He always had a plan to go on an adventure and most of the time, no one knew where he was. He'd throw his news paper route and stay gone the rest of the afternoon.

Buck often got overlooked when hell broke loose. Maybe because he was the baby. Maybe he really was the favorite. Once he started school, he made good grades for the first three years. That made my life better. I had often gotten in trouble for having good grades. I was told that I made them so that the boys would look bad on report card day. Report card day was always a very bad day.

The grace for Buck diminished later though. When there were fewer kids in the house to assault his turn came up. That made it more cruel. The message changed dramatically midstream.

The girls all thought James was dreamy. He was blonde like Buck and I and could do almost anything. He was fast on a bicycle and knew how to drive the midget racer and how to ride a skateboard and loved cars. One day he even painted the entire under carriage of Martha's grey Delta 88 royal blue with cans of spray paint. That didn't turn out funny at all, but we all agreed it looked great.

Not great to Skillet who beat him to the ground for it.

My heart produced no fruit or mirth and it wasn't really the funny list I was hoping for.

I was through being parked in front of my past. I didn't need to stay there anymore. I drove down to the end of the street and turned right, then right again on the road to the country club.

I needed to go there again and sort something out with that swimming pool.

twenty-six

DIRTY INNOCENT WATER

I stopped the Jeep in the parking lot and got out with my camera.

The broken fence looked like it was guarding an abandoned industrial site and nothing about it was inviting. The swimming pool that had taken my breath away for four and half decades was behind those nailed up vertical slats of wood. I walked to the south end first and then along the east side looking for a way to climb in, but after making one complete trip around the fence, I eventually noticed that the gate wasn't even locked.

Just walking through the discovery made me make a small smile, but as I opened the latch a storm was set off inside. On my right was the patch of grass that Buck and I had dropped our dime in one day. It was supposed to get us a candy bar to split and we lost it and had a big fight about it and I ran home and tattled on Buck and we both got a whipping with the buckle end of the belt for embarrassing the family.

I knelt down and looked through the grass for the dime I lost in 1967.

I prayed that day. In my room. After the punishment had been delivered I was exiled to my room to wait for round two to flare up. There was always at least a round two. Skillet had to catch his fired up emotional breath. Then he'd always summon us back in with his shrill from whatever room he was in. I don't know why I prayed that very time. I don't know why I prayed enough that I remember it now. I prayed to find the dime and I prayed to not cry. I prayed and the God I'd heard of continued His vacations in the tropics somewhere. He didn't hear me again. He didn't ever hear me about the orphanage I wanted the brothers and I to live in and He didn't hear me about the dime. I cried that terrible day. He didn't help me not cry.

I didn't pray for real much after that.

I didn't cry out loud this November day and even though I haven't prayed like that since, I did lean down and look once more for the dime.

The lifeguard chairs seemed like overkill for such a small pool. The high diving board was gone, and the low board for that matter. The pool furniture was white and broken and mildewed and strewn about and one piece was in the deep end standing below the surface in the collection of off-season rainwater.

I first stood at the side of the pool by the elevated lifeguard chair.

I stood there for all eternity before I realized that I was holding my breath thinking about it. I let the remember unfold there in the safe of the full cold sun barely hanging above the horizon. Then I relaxed my chest some and did not scold the cry that escaped my restraint. I tried not to cry much as a kid. It was dangerous, but this day I cried myself down to my knees on the poolside concrete. No one knew I was there and no one knew me even if they had seen me and I was grateful for both truths. Some things that hold on to a life have to be lanced or excised or murdered. Some are wimpy and run when chased. This was a face down variety. I touched the pool edge where I had tried to hold on over forty five years ago. I laid down on the concrete and kept my hand on the edge. I felt myself hold on for dear life. After a while I didn't want to hold on anymore.

I stood and held my own hands. The pool was no longer my enemy. I had since learned to swim and had stopped holding my breath in my dreams many years before. I did not want to be a prisoner any more.

I found myself tired and taller. I wanted to be sure though that the life of this loss was over, so I climbed down into the empty pool and walked down to the deep end where the dirty water of winter stood. I squatted down and wrapped my arms around my knees. I peered at the water. It was harmless. Dirty, but not corrupt. It had become murky but had gotten there clean. Straight from the sky kind of clean. It was not a threat. I didn't put my hand in it though, because of the murky that it had become. I waited. I was good. It was good. I unwrapped myself and stood. It felt like coming up from a baptism. It was time to go. I could be grateful. Grateful for the day it happened. For this day. For this pool brimming with empty.

TEARS ARE PRAYERS TOO.
THEY TRAVEL TO GOD WHEN WE CAN'T SPEAK.

—PSALM 58:6 (PARAPHRASED)

twenty-seven

WHY STAY

Growing up I often wondered why Martha stayed with Skillet. If anyone should have run away it was her in my opinion. I was only four and then five and six, and eventually seventeen and no number of years made me think it less. There were some things I surely didn't know. Didn't want to understand. The things that made her stay.

She was paralyzed by him. The surface of her had flinched for too many years. She was free of dignity. She turned to religion to help her cope and those factors combined to create an unusual kind of parent. A fear filled woman of God. She stuck to the quoting of scriptures concerning the sin of divorce. She gave her own interpretation to her merit. She wasn't all that unusual for a woman born in the 1930s. Divorce was the flagrant letter of her generation.

She lived in a state of nervous hope that each time he came home he might be in a good mood or playful even. We were all warned to be on our best behavior either way. If he was tolerable, no one wanted to be the kid that spoiled it, and if he was already on a tirade, no one wanted to be the kid that became the focus of his fury. We grew up believing that we held full responsibility for the precarious balance of this universe we lived in. God was in heaven. If we got baptized we

227

would be allowed over to His house after we had gotten killed by some unimaginable means, but He lived too far away from us to notice us in our now.

I don't know—even now—how she kept any sanity whatsoever in this environment. She was either pandering to his every anticipatable need or she was dodging his physical, emotional, and mental blows. Then she would pray. Pray things like forgiveness for what she had provoked him to do or that he would somehow find salvation in Jesus and become a new man. And then from time to time a wave of logic would wash over her and she would ask me if I thought she should leave Skillet. I would believe her temporary moment of sanity. I always said yes. She never left but she would tell him that I had suggested it. The days and events that followed those confessions to Skillet aren't memories I care to share with myself today. I did not change my mind though. The next time she asked, I did not change my answer.

We all knew that we wouldn't have gotten far should we have tried to run. He would have tracked us down and taken us out with one of the stupid little guns that he carried. The authenticating accessory. Or worse, he would have just dragged us back to whatever house we were living in and raged longer and louder and harder. I understood some of why Martha wouldn't leave, but I really didn't understand why she stayed.

I didn't have any of these reasons to run away. I live in a beautiful home, with a grand husband who is crazy about me. I loved getting daughters when Tank and I combined our families. I got two. Annie was the older. Nine years old when we met. And her blonde headed little sister Christy, who had just barely turned six when her dad started describing the yet unmet children to me as a matter of his favorite things to talk about. Sterling was my one child to contribute to the claim of parenting. Tank brought boys too. Ry was his dark headed sixteen-year-old. He is very like Tank in his appearance and temperament. A preserver of souls. A noticer. I enjoy them both for being like that. I wonder if they know that about each other. I will ask Tank. And AJ, the other blonde in the batch was a high school senior. Handsome like Ry and their dad. So that things weren't at risk of being boring by description of family units, Tank threw in his quiet, ambitious, kind nephew, Michael, who was a little older than the boys, but looked just like them. Someone he assured me we would be including always as his own.

Our family has grown in these eight years of being married. We've added daughters-in-law. We've added grandbabies. We've lost daughters–in–law to divorces. We've had greats and goods and terribles and we've buried grandbabies. My kids and grandkids are healthy and busy making their own lives.

I knew that at a safer place a few hundred miles east of here I had Tank. And I had these who we love. The ones who began trying to love me and know me. And I had Sterling, the one who no longer wanted to do either. Right then I did not miss them, but I could remember my tender for them when I paused to count back.

I hoped to miss them soon

HOLDING TO OFFENSE CAN NO MORE CHANGE THE
WORLD THAN CAUSING AN OFFENSE.

—SOMEONE SOMEWHERE

twenty-eight
LEVEL
BEHIND ME

The day had been long and lunchless, so I stopped in a barbeque restaurant on the highway to collect my thoughts and corral my emotions. The food was good. The building had been a grain elevator and lent itself to living in the past. I spread my works and writings out once again and my earphones full of music kept me company.

Over two hours later, I packed up my worldly things from the table and went out into the dark that a moonless night generates. The gravel crushing under my tires I left the safety of the parking lot and went east on Highway 114.

I knew that Levelland filled the space of my rear view mirror. I couldn't see it for the dark.

There were no other cars on the highway. It was mildly creepy actually.

The night sky when we lived here as kids had been astounding, and as long as I wasn't out in the dark by myself I was consumed by the matter of it. I needed to know if I had made it up in mind memory or if it really existed that way. I pulled off to the side of the road and got out to look up. I was struck at the ease with which my head actually moved up now. Just a few days ago, it simply would not have risen to any such angle as this.

There they were though. All of them. All millions and millions of them. And the Milky Way shadowing herself right across the distance of them. When we were kids, Pete was the great watcher of stars. We would get an old blanket out on the front yard or we would lie on the driveway and let the heat on the concrete warm our backs and look. James and Buck may have been out there too, but I mostly remember Pete.

Pete always saw all of the shooting stars. I don't think I ever saw one until I was much older. He knew some of the stars by name and some of the constellations and I was absolutely amazed by all of the information he had gathered.

That's the way Pete looked in shine. He just knew stuff that no one else did. He kept it all to himself until the perfect time would present itself for him to stand and deliver his knowings. Then he'd grin his incredible crinkly nose grin before acknowledgement was spoken. Most times the applause of a nod or a look his way did not come. His grin would turn and leave with him.

It was clear out this night and cold and present and I was scared about the dark and even though the stars were all looking right at me, I had to leave. The sky had done its job. Confirmed my hope. I had not forgotten. I had not exaggerated its color of forever.

The only thirty miles back to Lubbock was spent wondering about infinity and eternity and DNA and quantum physics and where should I stay tonight.

It was nearly eleven before I got to a hotel in Lubbock. The same room that had followed me since Laney. I sent Tank a text and he commented that I sounded good. He heard me and I loved him even more.

My thoughts were all a plethora of static pops when I laid down, so instead, I stayed up and wrote what I could put in words.

I had seen all these pasts. Or are they just one. People stay alive as long as I keep remembering them. So do, however their deeds. Mine too. Some things are better if passed over and some things are better once they have been spoken and exposed and allowed to die in the light. Mark the grave if I must in some fashion, but let them die. They are weary of themselves and I am weary of them.

My friend Sundy had tried to explain something to me about fear setting off a choice of flight and fight or forget. I had asked her about remembering all the encounters with me and boys and grown men. She said that those had probably needed all three coping mechanisms. I have chosen fight most of my life. Somehow it has seemed more noble. I think I have confused noble with something less worthy. I have used fight to cope for so long that I have changed its shape. I have turned it into a method for securing a bit of praise. I have wanted the brevity of admiration more than I have wanted the fixed and permanent of reclamation. The notion I had adopted was that flight was chicken—maybe forget was safest.

Some things do not merit my fight. It's some kind of crime really to use strength up battling for a thing or against a thing that I am fighting only because I am afraid.

Maybe flight is not chicken or abandon or forget. I think maybe it's a pause.

My own words finally bored me to sleep.

WHEN YOU TURN THE CORNER AND RUN INTO
YOURSELF, THEN YOU KNOW THAT YOU HAVE
TURNED ALL THE CORNERS THAT ARE LEFT.

—LANGSTON HUGHES

twenty-nine
NOT GOING BACK MORE

I woke up that morning in a panic of sorts. I couldn't place what day it was. I was ready to go home now and I didn't want to have missed our Thanksgiving Day. We never have it on the Thursday. We let the kids all go to their other family gatherings that day and we meet up on Saturday or Sunday. The alarming I felt seemed very much like a scene from the *Christmas Carol*. Like I should somehow stick my head out of the hotel window and shout at some kid to tell me what day it was, then send him off with a gold coin to purchase a giant turkey for Tiny Tim.

Instead I put on a ball cap and hustled down to the elevator, but there were people on it, so I used the stairs instead. I told myself that I would deal with issues of claustrophobia and crowds of people the next time I ran away from home.

I poured two cups of coffee, sweetened them with flavored creamers and went back up to the room to get my bearing. I was ready. I was stoked.

The Giant Journal was still opened to where I left off last night, or maybe it had opened itself in anticipation. I wrote my notes. The ones where I remembered the reasons I left home. I listed them again to myself. They were still there. Going away hadn't changed anything. It had changed it all.

Sterling was still a very angry young man. He hadn't taken the leave that I had. Martha was still going to have to host her own birthday party and I was still going to be the daughter that failed her. I still didn't want to trust this God purposed to love me. I will still be a social liability to my friends. I didn't get even an associate's degree in "fitting in" while on the road. I was still no one's good daughter. Skillet was still no one's good dad. I had not forgiven him. I had not adopted some hope of liking him. I had admitted that children love their parents. Sometimes love is all we can do and like is too lofty a goal.

There was a sweet chivalry to the bows my new present and my new past exchanged. We would be able to want to live together.

I finished my notes and closed the book over. I showered. I packed. I checked out. And this time I knew where I was going.

This day I am pointed east because it is the side of the world where the sun comes up. I am pointed east because where I live is over there.

The Creator guy in pursuit of me laid the fog feature to rest for another day. The road was all shined up and the sky was still sharp. I played the songs I liked loud and sang the words I knew and made up the ones I didn't.

I decided to use Highway 114 all the way home. It would take me through a dozen small towns and that was what I wanted. An interstate couldn't offer the transition.

Buffalo Springs Lake. Not far outside of Lubbock I saw the sign in Ransom County. Buffalo Springs Lake was another place of nightmarish quality in my catalogue. I don't know whose boat we had that day, but James and Skillet and I were fishing in a boat on that lake one day. I was probably three and all buttons were a temptation greater than my ability to resist. I'm sure I was warned but I don't recall that part. And I'm sure that Skillet was already in a bad mood, what with driving out there and putting the boat in the water with the help of a three year old and an eight year old. I only remember the part where I pushed a button I wasn't supposed to and after a bout of screaming from Skillet and some fierce back and forth slaps across the face I was thrown into the lake. Some people in another boat nearby were yelling at Skillet and he was yelling back and we were probably near the shore because James got me out of the water and up on to land.

I could drive down there. The next ramp would take me there and I could wrestle this one last West Texas born Skillet encounter. I slowed asking within whether to take the opportunity. It didn't seem the thing to do so I shifted gears and declined the exit.

I knew that the more I remembered, the more I would remember. Right then, I didn't know that the way I remembered would keep changing.

I was beginning my realize that in this life so far, I had not really even been in pursuit of tender or kind or things like grace. I had been managing a dance with it. I had claimed to want them. Grace to give and grace to give away, but that wasn't true. I just wanted visiting hours with a God I didn't like and with people I didn't want to be known by. Grace requires guts and I had the brave to be that naked, but I had traded brave for tough and fortify.

Grace seemed expensive. I would have to give up my angries and hurts and secrets and crimes to get grace. My known foundations were sure. Grace was a chance I wasn't ready to take. She may fail.

I had my safe system of generating drive with rebellion. I had bound myself with my determine to not become a sad and fear filled wife or mother or woman. Instead, I had shaped myself into exactly that.

I was afraid that if I conformed the rules would swallow me up into the grey of marking time. And I was afraid that forgiveness was temporary and performance based. A thing that took a lot of concentration so I could keep remembering with my mind what and who I had forgiven. I had spent my years trying to do good and trying to be good so that I wouldn't need forgiveness from anyone. And maybe not for anyone.

I had not found mercy for Skillet or Martha. I had used their behaviors to entreat or coax some pity from anyone who would listen, and even some bogus sympathy. These are depravities and arrogance.

I had studied and read and pretended to myself that I wanted to know about a God that was real, but I had substituted ponderings and difficult questions that couldn't be answered to my satisfaction.

The car was stopped. I probably did that. Stopped the car. I had pulled over inside someone else's city limit sign and quit. I could let myself wait now and remember more if I needed too.

I had been anxious to get home. Now I was ready to slow down again. I hadn't been ready to race home and deem my adventure worthy of the abandoning I had done.

All I had done so far was to remove the outer plastic wrap.

I cracked the door to myself and looked into the dark. The stories were lined up. Some were tapping their foot, some holding cups of coffee talking to other stories about how much they had in common.

They saw the light from the doorway where I stood and they saw me see them. The compartment of stories quieted to see what I would do.

I spoke from the doorway. I told them to keep their seats. I said I would get to each of them.

I went for a walk.

This one traffic light town was ideal. The most perfect resort for dropping off links of a chain. There was an old cotton gin and there were several cotton trailers sitting nearby. I walked in the short winter grass and felt the tears forming up. I didn't know exactly what called them up. I don't think I necessarily had the weight of sadness on me nor were they the kind of tears that flow with loss. Sometimes homesickness can make me cry and sometimes a thing can be so sweet that it makes me cry, but I couldn't be sure what these tears came from.

I had my camera and I stopped to add shots of the empty brick faced structure that used to be the Chevrolet dealership and a broken wooden building across the street from it.

I walked to the main downtown street that was two blocks long. Traffic was light, even for a very small town. I took another picture. This time of a door to a garage. The ease of the street made me wish for what I had wished for most of my life. I wanted to have had a simpler life. I wanted to be familiar with a life that had more predictability. One with less violence. One with love that I could recognize. A life where I could be certain when I had actually done something wrong or when that was actually just someone else's need to not take responsibility.

I WANTED TO HAVE HAD A SIMPLER LIFE. I WANTED TO BE FAMILIAR WITH A LIFE THAT HAD MORE PREDICTABILITY.

I had circled the two square blocks of town in the daze of the monologue. I could almost let myself believe that it was a dialogue with the God guy. That would mean though that I would have to give up some of my tools of survival. I would have to believe in a God who listened or talked or both. I would have to turn in my distrust keys.

The sidewalk I was standing on was my only surety. It was enough and I had to think to remember where I even was.

I realized that I had wandered over an hour. I needed light. And some clarity. And away from these one and two story downtown brick buildings. I needed to look at the horizon where I could see for sure that the world is round and I can't fall off. And a taco. I needed a taco.

Every small town has a Mexican food restaurant. They may not have a real grocery store or a pharmacy but they do all have a Mexican food restaurant and I found it.

All Mexican food restaurants order their menus from the same printer. They have the El Padre platter that feeds hundreds and the enchiladas and the less traditional fajitas, nachos, and quesadillas on the laminated page next to the tamales and chili rellenos. I only thought I wanted a taco. Apparently I wanted to feed the 5,000 because I ordered the El Padre.

The waitress had on a name tag and a rushed smile even though they had just opened and I was the very first and only customer. Maria brought me chips and salsa and looked hard twice at the Giant Journal on the table. I opened it to write while my predictable lunch was being prepared and she stopped by to refill my iced tea glass and take another look. I don't know if she was looking at the book or the person who might carry such a thing around.

I wrote down the new stock.

I know it's usually better to know what it is I'm looking for if I hope to find it. Going out to find a thing I haven't identified sets the stage for distraction and frustration, but it also lends itself to brilliant stumblings. I had not embarked with a plan. I hadn't embarked at all. I drove away from my house. Something I may have frowned on had one of my children done it. Actually, that's not true. I think spontaneous is righteous.

I have great kids. Some of them are Tank's. All of them are ours. I do not wish that blending our families had been easier. We all had to have a hurt to point to in order to get well.

I wonder if it's greedy for two people who love each other to want all the other people in their respective lives to embrace the union. Young kids and almost adult kids are walking along dealing with the tragedy of being the age they are and a dad or a mom decide that they will get married. Get married to someone who has other kids and other lives in another town and someone who has a mind of their own.

That's what we did. Tank and I were very much in crazy about each other and made all of our kids agree to the marriage whether they knew what that meant or not. I didn't even know myself what all it would have in store and I wasn't a nine-year-old. Nor a six-year-old.

Everybody stands to get hurt when someone in their immediate circle gets in love. And the ones in charge of caring for the young want to believe the little ones when they say stuff like, "I like her dad," or "She seems very nice."

Children want their care givers to be happy. That's what children want for everyone. They aren't equipped to determine the fall out on their own lives. The feelings of the ex-spouse that used to be the one in the "crazy about" seat is also the other parent that kids get to deal with. The little kids and the almost grown kids have to endure the vocal judgments of the one being left behind no matter how long ago the company parted from each other.

And those same kids tend to want to like the incoming family member whether they deserve to be liked or not because they want to belong to the new unit. They should belong. They need to belong, but it shouldn't be their own responsibility to make certain that they do in fact belong.

We asked that of six collective kids. We asked them to get married with us. It came at a price.

They are part of my history now. I would have never had this family except by way of this life. The story of me where I had just visited. Engaged. No, visited mostly or called on. I had no sooner written that down than the El Padre platter and side plates started showing up on the table and the Giant Journal had to be set aside.

The body knows what it wants. I should pay more attention to that. The heart knows what it wants too. I should pay more attention to that. The combination of crunchy and meat and cheesy was perfect and I ate some of everything before me.

Maria refilled my iced tea glass and paused longer this time. The she stepped out of her box and articulated her question once she had stilled my eyes with her look.

"Who are you?" she said.

I was intrigued. She didn't ask about the journal specifically and she didn't ask if I was travelling to meet family like the other inquirers had. She asked who I was.

I had travelled along-side myself for days wondering who I was not. I had hoped against hope that I wasn't a selfish mom and a terrible mother, or the pathetic product of violence that was destined to repeat it. I had considered seriously that I had behaved in ways in keeping with that of a contemptible daughter and socially destitute friend. I had chosen flight as often as fight with the Creator God that I had stopped praying to twenty-five years ago.

I had used ink to record conquering the swimming pool and 802 Mesquite. I had spent days and nights with my pasts. I had watched buildings make the lost days significant again. I had not said who I was to me or anyone else. I had only said who I wasn't.

Maria the waitress wanted to know who I was even if she had no idea what she was asking. I thought about dodging the question, giving a nervous chuckle in response, and over tipping her. But she wasn't leaving the table's edge. Her posture was casual and as firm as the question and she held the check in her hand as a hostage.

"A daughter going home." I said.

"That's who I am. I'm a daughter going home to my children and my husband and my present." I expanded.

She waited. I had nothing more to add. She kept her eyes on mine for some long seconds and then set the check down as she picked up my plate. She looked like she could accept that answer.

I did over tip her. Or maybe not. If measured against the tab yes, if measured against putting my back against an emotional wall and needing a statement—then no.

I put the Giant Journal under my arm on my way out.

thirty

ONE HUNDRED
FOURTEEN

I left the still nameless town. I was amazed at how beautiful this drive was. West Texas is red and has oil fields and usually counts descriptors like "boring" and "flat" as terms of endearment. This section was greatness. There were canyons and hills and farms and ranches with trees and I couldn't believe I'd never taken this road before.

Two hours of music later, I stopped at a roadside rest area that sat on the perimeter of a series of canyons and a creek. It was warm out and I was sleepy from eating a too big Mexican food platter lunch, so I took a break there.

The Giant Journal and the iPod and I found a fabulous sun trap on a flat rock and parked ourselves for a late autumn toasting in the midday warm.

The gratitude factor had stayed intact and I recorded with ease the wonders I was thankful for in my life miles from here. I wanted to ask who I was. I wanted to have someone to ask.

I didn't want to let Skillet absorb the way I felt anymore. He could maybe stay around, but not in that role. I didn't feel any desire to see him or like him. But now I didn't need someone to blame. I didn't want the endless energy supply that comes from the addiction to a deformed variety of anger that I had long used like an emotional amphetamine. I no longer wanted the level of anger where I feel right and think I am right and let right outweigh good and whole and life. The animosity that lies to me. That I loved believing because it gave me the wonder of self-righteousness. Justification for my behaviors and my stench and my paralyzed soul.

I wanted the ride of the life I was in to be the life I counted on. I wanted to have a new story. I wanted to integrate the meanness of yesterday with the fresh of this minute and know it was all the perpetual creation of me. The story where my children and my Tank and my humor help define me. Where I live because, not in spite of.

Right then I didn't want to fit. I began making peace. I began making a new definition of fit. I began to care about what I had and I began stopping the shame of what I had not. I looked at the silverless mirror and saw my profile. I asked myself what I am proof of. I saw that my coarse is my tender, that my ridges are my safe. I do not blend and I do not match and I am jarring and jagged and I want good and I want a few messy, recover seeking friends who see the build of me. A "band of brothers" who hear me see them and find it worthy. I am no more unique in degrees than any other creation. I am kind and curious. My intelligence variety is foreign and less familiar to people, but I want to begin living with some level of okayness with that.

I will offend. Always. I will know this to be an inevitable by-product of the collection of me. And I will not condemn. I will give thanks for mercy and seek out forgiveness and grace and give them away even when my ledger says I have none in the bank. I will write bad emotional checks and float the gap between deposit and withdrawal. I will know that I will offend less as my road gets longer and broader. I will not be ashamed of where I came from nor how I got through each new intersection even though I don't know how to not be ashamed yet.

I closed my Giant Journal, placed it under my head where a pillow should go and stretched out on the wide, dry stone. I looked through the hole between the leafless trees to the watching blue sky and let the angle of November light close my eyes to quiet.

Nothing provokes dreamery like an afternoon nap in the sun. I don't know what trip I had taken in my thirty minute dormancy, but it had the scent of ceasefire.

I waited to remember before I sat up. Not remember the dream. Just remember.

I wanted to go home. I wanted to get there on time. Not too early. Not too late. I wanted to keep watch along the closing hours of my holy war.

I gathered my companions up and went back to the Jeep.

I saw her through the window. Disappointment. Sitting in the front seat. She already had her seat belt on. Ready to go. I paused there on the narrow asphalt road.

I saw Him too. In the back seat. She had not made eye contact with me. She had just looked straight ahead, but she knew I was looking at her. He had been watching me look. My pause had become hesitation. The God that had ridden these days in the back got out. He opened the front passenger side door and held out His hand palm up. She waited. Took a shallow breath. She unbuckled the seat belt and put her hand in His. I watched … fascinated. I thought she was an enemy, but He treated her like a treasured friend that gets outgrown. He walked her across the lane and showed her a seat on a wood bench before kissing her on the head.

I felt bad that Disappointment wasn't going home with me. And I felt relieved. I felt adored that He would release me from this painful job of leaving her behind.

He climbed back into the backseat. He did not force His will. He did not presume. And He did not take her place riding shotgun.

I put my journal next to Him and closed the back door. With an ease new to my stride I got into the front seat, started the Jeep, and plugged in my iPod.

I saw Him in the rearview mirror. Humming the tunes I played, taking in the scenery of things He had invented. Crafted with His heart.

I was on my path back to the Sterling who had to also be set on a park bench.

His chaos is his. Not mine. I had loved him always. I like loving him. I always will. He will have to build his own new foundation or knock down the shack he has shaped, keep the land of his inheritance, and draw plans for the mansion of his dreams.

I will be grateful that I like loving him.

I will look for any truths in his hurlings and be honest in my responsibility and remorse. I will leave him with his freedom to square up his own insides.

I may not have turned out to be the mother he longed for. He may, and probably always will, have resentments toward me. Pains I have brought him. Reasons that he has soothed himself into believing have arrested his way into his unknown. We each have to make a decision to be mad at our parents or not. He has chosen. He can always rechoose if it suits him.

We each have to make a decision to be mad at our children or not. I have chosen and I am not.

I hear my slow exhaling sigh. It hurts. Love that is holy has some pain.

The first of three great ranches owned all my vision could reach on both sides of the highway. Red dirt and steep edged, dwarfed canyons.

Sparse shrubs. Beryl sky. Not skies. All one piece of wavy sapphire. I felt like I was running in place for miles as the borders of the highway played the same frames over and over.

Sterling will be fine. With or without me.

I catalogued this father, Skillet, and this daughter, Sammi, and made up my mind about a few things. And I did not make up my mind about a few things.

Skillet is no anthropic universe. He does not have the components necessary to sustain life forms.

Is it possible that he will ever get good? He will likely go on in a state of punishment. Punishing all for the sins of trying too hard to please. The sin of wanting too much to be liked by him.

I have settled for his punishments as if they were pieces of reconciliation.

Skillet's behavior has a life of its own. It can't just quit being. It needs an ending. Somewhere. A death to the carriage.

If he just dies one day and is neither punished nor redeemed, where does all that unfinished business go to live. I think I need him to reconcile with it. I am afraid that if he doesn't, the color of it will surely rest forever on me and on the brothers. The badnesses of his journey will have blurred the edges of my portrait.

He must believe with great conviction that if he told of his sorrow that he would have to trade in his breath and get death in return. I think maybe that holding on to his ground for dear life will be the death of him. How do I wash the void of him off of me. There are so many coats of it now. I am nearing the truth that I cannot save Skillet. I cannot make him safe.

I drive. I wonder.

I wonder how I know that Skillet cannot free either of us from his past.

If I forgave him, I'd have to admit that I love him. At least that I love him with the minimal love of any child solely by virtue of being born to him. I'd have to look at him and see more and forgive more. What if that turned into more love. Or an eventual hug.

That thought repulsed me. I shuddered. I cannot bear up to this weighty thought.

The lie is that it's easier to keep my distance and be mad about him once in a while. Like a secret stash of dark chocolate.

I have wondered if I picked him. Did I somehow pick Skillet before I came here.

When Sterling was about four years old, he said the most fascinating thing to me. It was Valentine's Day night. I always prayed with him at bedtime. I didn't want him to not like God, so I told him it was good to pray. I would place the palm side of my hand over his toddler sized chest and ask all the things a mother asks for her children. This night I couldn't. I had no will to pretend a line of words and wishes into heaven. Sterling's sisters had been born on Valentine's and left before I could even hold them alive. This night I was all about me. I was consumed with heartache and sad, so I just cupped my hand around one side of his gorgeous face and told him that I loved him. Big I said. I told him that I loved him very big.

He was watching me through my eyes. He took his hands out from under the duvet cover. He reached up to my face and waited for my thoughts to stop and see him. He said he was sorry that I was sad. He didn't know why. Then he announced to me in his little boy Scottish accent that when he was in heaven, before he came here, that he had told Jesus that he wanted me to be his mom.

So what then of that?

What if he did pick me? And what if I did pick Skillet? And Martha? Then that would make them the perfect parent pair for me. The perfect parents for my soul's stay in the human condition. The story of me that would not have been if I hadn't had them.

Peace with this is my mercy. But I am not all the way there yet. I am driving toward it. If I don't turn off this path I can get there. If I want.

The consideration gives me a gratitude that I can barely feel. Not at all describe, but hear. They were doing who they are for reasons I cannot grasp and I am who I have been so far in part because of their gene pool and influence. How then can I stay addicted to being mad at them. If I am unhappy about my progress in this life so far, I need to take inventory with me. Not them.

Not Skillet. He had a herd of demons to wrestle. I will try to not be afraid of him again.

And the Martha that waits for her birthday party on Sunday ... ironically on a Sunday? The next Sunday ahead of me. I am not her good daughter. I am not elegant or feminine or pretty. I do not fit the dream she had when she bore one girl among three sons. I may have been useful and ardent. I may have been funny and observant and excellent at rescue, but I was not the things she most wanted me to be. And I had not stayed close. I had stopped being in her company. I had stopped protecting her and covering for her. I had not called her or taken her to lunch in years.

And I still did not like her God.

And I still did not fit.

I still did not fit. In fact the whole business of running away meant that I fit even less than before. I had no friends who had ever run away. I would have no one in my club. No one to share runaway stories with. No one to nod, "I get it," when I mentioned with my words or my memory that I had been afraid. That I had been anxious. That I had been sad. That I had been a vapor to even myself. No one to know.

These rocks of my list are my fertile soil. My walk would be different and my eyes would be cast different and my aromas. I would be another person if Skillet had been another person. I would not have lived in the towns I did. I would not have met Sterling's dad or moved to Scotland or remarried the Tank of centering. I will want to want to choose grateful.

I stopped the Jeep again.

I opened both doors on the passenger side. The back door first. I made a glimpsing variety of eye contact with my eternal Passenger and invited Him out of the car as I held the door open. Then I stood behind the front door making my invitation very clear with the face up of my palm. He climbed into the front seat like a man who knows how to jump into a Jeep, and I closed both doors.

thirty-one

DAY OF THANKS

The official Thanksgiving Day had passed, but we got our kids and grandkids together on the Saturday of the long weekend.

I just wanted to have Thanksgiving no matter what the day.

I wanted to make my grandmother's dressing and serve it with too much cranberry sauce. I wanted to unsuccessfully make giblet gravy again and let my kids bring the food they were each good at making. I wanted to invite Sterling and wish he would come and wish that he wouldn't and wish that he would want to come.

Thanksgiving is the kindest of all the holidays. It is the pause of routine where I don't think about what individuals need. I consider us a collection. A gather over the most gorgeous and simple of meals. Scratch preparation and predictable foods that make the day complete. Dishes that left off would be missed whether anyone loves them or not. Food I have eaten every autumn of life since I got one. Portions I have scooped onto my plate in sizes of giving thanks. Rolls I have buried in butter. Turkey I have smelled for hours before tasting. The quiet anxious of wait and watch until it all comes together on the table between the seated and their iced tea glasses.

The day we sit at the table and lay down our agendas for a gentler couple of hours. Maybe more. Maybe longer. Maybe not, but we will pretend in the name of gratitude that we are a grateful people. A family grateful for this food. For the business of feeling hungry. For this day. For these others we own whether we like them often or not or never.

We will sit longer. We will eat more so we can taste it again. So we stay longer with the ones who want to sit at the table longer. We will laugh and we will look at each other hoping we will be better for this meal. And by our hope we will be better.

The dishes will have to be washed but no one will wash alone. And the football game will have to be watched even if we are mad about our team. And if the weather allows it the backyard will have to be surveyed one last time before the insignificant winter stretches its brown over the grass. Our own game of football will ensue for a time. And then the pies will come out. And the whipping cream whipped.

No one will ask for a special gift and no one will wonder where they will get enough money to do this day well. It will be about food. Food and lazy thanks and dusk will cause it to end in melancholy and a little emotional inventory will be taken by the older eyes.

Tank had collected the ingredients that make the day. He had hugged me deeply when I came home. He had asked no hard questions. He knew in his hold that I was okay enough and we had slept close to each other the night before the feast of belonging.

Thanks Day morning he put the turkey on the smoker before the sun even knew that dark would soon end. I was up early with him and made the things we would serve next to the anticipated bird.

The table was set. Places for all. All were filled that day except my treasured Sterling and his precious daughter.

We served the plates and moved closer together so that the black hole their absence created didn't suck anyone visibly in.

And we did the dishes and watched the football and we surveyed the acres we call the backyard. And the dusk bore the hazy end and everyone went back to their homes.

AT THE MOMENT OF COMMITMENT THE
ENTIRE UNIVERSE CONSPIRES TO ASSIST YOU.

—JOHANN WOLFGANG VON GOETHE

thirty-two
PETRIFIED PREPARATORY

The Thanksgiving dishes were barely dry before my thoughts were consumed with what was coming next. I knew I had a birthday party to attend for Martha the following day and I knew I still had wince about that. Only flinch I think. Not cower. And I knew I did not have a dread. I would go. One of my death grips had been taken hostage. Not executed. Not delivered from its own evil possession. A light had seeped in and even the dark was holding his hand to his forehead to thin the glare. The anticipatory paralyze of the future was now less debilitating. It did not arrest my beat nor my breathe.

A LIGHT HAD SEEPED IN AND EVEN THE DARK WAS HOLDING HIS HAND TO HIS FOREHEAD TO THIN THE GLARE.

My run had worn me out. Brought me life. Cracked a few harshes. Robbed me of my safer hurts. Gifted me with a fear that may be what the God speaks of when He beckons me to fear Him. A kind expectation of things to come. Things I can fear and trust simultaneously. Places I can go if I am holding the right hand.

I would go to the birthday party and I would not want to.

I needed to get something that might look celebratory of an eighty year stay. Looked like I had known her well for fifty-one years.

Or a frame. I could get a candle or a frame.

I am not a shopper. I am a buyer. I need to know exactly what I am going to find before I am motivated to go look for it. I didn't know what to go look for.

She doesn't need anything. Martha. Just about no one turning eighty has a thing they want for their birthday. They all say the same thing. They don't want gifts. They want family. It seemed a little late for that.

A gift. Something given. Not presented. Something set on the first table top I could find in the house.

This I could fulfill. I did not know how to be her family. I could not be her close daughter. So I would want to give her a wrapped token for the event. For the cause. Not so she would receive. I wanted me to feel better. Going empty handed was too much truth.

I had purchased items during my first couple of decades and handed them to Martha and Skillet. Christmas and Anniversary and Father's Day and Birthday and Mother's Day. I covered them all. Extravagantly. James had taught me how. He had a job all of his kid life. Always had his own money. Always bought things for everyone. Always been perpetually broke because he spent easily and often and big. The oldest brother may not be the trend-setter for present giving in every family but he certainly was in our houses.

That's where we grew up

Houses.

Addresses.

We lived in nice structures. Nicely furnished residences in good neighborhoods. Where our neighbors were church ladies and church lady men. Houses that were like book covers nice enough to avoid judgement. We lived in these houses.

Maybe we would have given better gifts if we had lived in a home. Safer houses.

Giving a wrapped purchase made me anxious.

Giving a greeting card made me sick.

I could not do it after a while of my years. Hallmark and all of his friends said things that were not true. Things I could not mean.

Sometimes I would think it was a good time. A good day. On those occasions I would very carefully choose a card. I would read the words over and over before I bought it, then read them more times before I signed it.

I would mentally practice my closing. The personal four or five words I might pen before my signature. I would know that my very signature was going to meet criticism and assessment because of some class Skillet had taken on handwriting and personality. I would know that my words would be deemed lies within the not too distant future. I would know that I was going to be told that my lame affection was not to be trusted. That I was manipulating him or them or her.

I would evaluate the possible responses before sealing the envelope with an anxious lick of my emotionally dry tongue.

I have always tried to find something they would know to have been expensive. Something that matched their house or their apparent lifestyle. Something they might describe with brag words to their friends or the brothers. A thing that would make it to one of the many shelves in our houses where they displayed proof that they had taste and money and smart children with taste and money.

The wrapped package was obligatory. The card was soul suicide.

Skillet was right when he said I was trying to manipulate them. I was a prostitute from my beginning years. I would do most anything to be liked by either of them. I would settle for any sign. I would slap the veins in the underside of my wrist and take it like heroin. I would stand still for their hug and do nothing that might disrupt the motion.

I had stopped buying them things long ago. I didn't go see them anymore. I didn't spend my money on them anymore. I didn't call their number anymore. I deleted their messages from my phone without listening to them.

On Sunday, I would be going to one of the houses we had all lived in and I would take something wrapped so that I could have an object between us. I could hold it close to me if they tried to receive an embrace of any kind or I could extend it toward them if they did not try to greet me.

For this birthday present I decided to find a fabulous antique frame for Martha's birthday and give her a picture of my whole family. Our blended collection of children and grandchildren.

I went looking for the perfect frame.

I found a pretty good frame. I think it pained me some that I didn't know what the perfect frame would look like.

I put the 8 x 10 photograph of our family of sixteen in the pretty good frame and wrapped it in Christmas paper. I don't ever buy birthday paper or wedding shower paper. If a present leaves my house wrapped—it's wrapped in Christmas paper.

I had a gift now. Or a present. I could carry it into their house. It would be my shield. The thing I brought through the door and held between us to limit the contact. She didn't know the people in the photograph but she could set it out somewhere to look like she did. If people came over, she could point to it and mention my name as if we are close and stuff. I didn't like that she would be able to lie some about that but as a mom I could understand the desire to do so.

I have remained a giver of good gifts. I love finding the excellent wooden box or the aged book with one grand paragraph and that smell of having been forgotten between the pages. I think about what things I want to present on an occasion. A birthday. A hope day. A getting married day. A Christmas day, I love the search. I like the find. Sometimes it's all I can do to actually give it away. It's my trophy for all the adventure. I find the most great thing and then have to talk myself out of keeping it. And sometimes I am so taken by the find that I cannot wait until the designated time to deliver and see the receive.

It happens best when I know the frame. The person or the milestone or the fate. When I have a vision of their time. Their current. Their wish for being seen as the thing they want to know as true about themselves.

When Sterling turned twenty-one, I collected all the notes I had taken over his time and wrote them down in order of his weeks and months and annuals under the sun. I had carried a camera for the length of his life and he was most often in the lens of my point. That year I chose the pictures that I loved most and printed them onto canvas cloth pages. I inserted them where they fit with his story. It took a couple of months of after work hours to put it all together.

The project had been amazing for me. I took stock of the hard things we had hurdled. The incredible things we had experienced. The moments he would never know had been expensive to me. The moments he gave me. The places where he had said or done the most profound and simple things. The words he had chosen to say to the most random of people in his path. The things he had been willing to learn. The things he had chosen to not attempt. The explanations he had for creation and God and color. The gorgeous hardy laugh I could hear in the photographs. The way I had felt when I was able to provide something I could not afford. Tell him about the assembly of his stay so far.

He opened the gift and knew what it was immediately. He said thank you before he even opened the first page. He turned the pages slowly. I watched him unpack the him that I know. I looked occasionally from the kitchen as he spent two hours reading the narrative. As he watched the pictures go by. He could not know how many hours and years of my life he held as his face looked through his documented days.

The notebook of him. A present I wanted to give. A gift I wanted to keep. Maybe hold onto until he had gone off to Wander Sea and returned. Be the keeper until he had become the receiver. The believer. The Seer. Until I could hand him something of himself that he had misplaced. The soul bones I had temporary custody of. I wondered if I should foster the collection a little longer. I still wonder if I should have transferred my him to him then or if I should have waited. Or if I should have never been so presumptuous to believe my perspective mattered more than a little. I could have kept them all. The thoughts. The facts. The angles of light and cast of shades and the stereo of soundtrack.

I wanted to remind Sterling of things he had never known. Things he didn't know he knew or didn't remember of his own run so far. The photographs showed him things he did not even know he had seen. His eyes too young to swallow the first glimpse of Ben Lomond across the loch I loved too much. The young of his grandparents when he was born. He had not gotten to see himself racing across the terminal at JFK airport when walking was new and nothing was in his way that wouldn't clear a path for him. His hear did not know that it had first followed the sound of bagpipes at three weeks old or listened to Wee Man turn his curious canine head at the baby's whimper that was his own. Renderings of him in word and color and black and white. He did not know that he had always known the smell of Scotch mist and 1,000 lambs in the highland pasture behind our house in his first spring of skin.

He didn't know that he had explained to me exactly why green was God's favorite color from a seat beside me on a train ride to Balloch. He did not remember the words he used when he prayed. He could not have seen the grin of his own making that proved joy always comes from the within.

I wanted to give him these things of him.

Twenty-one years of him from my side of his earth suit.

It was one of my favorite gifts ever to give away. One I could give and keep.

I think it would have been revealing, fascinating, breaking to know what Martha would have written down about me. Written to me.

So for this special birthday I would do the good thing—the right thing. I would go and I would let Tank hold my hand. But I would not let them see me having my hand held. The brothers. The Skillet. The Martha. They would not get to see me having my hand held.

They would not know.

They would not know that I did not want to be there and they would not know that my hand was held. That I was safe amongst them because my hand was joined.

Or they would.

Waiting for the birthday party day to come was a weight. Not the excited wait. The browner wait of doom. The emotional dusk wait of dread. There were no words for how much I didn't want to go to this birthday party lunch.

thirty-three

FAKING FELICITY

I would be doing enough faking it today so we didn't go to church first.

I chose my clothes deliberately. I would not be able to wear anything they thought appropriate or cute so I wore familiar. Familiar that gave room for flexibility should I need to fight or run or get invisible.

Tank drove us the one hour route to their house that was about fifteen minutes from ours.

I looked at him and wondered what all was going through his mind. Was he thinking that I was exaggerating things in my mind. Was he thinking of his own strategy of protect. Was he thinking we might make it home in time for the three o'clock football game.

I like him. A lot. He holds my hand when we walk from the car to any building. The movie. The grocery store. The Starbucks. I like loving Tank.

I looked at the wrapped package in my lap and knew it was the wrong thing to bring. I should have gone with something glitzy and expensive. Buy some favor. Should I leave this in the car and go in empty handed? No. Too exposed.

The wrapped package was not about the birthday mother. It was about protecting me.

Today Martha would no doubt make between two and seventeen mistakes in the kitchen that would set Skillet off. He would take them each as permission to throw things and slam things and cuss things and slap her. The number of times that the dinner had hit the floor before being set out on the table in my life were beyond count by now. I had no words within me or for me about how much it always scared me. Never sure when each episode would end or how, I had always dropped into the slinging hate of the kitchen and gathered the scraps of food and broken glass and dignity and tried to place them where they belonged again. I felt the relive set in and understood that I had spent chunks of my life shaking on the inside. Biting my mental bottom lip so that survive within me grew and no lip inside or out would be allowed to quiver when afraid was present. No one would know that I was afraid.

Measures of my stay on this earth had been sacrificed to afraidness. Time and safes stolen from me at gunpoint and knifepoint and for no point. I had marked the same robberies as they took place with the brothers. With the mother. It was the common blood in our veins. It had been my shame and my fail when I could do nothing about it.

I felt my present physical chin rise and place my face in position for what lay ahead.

I know in some ways I am afraid of falling short in appearance. It will be noted with a tip of their glances that I am still not gorgeous and still not feminine and still not a prize. I will be reminded in several ways that I don't dress like them. Then those comments will be followed by advice for my future wardrobe choices or an, "I'm just kidding," lie chuckle or a pause so that others would have time to join the subtle jeers. And I will make a terribly funny series of responses to defend myself and be genuinely and secretly glad that I do not match them.

And I know in some ways I am afraid of the space between the brothers and me.

The pitting of us against each other has taken an irreversible toll. We may each want with all of the brittle of our bones that the others all liked us but we do not say it. We do not show it. We do not try to sort it out and pursue it. We stay largely clear of each other in our adultness so that we cannot say our judge of each other. So that we cannot hear the judge we know is said over us.

The disdain and disregard and longing is apparent to the naked eye however. The glances to see if we remember each other. The hope that some glimmer of wartime buddiness will surface and the deep care of someone who knows what we each survived will embrace us if only in a pause.

I wish for the brothers and I know they wish for me. Wish is judgement after a while and doesn't bring a relentless pray. It is not hope. It lacks responsibility. It is a person telling another that they have been seen but they are still on their own. It means that I want someone to change their behavior so I don't have to explain them or excuse them or lower my expectation of them. Wish is not a breeding ground for mercy.

And I know in some ways I am afraid that I will say the things that I barely hide beneath the surface. That Skillet will do something mean or violent and I will break and yell at him and he will be sorry. And that I will not be sorry. And I am afraid that such an opportunity will not unfold and I will go home emotionally barren from having carried this child of justice for years without giving birth.

And I know that in some way I am afraid that I will walk into their house a fifty-one year old woman and immediately become a seventh grader under the influence of the parental cocaine. A drug that kills and consumes and drives the victim toward it with hateful desire.

The day was overcast. November Sundays all seem overcast.

We were there. In front of the shadowless house that smelled of dark from the curb's edge.

I held the wrapped package in my left hand. Tank held me with his gentle fold over my right hand. Both hands tied. Both hands ready to be fisted. Both hands in sight. Both hands not ready.

Tank rang the doorbell with his free hand and I stole one last warm squeeze before drawing away from him and from myself for the afternoon.

This had not been my house in thirty years. I did not want to walk in as if I was familiar. I did not want to walk in as if I belonged. I didn't want to walk in at all.

With the glass door between us and the roast beef birthday lunch, we waited on the red tiled front porch. We stood silent like a pair of tired Kirby® vacuum cleaner salesmen.

Pepe ran barking to the door. The tiny white poodle who met all the criteria to belong in their house. He didn't shed. He could be dressed up like something he wasn't when they wanted. He could be shouted at without remorse when his behavior was out of their order. He was their best friend. He was compliant and ever present and controllable. Purchased. They owned him.

Martha came into view walking to the door in her glad gait carrying a kitchen towel to wipe her hands. Her greeting was gracious and her relief that we actually showed up was masked in happy. Skillet rounded the corner frailly from the hallway and bore his gaunt onto my face to be sure I saw his minutes to live eyes. The same ones he had worn to family parties for years and years. I did not lock eyes with him despite his chase.

They each shook hands with Tank and tried to hug me long enough to feel hugged back and we eventually got past the marble floored entry.

I glanced back to mentally measure the distance to the door as we moved away from it into the living room.

Buck and Pete were already there. They had come in from out of town. Buck brought his girlfriend and his two kids. They had stayed at Skillet and Martha's house the night before. They were sort of welcome there.

Pete and his new wife had also come in the night before and stayed over at my brother James' house.

James and Norah hadn't gotten there yet. We weren't the first to arrive. We weren't the last. I would make certain that we were the first to leave.

The white tile floors were spotless and the evidence was abundant that Skillet and Martha had cleaned their always clean house thoroughly for the birthday show.

I was suffocating.

It was time to go.

I had been there four minutes.

Maybe I should pray.

No.

I will not pray. I will confirm and store the fear for later. That's what I do. I use pain that is real from things that are real for affection that is not real because I want to believe that people can heal each other. Because I do not want to pray to God. Because I survive better on the draw of being angry at Him. Because I have to keep myself in one piece right now. Because later I will find a safer place to recover from the afraid that this afternoon has brought.

I did not pray to God.

I looked for Tank. He was there. That was my only pray. He was my courage. He was being corralled into a conversation with Martha. He was good. He didn't feel unsafe. He didn't know my family. We had not spent any time with them since we got married. Nor before. He knew some of the histories. He knew my unsettle. He was my pray.

James had said that he would be at the birthday party. He told me he would. He must have told Martha he would. There was a place set at the table for him and Norah. So far he had lied. He had told me he would be at Skillet's birthday event last year too but he wasn't. I knew the chances were high that he wouldn't be able to make himself come today either.

The house was a creepy marriage of a Rod Serling and Norman Rockwell scene of people preparing lunch. The Sunday afternoon perfume of roast beef at a grandma's house filled the space and disguised the small talk as fond. Nothing was in the floor yet. Martha was dressed for a ball with an apron around her waist to protect the glimmer. Her hands rattled quietly with the clear mix of glad and sad and apprehension. Glad we were all four going to be there. Sad that it was so hard for us to come to her house. Apprehensive of Skillet's not yet revealed plan to cause all the day's attention to fall on him.

I saw her. She didn't look my way.

She had greeted me as authentically as she knows how at the door and gone back to the kitchen where she was preparing the curtain we would all hide behind at the table. She was seamless in the kitchen. Always had been. She was a very good cook. Skillet always claimed to be the better cook but he hadn't ever recognized that his food was laced with afraid.

Or maybe he had.

Martha cooked and it didn't have to be the best cornbread ever made in the years of the world so far. Skillet didn't cook unless there was a prize to be won or company to impress. Martha cooked with ease. It was like the only thing she did with quiet ease. She only cooked that way if Skillet wasn't present. It was her cathartic. Where she mitigated the harsh that beat down on her. The wrath unduly delivered on her from Skillet. The grief she couldn't feel as a too timid mother and frightened wife. The questions she could not raise to herself about what strength she had not used. I watched her stir today. The gait had changed. The day dreaming in the stir of the gravy was gone. The barely hope her rhythm held when I was little was gone. I hadn't seen her in the kitchen in two or more decades. I don't know if the change was slow or if one day her insides just left. Left like her children or left with her children.

I stood at the end of the kitchen and darted between the years.

My absorption was broken by the ringing of the doorbell. James and Norah arrived. I was glad for me. I was not glad for them. It had been an obvious struggle. They were not at odds with each other. James was in obvious struggle with himself. Norah had always given James gentle sound counsel on matters of his family. Then left him each time to do what he would. She is his Tank. His keeper. His watcher. His compass professor. Today his struggle was with himself. Much like my own except that James had remained more tender than I had. So he probably had not taken a giant inhale at the curb and raised a defiant chin. He had gotten out of his car and walked toward the same door I entered minutes before with his paced dignity. He had remained himself when he entered the house of current pasts.

He didn't hug either of them. His greeting was professional and warm enough. He did hug me. I insisted. An embrace of take and of give. An embrace of know. An alliance reminded.

James was the final and favorite guest child. Martha could begin putting the food out on the table. She could take the apron away and reveal her outfit for the day. She could smile and overlook Skillet and invite everyone to come to the table where she stood the best slight chance of being celebrated today.

So far he had not found any real reason to cause his inner bully to surface. Maybe he was keeping the little darling under the radar because of the spouses we had each brought. This might be his grand chance to disprove anything that anyone was saying about him in a negative light. He may need us to each leave saying he had mellowed or that he wasn't as mean as we remembered more than he needed to throw something. There are any number of ways to garner all the attention in the world of Skillet.

He settled into his seat at the head of the table and immediately began his maneuvering of the focus. He prayed one of his long and fruitless prayers while we chose to not kick each other under the table or look at each other with our unclosed eyes. Then he began one of his tearful paragraphs thanking us for coming. Forgetting completely that we were not there for him. It was Martha's birthday. He made certain that his voice maintained its pathetic. He made certain that we all saw that he couldn't pass the dishes around the table because weakness had overcome him. He made certain we all noticed that this may be the day he dies.

It was like a serious rock and hard place situation. If no one acknowledged all his claims and sentences then he would be forced to take his strive for attention to a new level. If we did give them notice we would be playing the game that we all hate so much. Having to decide between whole and peace can break an adult child's skin.

Pete was greatness. He had all manner of conversation topics. They neither detracted from Skillet nor drew address to Martha that might have caused his jealousness to surface. We managed to compliment the food, ask about jobs and run through some national headlines long enough to finish the meal.

James came bearing no gift. I couldn't tell if it embarrassed him to have followed through with that decision. Pete and Buck both brought gifts to Martha. Pete actually had a gift for all the women. Except me. He had guns for the men. Russian rifles that interested him greatly. Nothing for Tank. I guess giving everyone a gift makes it easier somehow. I handed over my wrapped picture of my family. I hated giving it to her. It was my family. I had taken my place on the street corner and sold my soul for a minute's worth of gratitude. Feigned gratitude. Or had I pawned myself for something worse. Something more like not being bad. Only a bad adult child would show up at a parent's eightieth birthday without a gift. Maybe I brought a gift to just avoid the ridicule of the silent eyed opinions. Did I bring a gift because lying was the lesser crime. A black and white photograph of the ones I called children and grandchildren and bonus children and blood. I gave them to someone who did not know them. I gave them to someone who would not ever know them. I watched Martha unwrap the framed figures I call my own and knew I had done a terrible thing. I should have brought a gift card.

By the time dessert was brought out, I had come to the end of myself.

I had become anxious beyond what my skin could contain. We had been there over two hours. I was done. I was spent, I was agitated. I was invisible. I was neon. I was dismissable and I was glaringly present. Some mean things had begun to unfold and I was the brunt of them.

There was talk several times of recreating a photo we had taken in the 80s with all four of us sitting on the hearth of the fireplace. I think James may have been tactical enough to have taken a Zanax® before he got there. He still seemed mostly okay to my observation at this point. Everyone else was busy admiring their gifts and thanking Pete for his consideration. Maybe that was part of the problem. I had no gift to admire. Either way this pose was not setting up and no photo was getting taken so that the day could be over.

I blurted out that we probably needed to go so we needed to take the photo if we were going to actually do it.

We finally sat down in our places of the past on the hearth. The picture was snapped. The brothers and I in the same places as before. Even the current dog matched the dog they had then. The picture was snapped and we all stood. I couldn't move quickly enough to the door. I do not know if I said good-bye. I probably did.

When we left I was more old. I was tired. I was lonesome. I was hurt. I was no closer to being an adult. I was not glad that I had done the seeming honorable thing. I was a fake. I was ashamed that I had lied about wanting to want to celebrate my mother's birthday. My mother was eighty years old and I was wishing I hadn't gone to her birthday party. I was ashamed of my heart toward it all. Oh my God, I was ashamed.

I was barely breathing.

I did not cry that night. It waited to rise within me. The cry. It waited for many days. I kept the weep away from my face long enough that it resigned.

I could not have known that over the next two years my life would become unrecognizable. Mostly unrecognizable to me.

November closed down. I had been a runaway. I had returned. I had attended the birthday party. I had remained the one who doesn't fit. I had remained the "mother unworthy superior." Evidence had confirmed again that I was not the daughter of choice. Nor the sister. I had resumed my life as the self-proclaimed casualty. I had packed my bag unwell and in a hurry and left for days and come home with a chance to see it all differently. To walk in the different. I could not gauge how different. I had no measure of what the different looked like. Looked like to my Tank. Nor in my mirror. But I knew in my fortitude that a shift had been made.

The month of December was disquieting.

Holidays when a family is broken are a shade of dark that surpasses dread. No number of strings of tiny colored lights make it bright.

HOLIDAYS WHEN A FAMILY IS BROKEN ARE A SHADE OF DARK THAT SURPASSES DREAD

Sterling was standing his ground of hurt and anger and distance. My crimes seemed to be indelible. Real events and imagined events were his hold against me. They were his hold over himself. They were his truth whether they were true or not. I had no defense. I had no speak in his company. I had no heart in his mind. In his world of energize by disdain I was the local power provider. The utility company of his angry energy.

I had taken inventory. Some of it objective. Most of it nor. I could agree that I had under done many things as his mom. I had overdone many more. I had missed things he tried to make obvious. I had been inconsistent. I had been present many times when it counted. I had been missing many times when it counted. I had not abandoned him. I had not hit him. I had provided for him. I had seen him. I had overlooked him. I loved him deeply. Curiously. Sincerely.

No matter what the real reality was I missed him in the mix of fact and fiction.

To be in Sterling's company was not good nor healthy nor restore but I did not know that. I still believed I could fix it. That I was the great and powerful Oz. That if we could just talk he would understand. And that I would hear him and I would understand. I still believed that it was all about understand. Everyone understanding me. Me understanding Sterling. Me understanding this man called God. Me knowing the future and understanding where all the roads were leading. I did not understand how fracturing the pursuit of understand was.

I was still sad and broken. And self-consumed. I had no gumption to be in Christmas cheer.

thirty-four

MAYBE NOT QUITE FINISHED

I agreed to attend an event in January, A women's event.
The very terminology grossed me out. I had been encouraged to attend this "women's Christian retreat event" thing for about three years, but thus far had managed to dodge the bullet. A church lady conference. I didn't know what it was and no one who has been to it tells much about it. They just mentioned that it would change my life and their eyes seem to mean it in the most sincere of exuberant understatements.

I knew I could use a change that would go on forever. Running away from home had brought some secrets to the surface, but I was still hiding from myself. Beyond the number of dollars, I wondered what it was really going to cost me. Emotional economies are a very different return on the cash investment.

I knew most of the reasons I didn't want to go. I don't do well with church lady people. I am a project for them. Someone to pray for. Someone to fix. Someone to shake heads about. Someone to talk about in whispers in the name of prayer.

I didn't want to go because I have done terrible and unforgiveable things.

I didn't want to go because I am terrible and unforgiveable things.

I didn't want to go because it was going to be about God and I didn't even like the guy. He was the king of the afterlife and absent in the current life. He was a narcissist and a forgetter and a very very poor Father. My personal experience was that He was all great at making stars and forgetting about their gazers.

I didn't want to go because someone might find out that I was not actually one of those Christian people. I had gotten baptized so I had a better chance of not burning with the friends of hell for all the rest of ever, but I was not a believer in this salvation thing as a life style. To me it was all barely more than folklore. Faith was not be trusted or relied on or built upon or claimed.

I wanted to go because my biggest customer was the one telling me I'd get a lot out of it. He and his wife had from time to time reminded me that I had not gone yet. It happens about once a month and I had managed to never find the time for over thirty-six of those months. I am a capitalist. I suspected that eventually it would have an adverse effect on my business if I didn't go.

I signed up in December and the thirty days of prep began. Reading the Bible and thinking through questions they emailed every day. I hated it.

There were fifteen other women signed up for this January trip. We had a common email thread and they were all using it to write in about what they were learning. They were describing who they are in their great and hurdle-ridden Christian lives in their fellowship-filled Christian worlds.

They wrote about how many kids they have and how great all things were. They used the church lady words in complete sentences. All I could see was little campers for Jesus all competing for the holy award before we even met.

I knew I was dead meat. I knew that my disguise of going to church some Sundays was about to be blown.

I quit the prep.

I was certain I would figure out a way to not have to go when the moment to go actually arrived. Kind of like a birthday party for an eighty year old.

The darkness darkened. The close in was heavy and dim. I had holidays yet to face down. And I had not recovered from the birthday party and this church lady retreat thing was frightening. And the admission of not being a good anything haunted my days and my nights.

Christmas Day was long. It was short. All the kids came.

We had breakfast together. We opened gifts. We opened presents. We had turkey and dressing and the same great foods of Thanksgiving. There was good in the house and there was sad and they stood in the others presence. They were emotionless in their encounters with each other and cordial with each other and suspicious of each other and I chose to carry them each on my hip like a barely toddler would be propped there.

Sterling and his daughter came for a very short time. They opened their gifts. I watched his little girl watch him for cues. For clues. She knew. She didn't know what she knew, but she knew.

They were not part of breakfast and they were not part of lunch. Her dad needed to see what he got. He came for presents. He came for gifts. His gifts. That's what hurt and angry people do. They appear on the scene. They bring their own air. And they suck oxygen out of everyone else's air. And they watch to see what they can take. And they watch to see what should be theirs. And they look to see what doesn't get given to them. And they give nothing back. And they take in such a way that no one is blessed by giving to them. And they leave confusion.

Sterling was punishing me.

It was effective.

I let him do it. I let it be effective.

The day finally came to an end. The family that felt the deep stayed as long as they could. They offered their protection in silence. They mourned from as close as I would let them. They prayed for Sterling. They did not pray for Sterling. They loved him. They did not. They had opinions about him. They had their opinions about me. And they did not.

I fought to keep a will. A will to enjoy the ones who wanted to be there with Tank and me and I came up short. I fought for gratitude and came up short. I fought to engage and have treasure and watch the littles with wonder and came up short. I scolded myself. It was nicest thing I could think to do for me. The scolding.

I made a note in my Giant Journal that night. "I may not be finished running away."

thirty-five

FACE TIME

January crawled by like a dread.

Sterling and I had little contact except at work. He was good at being late. I was good at getting furious. My furious didn't inspire any level of promptness within him. His lateness didn't inspire any level of appreciation for him within me.

He had been working for me since he left college at twenty. He's a very creative young man. So talented. When he is present on the job he is good at it. The customers love him most of the time. He is charming and winsome and talkative. The customers struggle with him when he says he will take care of something and doesn't. He can build most anything that requires a tractor and boulders and that has been a great asset to our landscape business. It has given him an area to call his own. But it has been difficult figuring out a work relationship.

I love seeing him work. When he started learning to talk his first word was "bobcat." He had a toy Bobcat® tractor that he carried everywhere. The scoop bucket had eventually fallen off of it from the many drops on pavement, all the scoops of sugar packets at restaurant tables and the many piles of dirt it had encountered. Everything in his world needed a good excavation. All tractors were the very best one he had ever seen. Every tractor driver was his idol.

When Sterling turned nine, I rented a tractor for his birthday present and bought him two loads of dirt to play with in the backyard. For two days he worked with that tractor and built a motocross track with jumps and whoops and banks. He made it look so easy to sculpt dirt with a tractor.

Taking that talent into a workplace had put a strain on us as mother and son in the personal arena as well. I don't know which is greater, the tension of parent and child or the tension of employer and employee. I don't know if I even care. I hate it all. I hate all the hurt and the miss and the disgust and the criticism and the attitude and the entitlement and the fact that he knows I will not fire him because he is married and has a daughter and wife to provide for. I hate being manipulated by those components and I hate even more that I built this dynamic and I hate the position I have put us all in.

I do things often with good intentions.

Sometimes there is no agenda. No expectation. Nothing in it for me. That last sentence may not be completely true.

Sometimes I have good intentions that are self-serving. Things that I think will help someone. I believe myself when I tell me and them that my intentions are pure. That I just want to be helpful because so many people have helped me. But then I realize that it wasn't pure. I have often helped because it also helped me. I have helped because I want to feel good about myself. Or because I want to pay back or pay forward. I have helped so someone can be grateful to me. I have helped because I have a conscience even when I don't have a God.

Right now I think it is a rare color of meanness to put people into a position of indentured slavement. I may be the worst purveyor of it of all time. Maybe helping is just how I feel good about myself. I do for someone. I provide them with an opportunity to make their lives better and then I get all high and mighty and disappointed and resentful when they don't follow through and when they don't make the most of what they were given to make the most out of.

Maybe Sterling is not any more disgusted with me than I am.

I had not found a legitimate and believable way out of going to the Church Lady camp.

So on a cool sunny Tuesday afternoon in January, I boarded the bus to what I had conjured up in my mind was a week ahead of me of holy hell.

I was bold about telling the people who so recommended this event that I hated them. A gorgeous couple who knew I was scared but had no idea why. They had no idea to what degree this was taking my life. They had no idea that I was certain I would be ripped to shreds. Customers or not. I told them I hated them. They laughed.

I was not laughing.

They knew not what they had done. They could not have known how many times church ladies and church lady men had tried to fix me into a tidier package. One that didn't cuss. One that sang the hymns. One that dressed like Christianity.

I was emotionally car sick for the entire six hours on the bus. I knew no one. No time for a nap. I was shot and I was wired. I was watching everything and everyone. I was suspicious and I was trying to participate and I was isolating. And my best covers were not cover enough.

We arrived late on a rainy dark January night to a beautiful ranch in the Hill Country of west Texas. I found my sleep spot and continued to take inventory of the faces. Searching for anything and anyone I deemed safe or at least equally alarmed about being here. I found no one. They either had better emotional camouflage or they were genuinely excited about the impending week with God and His constituents.

I had determined that I could intellectually muscle my way through five more days for the benefit of both those who had been so excited for me to go and for the sake of capitalism. They are, after all, my biggest customer.

It's not like any of them really thought I wasn't one of them, but they also knew I was nothing like them. What they didn't know though, was that in spite of all my church attendances and Bible study enrollment forms, I really did not like church. Nor its people. Nor its God.

This God had unwisely aligned Himself with fathers. Very bad publicity move as far as I was concerned. I had decided I wanted His heaven and no more. But I was not even completely convinced about that because one day I might run into Skillet over there and one life had been enough with him. I knew I didn't want hell and rumor had it that only left heaven. But to avoid the "firey pit of eternal sweat" meant I was going to have to like another father and risk him not liking me back.

> THIS GOD HAD UNWISELY ALIGNED HIMSELF WITH FATHERS. VERY BAD PUBLICITY MOVE AS FAR AS I WAS CONCERNED

The Boy I could like. This Son guy, Jesus, seemed legit. He had paid dues. He had left the comfort of some mythological throne in a forever sky and yellow precious metal streets to come see what the earth expedition was all about. He had gone through potty training and being teased at school about his mom's story to cover his illegitimacy. He had friends that gave him great love and friends that betrayed him and friends that didn't get him and friends that drank wine with him. He had something I could grasp with my mind and maybe my heart.

He had life and experience and a memory stick of recover and heal and enjoy. He came back fighting from every loss. He was scrappy.

I could like him. A brother. Like my own. Brothers I understood. Brothers that wanted good for me, got me, liked me, didn't like me, and didn't get me, and didn't want much to do with me. The brothers were real. Even when they didn't see me.

The Jesus hadn't invented fathers and He hadn't been one.

Then this business of a Holy Ghost. Almost an oxymoronic title really. Who was this? What purpose was He not meeting? Nothing to put my arms around with him. Or her. Seemed possible to me that this was supposed to be the mom side of the Holy family, but she had been snuffed into silence.

So there I was and the gig was about to be up. I was going to be exposed. I was afraid that my fraudulent church attendance would easily become apparent in this house full of women wanting to be better friends with their God. The type of women that I suspected would spend the week competing for the most Bible knowledge by quoting verses at the divinely appointed intervals made explicitly for their wisdoms to shine forth.

The thought of little Marthas everywhere felt like brain nausea.

I had nothing to bring to the table except my great dark past, my unredeemed losses, and my perfected distrust.

The first day on the ranch brought me no relief. In fact, I convinced myself that I was not going to survive all this pray and passage exposure that I was imaginaing. So by ten o'clock that night I was done. Completely done. Or maybe completely undone.

I said to one of the leadership team that I was leaving. I walked up to a stranger who seemed like a veteran and mentioned that I was going to go home now. I just wanted her to know that if they counted heads that night the one missing was mine. I let her know because it was the considerate thing to do. I assured her I would be able to find my way back home by morning.

Then I met mercy head on. I did not recognize it, but something within must have. My stride out the door was slowed by one who had crashed and burned on a trip sometime before. She circled to the front of my determined pace and placed her hand on my arm without invading my space. She just said, "Okay."

I stopped.

"Okay. I know you can't stay. I see that. I know that," she said.

She waited for me to hear her.

"But it is dark. It is cold. It is late. You have no phone. You don't know where you are. You have no car. Home is 300 miles northeast of here."

She waited for me to think about that.

"I'll stay until morning." I promised.

I reluctantly agreed to her plan and went to bed.

I was sure they would be praying for me. Praying that I would actually leave.

I didn't leave the next morning.

I don't know why. I didn't know why then. And I still don't know why today while I am writing these words down.

I didn't leave and things got harder. Things just got harder.

Maybe I stayed because things got harder. I can do harder.

By day three I had run into God.

The Real Dad. The Real Dad, His Brilliant Boy, and the Holding Spirit. The Triplets.

They showed up and I remembered them or met them or finally saw them or heard them or smelled them, and it was like being three years old.

I was star struck.

The Real Dad was star struck.

After a very long short day completely alone with the Triplets, I went back into the company of the other women who had spent their day doing the same thing. Everyone told stories of their day. I listened. I watched their voices and heard their eyes and said nothing. I had no words for it yet. I knew I may never. It was okay that I might not ever be able to say what had happened.

I said nothing. My quiet was the first time I had known sacred.

Known it.

And maybe even as I am writing this I am realizing that it is difficult to say it. Finding it difficult to describe what happened to me and for me spiritually and wholly because I have so long rebelled against the church language of Christianity that I have no translation for it. And I wonder if I should even write down that I am writing this down lest I affect adversely the mystique of penning a series of words that someone may make time to read. And that very thought makes laugh ... as if people who write don't know that they are writing and people who read don't know that writers are writing things down.

There are all these words used in churches that are supposed to draw me toward a decision of a believe in the God person. Just one believe. Phrases and ordered words that make no home in my system of consideration. And I cannot use them now as if they are good enough. As if they describe my actuality or my evidence. Words that do not ennoble accurately what I received. What awakened my remember and my brand new about the most entrenching profound I have ever laid down in the presence of.

So now I feel awkward using words that are not good enough. I feel incomplete in my truth if I say words so familiar in the church. Born again. Accepted Jesus as my personal savior. Washed in the blood. Converted. Became a Christian.

Really?! I don't even know what this means—"my personal savior."

All this time the Great Love was there for me. The Giver never changed. He never retracted His hand or His affection or His love. I had to approach the bench and point to the palm of His hand full of how He sees me and feels about me and what He has done for me and ask if that was all mine. Ask Him if this whole pile of affection was for me.

I had to look at the truths of my life so far and examine the undoings and ask where I would be if He had not been my God all along. Even if I had not wanted Him to be my God. Ask if He was a father. A Father. Let Him stay in my company long enough to answer me. Kindly. With dignity toward me. Toward Himself. Toward the Cross.

The Cross where He articulated His credentials. No longer a distant unreachable. He had come down from His King Chair and worn the skin around town. He had taken meanness and He had eaten good food and bad. He had been bullied and He had been adored and He had been misunderstood and He had cried out for help and He had been forgotten. And He had died a full bore unforgivably pain-filled death. And when He was ready He decided to not be dead ever again and the unforgivables were all available to be graced and mercied.

That day I saw that He understood my fierce rejection of anything resembling a father. He had not refused me anything because of it.

To His face I shouted my blames over the horrors of violence and violations and my buried children and divorce and belief in lies and the sad sexual corruptions I had chosen. I kept my own look cast down. And in a while I raised my fist and I raised my tear mapped face and asked without mercy for Him where the hell He had been in all these days and moments and years. And when I had destroyed all the fight I had, I heard Him whisper how He had wept that they had each happened. He did not defend or explain or promise better days ahead. He did not ask me to believe that He was sorry. He made no mention that He was not responsible.

HE DID NOT DEFEND OR EXPLAIN OR PROMISE BETTER DAYS AHEAD. HE DID NOT ASK ME TO BELIEVE THAT HE WAS SORRY. HE MADE NO MENTION THAT HE WAS NOT RESPONSIBLE.

He gave me a glance at His deep wordless sadness for me.

He described His own cry out into the universe and how He waited for His voice to echo back empathy. He described to me how His pain for me had pushed the edge of eternity to a further border. He showed me who I am to Him. Who I am to eternity. Who I am to this earth run. I am one He adores. One He had eaten up all crimes for. One He was always waiting to talk to. To hear from. One He has protected. One He has loved. One He likes. One He has rescued. One He had sent the Shepherd to find. One He has talked about. One He has been expecting. One who had arrived at His door right on time.

This exchange had nothing to do with going to heaven someday. It was invite for the now. The very minute of present. Know the Triplets. Know that the Real Dad is the Creator. The Guy who actually knows where this all goes. Big picture goes. Where the lead leads me. He knows what He means when He says that it's all about His Glory. His Brilliant Boy is the Obedience. The One who was fully man and walked out intensely the will of relationship. Trusting that the brutal life of rejection and being murdered would have purpose for the ultimate Glory Art Show. That He would become the incredible intercessor for souls both wandering and directed.

And the Holding Spirit is like a Mom—who brings life to the brand new. Brings comfort and remember and clear and conspire. The One who does not depart the walk. Who unfolds plans and redeems all day every day. The bench coach waiting to assist and instruct and encourage and take me out of the game when I can't take myself out. The third who has to be apparitional so He can settle on entire mass of miracles all at once. Nothing spooky. And certainly not muted and sent to the kitchen.

I could not resonate with the phrases I had heard my growing up years in a Baptist Sunday School. And being semantically challenged made it holier some how.

I could hear Him see me. I could hear Him see me choose to love Him back. Forgive Him for what He had not done. He is man enough to take it.

I got baptized in a cold river in January.

I loved the broken wholeness.

I came home new. Not better. Not on a better path with new understanding and better words. I came home a toddler. A very little kid with no new tools in my drawer save one. I was in love with the Triplets.

I had deliberately picked to love the Real Dad back. Outside of knowing that I didn't know anything else that I now believed.

I spent the month of February inventorying my old. My pasts were changing. I was walking in a new humble that was kind and encouraging and held great foreign. The variety of humble that keeps company. A humble that causes brave to quietly surge forward. A humble that has no condemnation and no curse and no exclusion. A humble that made me laugh and made me love apologizing. The substantial humble of run head first into very old questions and accusations and hear clear pictures of truth. Truths that showed me that I had never been left alone. Truths that tenderly revealed where He had been all the time. All along.

Each of the times. Each mystery. Each assault. Each terror and uncertainty. And that if He hadn't, I would not have survived long enough to reach this begin of thrive. The days of curtains being pulled back and the light being let in began. I didn't know if it would end. So many windows to look out from. So many things He wanted to show me. Tell me. Give me. Forgive me. Restore me. Bring to me. Serve to me as communion. So many fascinating doors.

I knew that my runaway had only started in November.

I met The Real Dad and His Brilliant Boy and the Holding Spirit and they let me remember as slowly and quickly as I wanted. The Triplets gathered for all my questions. They heard all my shames and carried them off as I brought them each to the table. They wept with me and spoke to me and waited for me and waited with me and the unwrapping of me and the unveiling of God began.

Things began to look so very different.

Sterling was not different, but I was.

I prayed for mercy. Mercy for me. Mercy toward Sterling. What I got was more accusations from him. What I got was him growing in aggressions against me. What I got was him catching any ear and explaining my crimes and humiliations and my very bad choices. What I got was more of his anger. And what I got was a very gentle heart toward him. A pained and changed heart. No new strength to endure. No supernatural ability to overlook the hurt that drew blood. No new wisdom to offer him. He gave no forgiveness for anything I offered apology for. No sign of him wanting to mend things between us. The Triplets gave me no permission to be offended. No permission to be justified. Just love him.

I still did not do social conform, but I was a different kind of different and still the same.

Skillet and Martha were not altered in any way but my sight of them had shifted. I was less afraid or more empathetic or less angry. I was no less distant. I did not know where that would take me but I knew my safe collection of unkindness toward them had begun its fade.

Everything changed some and some things completely and some things I have yet to let change more than just some. Things I had not gotten ready to rid myself of yet. I found myself still unable to lay all things down. I was on my way. I know I slow myself with my anvils of guilt and blankets of protection. The knowledge not enough so far to break all the years of gathering controls. The broken heart I had earned and rooted me in was not fully reliable in this kindergarten stage.

I was walking in experience. Running in trust. Sleeping in restore. Catching realities. Realties that proved out no sin and no crime nor the exposures of them could make me dead. I had been so very afraid of the results of people finding out. Finding out things I had done. Things I had said. Things I had inside my soul. How much I hated their God. That I had faked being a believer. That I had prayed for terrible things. That I had walked in vile and stored secrets in dark closets. Now those things were hung out to dry. Laundry in the wind on the front porch. All could see. And I did not die. Admission had not taken my life. It had gotten me born.

I was walking among miracles now. Everything was a miracle. Everything was intense. Intensely painful and intensely alive and intensely gentle and intensely His. I was walking among forgiveness and humble and freedom and anyone standing near me was in the presence of a miracle. I had gone from abandoned to belonged in a week. Or a minute in the middle of a week.

I prayed like a kid. Like the days when I prayed with all my might for the brothers and I to become orphans. I was an awkwardly elegant toddler for Jesus.

I still had my job to go to everyday and laundry to do and birthday cards to buy and car payments to make and children to stay in touch with. Nothing was different and everything had changed.

THE REAL VOYAGE OF DISCOVERY
CONSISTS NOT IN SEEKING NEW
LANDSCAPES, BUT IN HAVING NEW EYES.

—MARCEL PROUST

thirty-six

THE NEW SONG

Three of the women who had been leadership types on the section of my runaway journey at the ranch were turning fifty years old this same year. They were all very good friends to each other. They had changed my life and I wanted to do a grand thing back. I could never repay them for their walk but I could try.

Turning fifty is a kinda big deal. It may not merit respect to those younger or those older, but it does seem to give us permission to respect ourselves. Maybe respect ourselves more or maybe just respect ourselves for the first time. We lumber and wade through all manner of emotional muck to get there and mental mire to get there. We have a long list behind us of graduations and overcomes and overwhelms and incredible tears and "pee your pants" laughs. Parts of us in one piece. Parts of us missing in action. None of us still sporting a bikini. Maybe none of us wanting to.

Fifty may not make us wise and sagey just yet, but it is not forty, and it is not thirty.

I told them that I wanted to help them remember turning this number always.

"How about I take you on a trip!? How about Paris or London?"

Their blank stares were sincere.

"Which London?" one said.

"The London that lives in England," I said

So we all went to London to celebrate. I know London well. I had visited dozens of times and had lived there briefly and it is a town that I adore. Tank and I had gotten married there. I had been evicted from my home there and closed the door on my first marriage there. It was a town of a million memories and joys and experiences and darknesses.

We picked dates at the end March and I booked flights and booked a hotel and we all went for a "five day" weekend. Seven of us went to celebrate the birthdays. I was now a veteran at running away for days at a time and chuffed to share my manual on how to do it.

The hotel was great. The weather was mostly great. The food was British. The plays were entertaining. The James Bond movie being filmed was very cool. And the company of chicas was righteous and timid and bold and curious.

The next shift in my own indefinite runaway life began on the flight home from that trip.

I build play lists all the time. I love music. Some lists are cowboy music and some are blues and some are oldies. My favorite is the genre of singer songwriter. The people who take strings and lanes of rhetoric and make them say what I can only know I feel. They read me and reflect me back to myself in brutal empathy.

I boarded the plane and put on my tunes and settled in for the ten hour flight home. Real Dad had other plans. He gave me a song that afternoon. And a mission that I did not want.

The song was by Rascal Flatts. I listened to it and started crying. I listened to it and wondered how it got to my playlist. I listened to it and wondered why I had never heard it before.

It is a great song. But it says, "I'll be with you."

The message was so very out of left field. So very random. He was so very clear. I don't know how I knew what the message was or why Skillet would be on the mind of the Real Dad as I was travelling home from a chick trip. I didn't even know what to call it. This relationship with the Triplets was so young that I didn't understand how He speaks, but He told me I would be the one with Skillet as he wound out of this life. He would not be alone when he left. He would not be by himself. I would be his provision for company if not companionship.

I cried for almost the entire flight. I know my new friends were puzzled or concerned or both, but I could not explain what the tears were. I didn't honestly know.

For the next twenty months I would go see Skillet each time my God asked me to.

I was not happy to do it.

I asked why. I asked what I was supposed to say. I asked what I was supposed to achieve. He did not respond to my questions. Each time I was sent I asked the same things. Each time His lips fell silent

He just said go. Go now.

The first time was hard. Each trip was hard. I don't know which one was the hardest.

I knew I wasn't willing to go see Skillet if Martha wasn't home so I called first. It was an awkward call. Skillet answered the phone. He was more surprised than I was that I was calling. He said that Martha was not home that evening. She had gone to church. Skillet had stayed home because he didn't feel good.

I was thankful that she wasn't home since my condition had been that I would not go if she was not home. That was my control with God. My compromise. The deal I struck. Nothing surprises Him. He knew that

I was going to ask for that. He agreed to the concession. The terms of our agreement were made.

I had escaped the court's sentence.

On Monday the Real Dad spoke again. He told me to call today. Call and Martha would be there and to go.

I reluctantly called. She was there. They both were. He never went anywhere without her anymore because he couldn't really drive. My heart sank and my insides went sick and my mind got paralyzed and I got in the car and drove across town to their house.

I told Tank I was going. I told my excellent friend Sundy. They both balked. Sundy agreed to pray but I didn't ask her to describe that pray. I didn't ask Tank to pray. He may have done it anyway. I didn't ask that either. I knew that he would be home when I got back.

If I got back.

I was afraid. Afraid of the reality that this visit could go very badly. That mean and terrible things could get said. Said by me. Said to me. That more distance and bigger walls were probables. The traumas of the past provoked irrational conjurings inside my head and once I parked in front of their house I could barely open the door of the Jeep to get out.

The front door was open. The glass storm door stood between me and the smells of the house of history. The house of unpredictable. The house of screams and quiets and laughs and strikes and achieves and unforgetables.

I stood on the red tiled porch and looked at my own shoes. I asked my feet how they carried me from the street to here. Silence came from them. They stood still now. I raised my hand and watched my own finger press on the doorbell. My last visit here Tank was at my side. My hand had been buried in his. Now my hands were on their own and they were split from the parts of me that did not want the doorbell to get rung.

It didn't take long for Skillet to appear. There he stood in his feeble. Wearing gym shorts and no shirt. No shoes. He was making certain that I could see him in his gaunt. He was not going to risk having his impending death from nothing in particular overlooked.

The games began.

He hugged me. I resisted. He knew it. I placed the flat of my hand on his back and his skin was warm and old like a worn down velvet soft.

His face was posed and his unclenched teeth stared at me when he smiled in victory that I was there. Martha soon came to the entry of the house and tilted her head as she welcomed me and thanked me and hid her watch of me. She too knew that this could go very badly. And we both knew that if it did, she would be left in this prison with him and that I would drive away and abandon her.

I stepped further into the house behind them as they led us to the couches in the less formal part of the living room. They offered me a specific place to sit and they took their positions. Neither asked why I was there. They launched a little into their agenda for the evening. They didn't know what I was there for so the best defense they could think of would be an offense. To give me stuff. Their stuff. They described things they wanted me to have and the travels around the house began almost immediately.

We stood within minutes of sitting and Martha opened a door to a curio cabinet. There she took out items I had given them in prior years a life time ago. She held them out my direction. She had bags ready to put them in and newspaper on stand-by to wrap the breakables in.

We moved slowly and for me it was hard to breathe.

They each began selecting things from the further back past and telling me what they were. Then Martha would hold it out toward me in offering and reach for another piece of newspaper to wrap it in before I could give an honest reply of receipt. They gave me two hand painted, cat shaped, porcelain ashtrays that had been Aunt Mary's. They fit into her hand so that she could carry her cigarette with the brown Bakelite filter on it in one hand and the tiny ashtray in the other. A lady would never flick her ashes on the floor. They gave me the topper off of their wedding cake. I couldn't imagine that any of us believed I wanted it, but maybe in the real family world the daughter keeps these things. Martha wrapped it and put it in the bag as well.

We went into Skillet's office and the first thing he gave me was a miniature bail of cotton exactly like the one I had been given on my runaway a few months prior. I had looked at that bail in his office for over forty years never being allowed to touch it, and something about it had always attracted me. The size or the white cotton bound in burlap and tiny metal binders had captured me for so long. So here on this April Monday night I was offered some kind of right of passage into adulthood when he handed it to me.

It went into the bag of confusions.

We looked around the office. All three of us. Some anxiety was present. I was nervous about what they would offer me next. They were nervous about whether I would want it. I was nervous about saying no. I was nervous about saying yes. A framed document on the wall was pointed to. The letter of discharge from the army for my grandfather in World War One. Skillet took it down and purposely pointed to the dates on it. Nearly a hundred years have passed since Pa had been a soldier. He hung it back up unready to hand it off and promised that it would be mine when the end came for him and Martha. Instead he gave me the government-issue New Testament that he had carried in the Korean war and he gave me the one his father had carried into the army. Skillet had been a Marine. To his mind the Army was for half-wits and lesser men.

There was nothing much else for us to discuss in the office. It would mostly be for them to give the boys if they hadn't already done that. The office was mostly man child items. Pete and Buck had no doubt staked their claims and received their assigned fortunes. James had made it clear that there would be nothing that he would ever want from their estate.

In the next room there were two antique chairs that they said I could take on my next visit if I brought over a truck.

I hadn't even left and they were already planning that I would come back.

On the bed there was a big bag of things Martha had set out. Things she must have been planning for a while to make sure I had. I had only given them about an hour's notice that I was coming by so I know she hadn't put them together this day.

I was still very much in a state of untrust. Earth so far had not given me much reason to trust. Trust the air or the series of faces or the sun to set without making Skillet mad about something or all things. So this moment was intensely lack of trust. I had seen sides of my parents that a kid should never see. It had made an unrest in my soul that alerted my unwillingness to have believe in them from the time I was little.

She had things that her mother had crotcheted. Pillow cases and doilies for table tops. And they gave me two pictures. One of Skillet's oldest sister Aunt Mary holding a cigarette in one hand and one of those ashtrays in the other. One of the pictures was of Pa, Skillet's father, when he was about six years old. It's a family picture with several of his siblings and his parents. I loved getting the pictures the most.

301

I thought we were finished for the evening. I felt that relief of departure closing in but I was wrong. They had one more cabinet of histories to be considered. There were four glasses in the cabinet. 1950s sized ice tea glasses with gilded cotton bolls painted on them. I remembered them from our kitchen shelves in the houses we had occupied before. They had always been off limits. Skillet loved theses glasses. At one time there had been six of them but I don't know exactly what events had brought the missing two to their premature demise. Skillet took the remaining four out and presented them to me. I didn't want them. Or maybe I did. I was afraid of them. I wasn't sure why.

The glasses were the last thing to be wrapped and put into one of the bags for me to carry to my own home.

Now it seemed we were finished. I had made the assumption that this was to be my only visit and I was surprised and grateful that there had been no fight and no questions about my staying away from them for these most recent decades.

Martha carried one of the packed bags out to the Jeep and was trying to over help me put them in the back seat when one of the glasses was knocked out of the bag. It was wrapped in newspaper but the sound of shatter could not be muffled and we both knew Skillet heard it hit the street. We did not look at each other. We did not look his direction. Her fear was physical. Her face went completely colorless in the night street light. She cast her eyes downward but not toward the broken object. They were cast toward her broken soul. Her slightly shaking hands had become disoriented. She did not know what to do with them. She did not reach for the wrapped piece on the street and she did not really finish putting the bag she was holding on the seat. She backed away from the car door and waited. A different stall out than a pause. She was not considering what to do next. She was considering what she had done. The shame was heavy and intense and made my insides sick and my tears surface. I should protect her.

I should take the blame. I should go to the porch and show Skillet what I had done. Then I should go inside and place the deceased piece of history into the trash bag with a little bit of ceremony so he knows I am deeply remorseful.

I did not.

I touched Martha's shoulder with as much compassion as I could. Albeit contorted affection, I did care. I cared that she was going to walk back into a terrible war zone but this time I would not go back with her. She was on her own. I might remember to pray for her. I might not.

Skillet in his staged weakness was still standing on the front porch. He did not shout from there. He may have clenched his teeth in preparation for her re-entry to the house. He may have added the accident to a mental list of other intentional travesties she had committed against him deliberately that very day or over their lifetime together. He did things that way. He gathered things all up and called them all attempts to embarrass him or hurt him or inconvenience him or cost him money.

Everything that happened in the whole world was perceived as against him personally. There are no accidents. If the brothers or I got sick we did so to make his life more difficult. If we forgot to do something. If we lost something. If we got more of a laugh than he did. If we knew about something that he didn't. All things were done to persecute him in some way.

The accident with the glass was the same.

She would pay for her atrocities.

I picked the wrapped glass up from the street as quickly as I could and told her not to worry. She would anyway. She has to. It may not be worry. It may be more of a bracing of herself.

I put the now broken glass back into the bag that she hadn't finished setting into the seat and pushed the sack back to a safe place. She had offered to take the mishap inside and throw it away. I couldn't let her. I was protecting us both. I don't know who I was protecting more. Taking the precious pieces into his company would prolong the cruelty he could deliver. I took the glass to my house where no one would get injured over the shatter.

I gave her a hug and wondered what would happen if I took her home with me. She didn't hear my embrace and she thanked me for coming by much like we thank the plumber for fixing the kitchen sink that was leaking. I think she wanted to want to thank me without words. The kind of gratitude that runs between people who know each other well. But we do not. She knows me as the younger Sammi. The child probably. The one who abandoned her and the one she knows does not understand all of the things we experienced together separately.

I had climbed in the Jeep and put the key in the ignition before I realized I was bleeding. Not just internally. In picking up the glass with its painted on cotton I had cut myself. I counted it significant. I counted it a picture from the Triplets. I saw the blood and the white skin and knew I was being reminded of forgive. Reminded of redeem.

Three glasses left now. One for each of the Trinity I thought and smiled.

The evening had gone on forever.

I drove home and wondered if this had been the plan of our God. The God I call Real Dad and the one Skillet calls Peer and Martha calls on often with her certainty.

Nothing had been achieved. No begin had been birthed. No dialogues to shift the past into mercy. We had shuffled around each other like animals marking territory. We had not argued. We had not enjoyed. We had not endured well but we had endured. The April Monday night had come to a close and the urge to ask what had happened to the chance to love and be loved had been suppressed.

I was deeply sad. I was deeply glad the duty had passed. I was intensely lonesome. I was the orphan I had prayed to be so many decades ago.

I did not know that night that there would be dozens of visits ahead of me.

I did not know how deep freedom could become with obedience.

The reality that faith is very different from trust was beginning to shape within me. I had fallen in love and forgive with the Real Dad and the reward for that was to be sent out into the war zones and the mine fields.

This Dad God was proving to be interesting. Interested. Giant. Personal. He was making me whole every time I asked. Maybe every time I didn't. As whole as I could contain in the moment.

IF ALL YOU CAN DO IS CRAWL,
START CRAWLING

—RUMI

thirty-seven

GETTING DEAD

I had learned over the past twenty months to listen to what was being said in the less audible sounds of notice. I had not been very responsive to nudges before, so they had become more like shoves and gentle bulldozes from the Creator. The Creator who I had reconciled with during these months.

I made the phone call.

That phone call. Some people get the phone call. I made it.

It was late morning. Too late for more coffee. Too early to wonder what would be good for lunch. I was making my way through an ordinary day of breathing and eating potato chips and doing what I do for work when I understood that I needed to make the call. I rang Skillet's house. A pleasantly voiced female answered the phone. That I knew of, I didn't know the person that belonged to the voice. It wasn't my mother. I didn't ask her who she was even though she had answered the phone in a house that was not her own. I felt hurried. Impatient but not irritated. I asked to speak to Martha.

"She can't come to the phone right now. She's in the other room with her husband. He only has a few minutes to live."

I heard the words. The words she so quickly and restlessly expelled. At the time I didn't wonder what it might have felt like to deliver such a report. Now I do. I wonder. To deliver such a truth would be a mix of care and burden and sad and honor. I barely heard the dimensions and the responsibilities and the unusual grief of what the sentence meant for me. I inhaled short of fully with my shoulders and my heart before responding quickly.

"This is their daughter, Sammi. Tell Martha I will be there soon." I knew my words were true. I knew my commitment had been made whether I wanted to be there or not.

I'm sure she said okay. I don't remember if I actually waited for her response. I knew she would be understanding toward me even if she didn't understand.

Urgently I left the job I was working on. Right then I had a place I needed to be. Maybe a place I wanted to be. Near Skillet. Near obedience. Near privilege.

When I started this run away from home two years ago I would have spit hate daggers on someone if they had suggested I might end that escape here. Heading back to the home of the begin. To the ones I hold liable for beginning my human experience. But I don't spit so much these days. I have laid daggers down. I have pawned my hates and used the coins to buy the ashes. Ashes that have begun bearing signs of life.

Small hardy plants of life not ready to bear fruit. They had been forming and shaping and taking tender root since my drive in the direction of west—when my adventure was still young. Life forms that now seemed eager to seek the sun of mercy on this ordinary November day. So today, the light my soul sickens itself for, summons itself toward, will be death. Skillet's death. I have peace and panic on my side. I wonder if I will get there in time. I wonder if I want to. I wonder if getting there in time means before he leaves or after he's gone. What will it be like. Will he say anything to me. Will I have anything to finally say to him. Will Martha need or want me near. Near her. Near him. I can't do it wrong. That is the peace among the hurry. Among the alarm. Whatever happens in the deliberate will be right. Will be well.

On a regular day these are regular streets that lead to regular destinations. Today they seem to have too many red lights and not enough red lights. Today they seem to have no options and too many options. Today these roads that need to go south seem to snake east and west like a path on a mogul ridden black diamond ski slope. I want to get there now. To their house. The house they live in. The house he will not live in shortly. I want to get there maybe never. I forget even that I'm driving. Then I remember and see that in my own absence I kept going toward their house until I had gotten there.

I stop out front with no idea how long I will be parked here. I don't know if my mother is already a widow or if I will stay with her until she becomes one. The reality sinks into my bones.

I walk. Or I creep. I vertically drag my deliberate steps the thirty feet of paved lead walk from the curb to the front door. The pathway is bordered with a thick blanket of beach colored dormant St Augustine grass. There are green hedges and browning yellow chrysanthemums standing still in the flowerbeds and the twelve inch bricks of red lay together to cover the swept front porch.

I don't ring the front door bell. That's a first. For all of my adult years I rang the doorbell. Even though I lived here for ten growing up years, the house is less my childhood home and more Skillet and Martha's house. I always ring and wait for them to open the unlocked doors. One of heavy wood with two vertical panels of lead glass in the top half. Then the more exterior all glass door that let's them see the outside and keeps them entertained with passing cars and the odd territory sniffing dog to notice.

The wood door is already propped to a welcome position. I opened the glass storm door and entered Skillet's next to the last world.

The white shades of the tile floor were overcast. Weary. Clean and sheenless out of respect for the hearts of the whelmed residents. The long glass top table and its dark wood legs stood planted below the bottom edge of the mirror that I did not look into on my right. The decorations of crystal vases and silk flowers stood fragranceless on the end of the table where they wouldn't block the view of the framed mirror. The elegantly pale rug, perfectly squared to the burnished baseboards, softened the sound of my steps until they stopped.

I had paused. Or I quit walking in. Was he gone yet. I stated it to my inside self but I did not ask. I didn't say any words aloud. My breathing didn't change. My heart waned barely. I didn't know if anyone heard me come in. Usually Pepe would have come charging to the door barking that little dog protest at the intruder. No Pepe this morning.

I heard the front door finally come to a close behind me and resumed my forward motion of steps into the den of proof that this was home for someone.

A woman came to greet me from the kitchen. I presumed her to be the same who had answered the phone earlier. My pace was sure but not hurried as it carried me toward her and past her. She smiled. The tragic smile. I don't know if she spoke. I don't know if I spoke or spoke back or made any attempt beyond acknowledging her wondering sympathy within the simmered expression.

I knew she didn't understand. I knew she knew their version of the history. I knew she knew I had long been the daughter who didn't come around. My many years of absence still out weighed my more recent nearly twenty months of visiting. She had no doubt been one of Martha and Skillet's confidants. Those friends we all have who hear our griefs and moan at the nothing with us in our helplessness. The people who acknowledge our pain and take our side. The people we don't introduce to the ones we blame for our heart ache because we cannot risk losing any sympathies. Something that could happen if our friends meet our enemies and don't see it the same way. The enemies who are not the enemies anyway. They are the ones who provide us a way to acquire compassions and pities when we don't actually long to be whole. Those who are around making sympathy flavored stew when we are starving for a short-sighted relief from pain inside. What if our allies met the enemy and did not determine them to be so cruel after all. We cannot risk such casualty. A loss we cannot bear might be born so we do not introduce them.

I was still in forward motion toward their bedroom as we recognized each other. I saw her posture of protection of them. I was grateful that they had found comforters along the way. It had been a pain filled two decades or three or five. The count varied with the counter.

Stepping from the cold white tile floor onto the pride colored carpet of their bedroom I made the transition from getting there to being there. Physically anyway.

Skiller was laying on his back on the right side of the king-sized bed Covers pulled up near his chin. It was clear from the turned down cuff at the top that he had not placed them there himself. The shallow ridge of his arms rested underneath, neatly positioned in straight lines near his sides, but not touching his body. His head was centered stiffly on a large, soft pillow. His patch of white hair covered small amounts of the skin that stretched tight over his skull. His eyes were open. So was his mouth. His skin was old man colored. Highlights of age spots and sags and creases. Hollow the dominant feature of the form of him. Sunken eyes that couldn't blink held the fright within him.

He didn't speak. Speech had gone from him. But he was still inside the scraggy carcass that contained his last signs of life. His dread matched mine. Some things we were still the same about. Blue eyes that lean toward granite late in the day. And the curse of being aware that more than one thing can happen in the same square of space and time. We have other commonalities as well.

Pepe was here on duty. Their small white poodle was clearly not certain what that meant; what duty meant or death or the grey of the quiet, but he seemed sure he was supposed to be there among the leaving and the living.

Martha was sitting up on the passenger side of the bed. Her Bible opened to a portion that she had been reading out loud. To him. To her. To the air that brought her comfort. She stopped when I came in. My arrival not a surprise. Her worry pace quickened for a moment when she saw me. Her understanding of the The Big Book might not have a wisdom to cover my arrival. She wasn't sure of my agenda. She wanted to want me there. But my being there confirmed that his end was close. My being there would be something to explain to those who had believed her descriptions of my abandonment of her and my father, Skillet. My being there would free her up again. Like in my little kid years where I would step in and she would be released from managing him. Him and his mysterious rages. He would not rage again. But she did not want to care for him alone. I could do that. I could care for him with her. Release her to go to the other room. To busy herself through the storm of gratitude and grief that was already altering the emotional barometric pressure of their house.

I had gone to his side of the bed. I hadn't asked to come in. I hadn't asked to enter their last paragraphs together. I had made a peace with the weight of knowing I would be there. Most of her knew that. Most of me knew that. She watched to see what my compassions were. Always vigilant to protect herself. The pattern of being careful to not let anything in their ring that would make him mad had long been a variety of her guard. Even now. Even when the threat is gone.

I put the palm of my warm right hand that still smelled like outside on his cool motionless forehead and brushed back the small span of his hair. I held it there a measureable amount of time before I kissed the skin above his all but gone eyebrows.

He acknowledged me with a sound in his labored breath. I watched his throat struggle to make sure I knew that he knew I was there.

I would be there to hear his last quiets of time. I would be there boldly. Fully. Humbly. Gently. Obediently. Relunctantly.

"Hey man," I said.

She watched the brief exchange and her guard became gratitude. Gratitude toward her God that I was there. Gratitude toward me for coming. Her hand on the open page relaxed. Her gapped fingers slid across the ancient words and I saw her grant me permission to take over without saying the words.

She said, "Thank you."

I know I smiled for her. To her. She looked down at the Old Testament passage again as if she could be lost now. She no longer wanted to read. She was no longer on duty alone. She touched his arm with the blanket between them and tears made it to the surface. She said a few sentences. Predictable things. I listened. I listened for information and for heart. Some of each were present. I watched Skillet while she talked. His face was frozen in haunt. His unsteady pulse visible in his neck. His breath lacked rhythm. The automatic of it all gone from him. Visible concentration now required for each draw. For each release. The oxygen travelling into his system through uncomfortable little tubes in his nostrils. Clear tubes tied to his ears without him being able to do anything about any of it. He could listen though. And he was hearing her.

She commented that she had prepared for this time for what seemed like ages, but now she wasn't ready for it. She looked down at the nothing. She lingered her sight there. Then she moved her mindless cast to her own hand on his covered arm and briefly to his locked face.

Her sadness succumbed to things she would rather think about and she awkwardly excused herself from the room of a muted life.

I watched her go out. Her pace was valiant and purposed on things she needed to do elsewhere. He couldn't see any more, no job left for his eyes, but I saw him watch her go out too. His wonder evident. Would that be his last look at her. One where he couldn't see her. A look where his eyes could not turn her direction. Would that be her last glance on him. Too much had gone wrong in their sixty-four years as husband and wife. Now with his body all but paralyzed into a state of stark, no more angers and no more unrepentant apologies would be offered. Regret has an odor. It smells like forever. It smells like dense. Forever weight draped on cold links of metal chain over an un-collard neck. Even laying down brought him no relief from the ache of heavy. No one left to blame. Blame no longer a way to get out of his jail. Blame no longer a comfort.

> REGRET HAS AN ODOR. IT SMELLS LIKE FOREVER. IT SMELLS LIKE DENSE. FOREVER WEIGHT DRAPED ON COLD LINKS OF METAL CHAIN OVER AN UN-COLLARED NECK.

I told him that I was going to go to the other side of the bed and I took my hand from the warm spot I had made on his thinly skinned skull. His eyes that could not move strained to tell me not to leave. With a voice that carried more charity than I knew I had for him I assured him I wasn't.

I got up on the bed near him. I leaned on my left side with my arm extended to brace me. Physically. Emotionally. Not knowing what to say, and not ready for silence, I told him I would begin again reading the page that the Bible beside him was opened to. Psalms. Psalms 27. She said that was their scripture. The one they liked. Maybe it was.

Maybe it was hers or his and the other just adopted for the sake of agreeing on something in these final months or weeks or years. I hadn't heard either of them mention it before so I didn't know how long this favor had been in place.

I read it to him. I started each of the sentences with my eyes on the print and finished them with my eyes on his breathing. Aware that each could be the last or the next to the last and not certain which I preferred it to be.

The verses came to a numbered end as if they were days. Skillet drew a graveled grab of air, then another, and after a long pause another. Now I knew the watch could be long. More than minutes. I had willfully abdicated to this last ride so within an hour of arriving I settled into my stay.

I texted Tank to tell him where I was. Who the clock was running out on. What things I needed him to take care of while I kept my keep. He texted back that all was good. That he loved me. That he was sorry. That he was glad I was there.

I had closed the Bible hours ago. I laid there on the bed. Close to his frailty. I had placed my hand over his. The thin blanket between us was something of a metaphor for the reality of layers between us. The blanket and the sheet that kept him warm also kept us from actually touching each other. The layers of woven cotton were soft. Clean. Comforting. These layers made it possible for me to reach out to him. I don't know if I would have been able to hold his hand if there had been no layers.

He had relaxed what little he could. I could see him roaming the waves back and forth between exhaustion and quiet and scare.

The room was loud. The room lay still.

I sent my brother James a text to let him know. And one to Sterling the still estranged son of mine. I let Sterling's dad, Robert, know in case he wanted to come by or wanted to be there in some way for our son.

Martha was in touch with her other sons. Pete and Buck.

Robert would want to know that his only father-in-law was calling it a final day. The man who had not been a grandfather to our son. The man who had ridiculed him and never known him was going to die and Robert would want to know.

The list of those who might want to say good-bye was probably complete. He had narrowed it down to a few friends. Good friends. But few. Skillet had alienated more people than he had drawn. His prejudices and criticisms and judgments were not inviting. Now the door was closing and most were willing to let it.

James had no interest in coming over. He had made his peace. Or maybe made peace with the idea that there would be no peace.

Pete would be coming the next day from Huntsville where he and his wife lived.

Buck and his wife would be coming when his kids got out of school. But not today either.

Tank came by. He stayed in the room with me for a while. He left to take care of some things I needed done at work. I was good. He knew I was good. He had come to see for himself. I loved that he wanted to see for himself that I was good.

Martha didn't come in very often. She was busy in the kitchen and in the other rooms. Busy with things that kept her in motion. A neighbor came by. Two more friends from church were there for most of the afternoon but they didn't come in to his room. Sundy came too. And there was a hospice nurse. A young woman with a beautiful face and an attentive soul.

She would check his vital signs sometimes and we would change his diaper and we made conversations that were brief.

Mostly it was just me and Skillet there in the room together.

Me and Skillet and all of our unstarted conversations. Me and Skillet and our variety of peace. Me and Skillet and my hand resting over his with the metaphoric layers between us. To hold us together. To make the distance comfortable.

I couldn't tell if the hours were long or not.

I watched him breathe. I watched him not breathe. I heard him not be able to cry. I spoke some. I wished for him to hear tender as the last tone of earth. He listened when I spoke. He rattled motionlessly when I didn't.

Skillet's face was now terrified. No peace. Something left to say maybe. Something left to ask. Something left to confess. I didn't know. Something short of complete kept him in terrified.

His breathing was no better. It was never going to be better again.

No one has words. No one wants to have words. No one wants to be the one with no words. It is painful. And it is pain filled. And it is pain free. And it is life going to death and that is where the new life will begin if there is any chance for a new life to begin at all.

It is both bitter and not.

Then things take the turns that death causes. A strange and familiar fear that we have forgotten something. Like leaving an iron plugged in after we have driven four hours from home. Did we forget something among the things of the dying. Because once the dying are dead there is no going back. So do we wish for more time. Will more time give us enough time to remember whatever it is that we forgot anyway. And if we do remember will we remember the courage to say it. The courage that we haven't had for the length of the lifetime we have had with the dying anyway.

When all they can do is hear how do they say anything again. Can we say anything with our hear that maybe we could have never with our words or our eyes or our sighs or our clenched teeth and clenched fists and then what happens when we release the fist and relax the jaw. Will the words we loosen on the world be of sorrow and compassion and heal or will they be of the things our hearts hold more dear like the prison of anger and the power of disappointment. Will we be better for the saying or better for the withholding?

It seems like several deaths are impending among the dying. The deaths of possibility and the death of probability and the life of the unknowing will live on forever once the breath is completely exhausted. Did we use the final times well. Did the clock rob us or did the very lack of the clock called years wipe it all out before we knew how to count time as valuable as it is.

I wish he could scream. I wish he could scream for mercy. I wish he could scream regret. I know that it is my fantasy that he wants to be forgiven.

Skillet could not scream. I could not scream on his behalf.

Tank came at night. For two nights he slept in the chair on the side of the bed I was on.

He brought my speaker and my iPod and I played the list of songs that brought me comfort and courage for Skillet.

I talked to the leaving Skillet. I told him everything that the Real Dad told me to tell him about the brothers. His sons. Things he may have missed about them. Things familiar to him. I told him they were good guys. I told him how they were like him and how they were not. I changed his diapers and watched his breathing and watched him stop and start again.

I loved watching the Triplets love Skillet to the other side.

No matter how Skillet had managed his time on Earth, it would not change who God is. The Son in Him admitted that death is hard and painful. For the dyer and for the stayers. The Holding Spirit did the Holy Holding. Held Skillet with my hands and held him with the way He changed my heart for this very time. And the Father God never stopped loving his boy, Skillet. No matter what Skillet had done or rejected or said or turned away from. No matter how many times Skillet had tried to measure up or be good for a time without success, the God was not going to leave him. He would not exit this plane alone.

I don't know where Skillet went on to when he left. I do not understand the justice of God and I do not understand the fraternal twins called Grace and Mercy. I do know that I am not mad anymore. Skillet's choices and violences have had a deep effect on my life and I am not mad. It is my testify.

What I was allowed to do was witness the gentleness of my Real Dad who couldn't not be love. He had never stopped loving Skillet.

GOD WILL TAKE YOUR MISTAKES AND
TRAGEDIES AND MAKE YOUR LIFE BETTER
THAN HAD THEY NOT HAPPENED

—TURBO BIGGERS

thirty-eight

REMEMBERING HIM

Exactly two years before Skillet's last night of struggle, I ran away. I thought at first that it had been for about six days.

I was off by 725 days.

I had moved from one event to another, from one location to another, and from one piece of my heart to another. Searching one step forward and two back and sometimes three forward.

I had spent time remembering things I didn't want to remember. Remembering things that had been done to me that I had loved calling unforgiveable. Remembering things that I had done that I had hoped would either be forgotten or be forgiven without my asking, or that I would be exposed for and tried and found guilty and punished appropriately for having done.

I had spent lots time at the King Chair and with people who loved being in love with the Real Dad, The Holding Spirit, and the Brilliant Boy. I had been envious of them and curious and drawn in.

I stopped looking for evidence. I stopped looking for proof. I had stopped drawing energy from being mad and being justified and needing punitive action to be taken against my damagers and against myself.

I began to take the business of forgive and be forgiven seriously.

I saw for the first time that salvation was not about a ticket to the nice side of forever. It's about eternity starting now. It's about a journey of being fascinated that goes on for always. About knowing I am the only one who can love the Triplets exactly like this and that we both want that.

That my job is to keep remembering. Remember the pieces of the Maker that He sent me over here with.

When He says He created me in His image it was the never-before-made mix of percentages of His character. The true thing is that everybody is His likeness and just knowing that has changed how I see people. How I see me.

When He says that He is in the business of restore and reborn, it's because He is taking me back to who I am. Who I was before things got robbed from me for another's use or purposes less than holy. The who that he spoke into being.

He just wants me to do this journey in remembrance of Him.

I will be willing to take on His forgiveness and I will be willing to say this testify as well as I know how. The testify of being carried through what was done and what I have done and how He carried those I have hurt and scarred with as much tender as He carried me.

After Skillet was gone and buried and Christmas had passed, I went back to Cotton Flatts and eventually found the boy and the pictures he had drawn. The ones on the back wall of the hardware store where I bought the level that took me to Levelland.

I thanked him and I thanked his dad and I thanked my Real Dad.

Then I drove to the orphanage in Lubbock where I had prayed to live so many times as a little kid. The same place where I had stopped my pray when I thought He had not heard me since the brothers and I had never been able to live there.

I thanked the Triplets for my life of unnoticed provision and protection. I apologized and felt them say, "Aw, that ain't no big thing," as He punched me lightly in the shoulder with a grin.

And I drove to Levelland to take one more picture of the house on Mesquite. I knew it would look so different now. It did. It's just a home now where someone else lives. No longer a brick and mortar keeper of dark secrets.

Then I went back to the swimming pool that had terrorized my decades and my dreams. It was gone. They had torn it out after all these years. Skillet did not drown me there four and half decades ago and his ghost cannot drown me now.

WE SEE ONLY WHAT WE KNOW.

—JOHANN WOLFGANG VON GOETHE